Beyond Imagined Communities

Beyond Imagined Communities

Reading and Writing the Nation in Nineteenth-Century Latin America

Edited by

Sara Castro-Klarén
and
John Charles Chasteen

Woodrow Wilson Center Press
Washington, D.C.

The Johns Hopkins University Press
Baltimore and London

EDITORIAL OFFICES

Woodrow Wilson Center Press
One Woodrow Wilson Plaza
1300 Pennsylvania Avenue, N.W.
Washington, D.C. 20004-3027
www.wilsoncenter.org

Order from

The Johns Hopkins University Press
Hampden Station
P.O. Box 50370
Baltimore, Md. 21211
Telephone 1-800-537-5487
www.jhupbooks.com

2 4 6 8 9 7 5 3 1

Library of Congress Cataloging-in-Publication Data

Beyond imagined communities : reading and writing the nation in nineteenth-
    century Latin America / edited by Sara Castro-Klarén and John Charles
Chasteen.
        p.   cm.
    Essays from a meeting of Latin American scholars held in the spring of 2000.
    Includes bibliographical references and index.
    ISBN 0-8018-7852-7 (hardcover : ak. paper)—ISBN 0-8018-7853-5
(pbk. : alk. paper)
    1. Latin America—History—19th century.   2. Nationalism—Latin
America—History—19th century.   3. Identity (Psychology)—Latin America.
4. Ethnicity—Latin America.   5. National state.   6. Anderson,
Benedict R. O'G (Benedict Richard O'Gorman), 1936– Imagined communities.
I. Chasteen, John Charles, 1955–   II. Castro-Klarén, Sara.

F1412.B49 2003
320.54′098′09034—dc21   2003014646

ABOUT THE CENTER

The Center is the living memorial of the United States of America to the nation's twenty-eighth president, Woodrow Wilson. Congress established the Woodrow Wilson Center in 1968 as an international institute for advanced study, "symbolizing and strengthening the fruitful relationship between the world of learning and the world of public affairs." The Center opened in 1970 under its own board of trustees.

In all its activities the Woodrow Wilson Center is a nonprofit, nonpartisan organization, supported financially by annual appropriations from the Congress, and by the contributions of foundations, corporations, and individuals. Conclusions or opinions expressed in Center publications and programs are those of the authors and speakers and do not necessarily reflect the views of the Center staff, fellows, trustees, advisory groups, or any individuals or organizations that provide financial support to the Center.

Contents

The Critics

Introduction: Beyond
Imagined Communities

John Charles Chasteen

Benedict Anderson's memorable formula, "imagined communities," be-came a central reference point in both historical and literary studies of Latin America during the 1990s.[1] So, in the spring of 2000, a group of Latin Americanist scholars met to take a critical look at Anderson's narrative of how national communities were imagined into existence in that part of the world. Such a critical look seemed especially important because the imaginative creation of Latin American nations figures importantly in Anderson's account of "the origins and spread of nationalism." Another motivating idea of the conference was to foment interdisciplinary dialogue. As disciplinary boundaries famously blurred in the 1990s, both critics and historians had set to work on the same topic—national identities—but because of disciplinary habits, they rarely communicated with each other. Much

The authors would like to thank Joseph Tulchin, director of the WWICS Latin American Program, for inspiring the conference and providing the necessary resources to make it a reality.

1. Benedict Anderson, *Imagined Communities: Reflections on the Origin and Spread of Nationalism,* 2d ed. (London: Verso, 1991).

could be gained, it seemed, if they did. We started from the premise that evidence of nineteenth-century nation building in Latin America is mostly textual, and texts are the special province of critics, but that nineteenth-century
texts must be historically contextualized, the specialty of historians.

The result of our encounter, this book, represents a collective assessment
that may be surprising to some. Taken as a whole, the essays gathered here
provide little support for Anderson's assertions regarding Latin America unless those assertions are substantially qualified. All the historians present at
the meeting agreed on that point. The literary scholars, on the other hand,
suggested persuasively that Anderson's overall interpretation—his broad
historical search for the imaginative contours and, especially, the affective
power, of modern nationalism—does provide valuable insights for Latin
America. Newspapers did not define "national space" on the eve of independence, as suggested in *Imagined Communities,* but they did work that
way later in the nineteenth century.[2] Anderson's crucial emphasis on the relationship between print culture and nationalism will probably continue to
inform historical and literary studies of Latin America and, no doubt, many
other parts of the world, for years to come. The result of the conference,
then, was a survey of the various fruitful paths that lead away from the starting point provided by *Imagined Communities.*

Before turning to the essays produced by the spring 2000 conference on
Reading and Writing the Nation in Nineteenth-Century Latin America, let
us make a systematic approach to the matter of Latin American national
identities. Our agenda follows: first establish an explicit frame of reference,
some background on the evolution of collective identities in Latin America;
second, provide detail on our assessment of Anderson's seminal book as it
relates specifically to the study of nationalism and national identities in
Latin America; and third, a look at how new studies of the problem are going beyond *Imagined Communities.*

In 1800, on the eve of the wars of independence, Spanish and Portuguese
territories in America were brimming with an ethnic complexity destined to
complicate future attempts to create cohesive national communities. The
Iberians themselves were a diverse lot. Symptomatically, the Spanish colo-

---

2. On newspapers, see François-Xavier Guerra's contribution to this volume and
Fernando Unzueta's "Periodicos y formación nacional: Bolivia en sus primeros años,"
Latin American Research Review 35 (2000): 35–72. While Guerra persuasively questions the importance of print media in defining national identities before independence,
he affirms its function to that effect during the wars of independence, and Unzueta does
the same for the first republican generation.

nizers of Latin America often referred to their homeland in the plural, speaking of "the Spains."[3] The northern half of the Iberian Peninsula, with its regional languages or dialects, and the southern half, with its strong Moorish influence, presented a veritable mosaic of cultures. Immeasurably augmenting this diversity in the New World (so-called, and not without some reason given the unprecedented societies created there) was the confluence of Iberian with African and indigenous American populations. Indigenous people and enslaved African people together comprised a majority in the region as a whole in 1800, and these non-European groups were even more ethnically complex than the Iberians.

The slaves—particularly numerous in Brazil and the Caribbean—were from widely separated parts of Africa and represented countless ethnic affiliations, grouped in colonial usage often by their African port of origin in the slave trade or by broad geographic terms, including Congos, Benguelas, Mozambiques, Angolas, Mandingos, to name only a few. These groups, each of which lumped together a number of African ethnicities, were usually called "nations," *naciones* or *nações,* in Spanish or Portuguese. Completely uprooted from their native villages, kin groups, and tribes, enslaved Africans were forming new identities as they gathered to dance and socialize as Congos, Benguelas, or Mozambiques on Sundays and church holidays. In the festival of Corpus Christi, when official symbolism called for a parade representing the constituent elements of the imperial body politic, African nations were expected to display their "national" dances in the streets. Overall, African slaves and their descendants in Latin America preserved more "Old World" antecedents in their "New World" identities than was the case in the United States—perhaps because the Iberians allowed them greater freedom, as has often been claimed, but surely, too, because of a greater intensity and longer duration of the slave trade.[4]

Indigenous people formed the demographic core of the Spanish American population before independence, and they too represented many different "nations." In the sixteenth century, indigenous people had been segregated by the Spanish crown into a "Republic of Indians"—not a separate

3. See François-Xavier Guerra, "Identidad y soberanía: una relación compleja," in *Las revoluciones hispanicas: independencias americanas y liberalismo español,* ed. François-Xavier Guerra et al. (Madrid: Editorial Complutense, 1995).

4. Good looks at the phenomenon in widely separated parts of Latin America are George Reid Andrews, *The Afro-Argentines of Buenos Aires, 1800–1900* (Madison: University of Wisconsin Press, 1984); and Fernando Ortiz, *Los cabildos y la fiesta afrocubanos del Día de Reyes* (Havana: Editorial de Ciencias Sociales, 1992).

territory but a parallel society organized in administratively designated "Indian towns" where Iberian colonizers were not to intrude. Despite the colonizers' constant use of the umbrella term "Indians," indigenous people were slow to assign much importance to that category, which assumed a common identity among indigenous groups who felt as remote from each other as might Scots from Slovaks or Sicilians. For the most part, indigenous people presented themselves as Indians only when that brought them a specific advantage in interactions with the colonizers. Otherwise, they long remained Nahuas or Aymaras, Quiché Mayas or Tupinambás, according to their own sense of ethnic identity.[5]

Not only did the colonization of Latin America bring together three racial groups, each of which was riven internally by ethnic diversity, but additional ethnic differences also emerged as a result of the process of colonization. For example, the process of colonization displaced many indigenous people and separated them from their tribal origins. Indigenous migrants in the Andes, called *forasteros,* created significant population shifts as old communities withered in the face of colonial exploitation and new ones sprang up elsewhere.[6] Centuries of Portuguese slaving and missionizing in the Amazon region created a floating population (literally and figuratively) of detribalized indigenous people called *tapuios,* who lived independently along the banks of the fluvial maze, moved about in canoes, and often spoke only Nheengatu, a kind of Amazonian Esperanto, a composite of indigenous languages cobbled together by Jesuit missionaries and spoken, at one time, throughout Brazil.[7]

Racial mixing was another source of new distinctions born of colonization. The Spanish and Portuguese invaders were overwhelmingly male, and large numbers of biracial children resulted from their sexual encounters with African and indigenous women. The rapine of conquest played its ugly part, but the historian also encounters frequent tales of helpless Iberian castaways who were adopted by indigenous people and fathered literally scores of children among them. The Iberian crowns generally tried to discourage this racial mixing, even prohibiting it legally in some cases, but they never

5. It is interesting to note that, by the same token, most indigenous terms for "outsider"—such as *misti* in the Andes—crowd nonindigenous people into a single category as well.

6. Karen Vieira Powers, *Andean Journeys: Migration, Ethnogenesis, and the State in Colonial Quito* (Albuquerque: University of New Mexico Press, 1995).

7. See Carlos de Araujo Moreira Neto, *Indios da Amazônia, de maioria a minoria (1750–1850)* (Petrópolis: Editôra Vozes, 1988).

succeeded in stopping it. People of mixed race occupied, at first, an uncomfortably marginal position—not European, not indigenous, not African—but by 1800 they constituted perhaps a quarter of the population. Mixed-race (Spanish *mestizo* or Portuguese *mestiço*) became, not a single category, but a congeries of categories corresponding to each individual's particular combination of ancestry. Progressive intermarriage multiplied the possibilities in each generation.[8]

Race mixing thus inexorably undermined the caste system through which the colonizing powers tried to govern. The right to wear certain clothes or occupy certain offices, for example, was reserved for whites. Indigenous people had to pay a special head tax, and so on. Children born to parents of different caste fell between categories and confounded the system, so more categories were created to accommodate them. The strains were most obvious in Spanish America, where official racial categories multiplied alarmingly in the late colonial period, reaching a half dozen in common use and several dozen in theory. What category for a person whose grandparents were a Portuguese, a Benguela, a Tupi, and a mulatto? While some have viewed this as the zenith of the caste system, it was more like a desperate last hurrah.[9]

In addition, over the course of three centuries of colonization a substantial class of American-born whites, the Creoles, arose, and comprised a very irregularly distributed fifth to a quarter of the population. In the eighteenth century, reinvigorated Iberian monarchies tried to tighten their imperial control over their American colonies, and men born in Spain or Portugal— detached from local roots and presumably more loyal to imperial purposes—seemed better agents of those purposes. An administrative policy of systematic preferment for European-born whites raised bitter resentment among the American-born whites. The general ideology of European colonization in America included ideas about the biological superiority of European organisms—crops and animals, as well as people—as well as the notion that transplantation of European organisms to tropical America brought inevitable degeneration. Spanish *peninsulares* and Portuguese *reinóis* (as the European born were called) never tired of citing the profligacy and in-

8. Magnus Morner, *Race Mixture in the History of Latin America* (Boston: Little, Brown, 1964) has long been the standard account.

9. Claudio Esteva Fabregat, *Mestizaje in Ibero-America* (Tucson: University of Arizona Press, 1995) is more quantitative and more recent but not an improvement on Morner.

dolence of American-born ne'er-do-wells as a case in point, and they often added innuendoes of racial impurity to their imputations of environmental determinism.[10]

Finally, a profusion of Latin American provincial identities grew up during the colonial period. To begin with, the Spanish had gravitated toward large indigenous populations, and their most successful tactic of colonization involved, in essence, taking over preexisting indigenous tribute systems, so the indigenous "provinces" that organized those tribute systems carried over to the colonizer's administrative map. This gave some provincial identities in Spanish America pre-Columbian roots—roots that, on the other hand existed nowhere in Brazil, where forest- or plains-dwelling tribal people had no such large tribute systems to be co-opted. The Brazilian provincial map was initiated by a different process of colonization, parceling out neat parallel strips of fertile coastal plain for sugar plantations to be worked by uprooted African slaves. With or without an indigenous substratum, Spanish American and Brazilian provinces had been given more or less permanent shape by 1800.[11]

In the last years of the colonial period, feelings of territorial belonging among Spanish Americans and Brazilians were more focused on provinces than on larger administrative structures such as viceroyalties. Significantly, common names designating people's place of origin referred to provinces rather than viceroyalties. Inhabitants of the viceroyalty of New Spain would identify as *poblanos* or *yucatecos* or *veracruzanos,* for example, according to their province of birth, avoiding the forced, erudite-sounding name *novohispano* that corresponded to the viceroyalty of New Spain as a whole. On the eve of independence, most people in Spanish or Portuguese America said *patria* (fatherland) for the province where they were born.[12]

After 1808, the movements for independence gave the word "patria" its modern meaning. Now the patria could be of any size, from subcontinental Brazil to province-sized Uruguay, but always it was a territorial identity that

10. Anthony Pagden, *European Encounters with the New World from the Renaissance to Romanticism* (New Haven, CT: Yale University Press, 1993).

11. The primary subsequent change has been the gradual subdivision of large provinces as populations grew. These subdivisions have added new lines to the map and created new provinces, but almost never have old provinces and local identities been erased. See James Lockhart and Stuart B. Schwartz, *Early Latin America: A History of Colonial Spanish America and Brazil* (Cambridge: Cambridge University Press, 1983).

12. Roderick Barman, *Brazil: The Forging of a Nation, 1798–1852* (Stanford: Stanford University Press, 1988).

coincided, or was supposed to coincide, with a single nation. The territorial limits of the patria defined, or were supposed to define, a sovereign people, the essential foundation of republican legitimacy. Those born within it felt, or were supposed to feel a powerful affinity. Those who shared the new national identity shared, or were supposed to share, the rights and obligations of citizenship, including a relatively broad male suffrage.[13] The nationalism associated with this definition of patria—more aspiration than fact at first—is the nationalism to which Benedict Anderson refers in his chapter on Latin America, entitled "Creole Pioneers." A period of turbulent struggle created a dozen such aspirations on a republican model between 1810 and 1825 (when the continent broke away from Spain and Portugal) and continuing struggle created a half dozen more aspiring nations before mid-century.

The wars of independence themselves powerfully shaped national identities in Latin America. Every successful independence movement in the hemisphere played the nativist card, proclaiming "America for the Americans!" The spread of nativism reflects above all its tactical utility for leaders of independence in situations of decolonization. With rare exception, patriot leaders were members of the native-born white minority who sought, not to remake colonial society, but to assume control of it themselves. Independence promised them above all the opportunity to wrest political and economic privileges away from those born in Spain or Portugal. Their main problem was the other four-fifths of the population—the slaves, mixed-race, and indigenous people whose continued subjection defined those privileges and who had scant incentive to endorse the narrow interests of the native-born whites. Feelings of inclusive belonging were weak in this situation. The nativist formula—America for the Americans—addressed this difficulty by rhetorically asserting affinities among the vast native-born majority in contradistinction to a vulnerable, neatly defined enemy. Focus on a common enemy had tremendous political utility in the creation of broad political alliances because, unlike problematical aspirations of national solidarity, anti-Spanish and anti-Portuguese sentiments were something (Latin) Americans of all social classes did indeed share. Thus, the nativism of the military struggles against Spain and Portugal was largely an "Americanism" that differentiated little among American nations.[14]

13. See, for example, Hilda Sabato, *The Many and the Few: Political Participation in Republican Buenos Aires* (Stanford: Stanford University Press, 2001).
14. Guerra, "Identidad y soberanía," 229–231.

Bolívar drew the nativist line with paradigmatic clarity in his 1813 declaration of "War to the Death," promising clemency for all of American birth, though they oppose independence, while announcing no quarter for the European born, though they seek neutrality. Mexico's wars of independence began with a massive insurrection of peasant armies that marched under the banner of Mexico's Virgin of Guadalupe and shouted "Death to the Spaniards!" as their principal battle cry. Nativist agitation remained the most volatile aspect of Mexican politics, the country's political "hot button," for a long decade thereafter. Likewise in Argentina, nativist identification with the independence movement carried over strongly into the politics of the 1830s and 1840s.[15] Peruvian elites were the slowest on the continent to embrace independence precisely because indigenous rebels had already used nativist themes to convulse much of the Andean highlands during the 1780s in the famous revolts led by Tupac Amaru. But after patriot armies from Venezuela and Colombia defeated and captured Peru's last Spanish viceroy in 1824, the Peruvian elite found nativist postures useful in expelling Venezuelan and Colombian armies as foreign interlopers. In Brazil, nativism provided the central logic for separation from Portugal in 1822, and then brought the downfall of Brazil's first emperor (Pedro I, accused of surrounding himself with ministers born in Portugal) nine years later. During the years 1835 to 1845, a string of provincial nativist uprisings temporarily imperiled the territorial unity of Brazil.[16]

Once the Spanish and Portuguese presence had been purged, nativist agitation focused on finer distinctions, now differentiating "us" from "them" among the native born. Thus, Argentine populists baited cosmopolitan elites (Francophiles or Anglophiles) despite their native birth.[17] At issue now, in addition to birth, was culture. Without exception, the aspiring new nation-states had been founded on a premise—a fiction full of ulterior motives, but still a key premise—of profound cultural affinity. Now feelings of affinity

15. An excellent overview of Latin America in this period is provided by Tulio Halperín-Donghi, *The Contemporary History of Latin America* (Durham, NC: Duke University Press, 1993).

16. John Lynch provides the standard English-language synthesis of the independence period. For more on Central America, see Ralph Lee Woodward, *Central America, a Nation Divided* (Oxford: Oxford University Press, 1976). On Brazil, see Barman, *Brazil: The Forging of a Nation.*

17. A famous literary evocation of this bating is Esteban Echeverría's short story, "The Slaughterhouse," now standard in the Argentine canon for the early nineteenth century.

had to be nurtured if the new nations were to survive for long. The years between 1830 and 1850 were dominated by an identity politics that has always been hard to explain in terms of formal ideology or economic interest. Patriot leaders ruled almost everywhere in Latin America for a generation after independence. Gradually, the wars of independence and their heroes became important reference points in the imaginative construction of new nationhood.[18] In addition, clothes, accent, music, dance, and food gained salience as markers of national identity. Nativists produced a lot of political satire in dialect and directed suspicion against anyone heedless of national customs. Such heedlessness betokened lack of patriotism or even suspicious foreign influence.[19]

Of course, traditional folkways varied considerably from province to province, and virtually all the new states contained more than one province. If folkways defined a nation, then many provinces could aspire to nationhood for themselves, and more than one nativist movement attempted to form a breakaway republic. Several such breakaway attempts failed in Brazil, although one, the Republic of Piratini lasted almost a decade. In Spanish America, many second-stage breakaways became permanent: Venezuela, Ecuador, Honduras, El Salvador, Nicaragua, and Costa Rica. Yucatán failed in separating from Mexico, but Texas succeeded. As for Colombia, its intense preoccupation with regional folkways corresponds to the quasi-national status of its federated provinces in the mid-nineteenth century. Even leaders without a regionalist agenda (much less secessionist ambitions) often gained political legitimacy by demonstrating a personal affinity for the folkways of their province of origin.[20]

Spanish American and Brazilian nationalists have continued, ever after, to elaborate nativist themes in everything from history, poetry, and fiction, to music and folk dance movements. The systematic designation of "typical" dishes and peasant costumes, for example, the energy invested in them, and the pride with which they are displayed to foreigners, go far beyond

18. Pantheons of independence heroes are among the clearly modular aspects of Spanish American nationalism. For a broad interpretation of their importance in world nationalism, see Anthony D. Smith, *The Ethnic Origin of Nations* (New York: Basil Blackwell, 1986).

19. See, for example, John Charles Chasteen, "Patriotic Footwork: Social Dance and the Watershed of Independence in Buenos Aires," in *State and Society in Spanish America during the Age of Revolution,* ed. Victor M. Uribe Urán (Wilmington, DE: Scholarly Resources, 2001).

20. Halperín, *The Contemporary History of Latin America,* 74–114.

analogous activities in the United States. The ethnic and geographic diversity of Latin American rural life provides the raw materials for these markers of collective identity, but a history of political nativism gives them special prominence.[21] In addition, the energetic elaboration of these markers of identity responds to a continuing need for evocations of nationhood, because the construction of really inclusive national communities has been arduous and halting.

Overall, Latin America's contemporary nation-states consolidated themselves only after 1850. The onset of export-driven economic growth, a regionwide trend from the 1870s on, helped unify national elites. Export growth produced newly robust tax revenues, providing resources necessary for the creation of social infrastructure and state institutions like effective national bureaucracies, school systems that reached beyond capital cities, and disciplined armies and police forces. New technologies of weaponry (such as long-range rifles), of transportation (such as railroads and steamships), and of communication (such as telegraph lines that connected Latin American capitals to Europe and to their own hinterlands) strengthened modernizing central governments. Latin Americanists have tended to emphasize the importance of state consolidation as a precondition for inculcating a widely shared vision of national identity. Many would go so far as to say that "true nationalism" is a twentieth-century phenomenon in Latin America.

Anderson's chapter on Creole pioneers fits uneasily into the framework just sketched. Most importantly, Anderson's premise that a national consciousness preceded the wars of independence and defined the boundaries of the resulting independent republics is entirely at variance with the consensus of Latin Americanist historians and critics.[22] Latin Americanist historians and literary scholars insist that these nations remained more aspiration than fact for many decades after gaining independence between 1810 and 1825; that, contrary to the situation in Europe, "states preceded nations" in Latin America; and that, reversing the more familiar model of irredentism, they long remained "states in search of nationhood." In most tellings,

21. Angel Rama, *The Lettered City,* trans. and ed. John Charles Chasteen (Durham, NC: Duke University Press, 1996), 50–73.

22. Anderson's entire view of Latin America rests on a breathtakingly narrow evidentiary base, relying, for the most part, on just two books. By all appearances, Anderson's chief sources on Latin American independence are John Lynch, *The Spanish American Revolutions, 1808–1826* (New York: Norton, 1973), and Gerhard Masur's egregiously outdated *Simón Bolívar* (Albuquerque: University of New Mexico Press, 1948).

Latin American nationalisms were elite projects that gradually "deepened," in social terms, only after the collapse of the 1870–1930 export boom, which had maintained landowning oligarchies in power without need of a vigorous nationalist ideology. Only in the mid-twentieth century, runs the Latin Americanist consensus, did mass political participation make nations compelling communities in the imagination of most Latin Americans.

In *Imagined Communities,* the chapter on Creole pioneers outlines two specific mechanisms whereby a national consciousness supposedly emerged much earlier during the eighteenth century, and became robust enough to define the limits of new republics in the early nineteenth century. In the collective view of the Reading and Writing the Nation conference, however, Anderson's argument does not bear close inspection.

The first of these mechanisms is the circulation of colonial bureaucrats. Beginning from Victor Turner's work on the meaning-creating quality of journeys, Anderson argues that colonial bureaucratic careers were circumscribed by territorial limits that later defined nations. For example, according to Anderson's argument a Mexican-born colonial functionary might be posted to Tampico or Guadalajara or Oaxaca, but never to Havana or Guatemala City. As a result, the functionaries came to understand these limits as defining their political community. This is an interesting idea that must have a kernel of truth. Creole bureaucrats no doubt had careers that were much less wide-ranging than did Spanish- or Portuguese-born bureaucrats within their respective seaborne empires. But did Creole functionaries range uniformly within colonial territories neatly coterminous with the later independent republics? Just what were the bureaucratic posts upon which Anderson places so much interpretive emphasis? Roughly what numbers were involved? Anderson provides not one specific example and not one iota of evidence or documentation in support of his assertion. One might argue that all the evidence is not in, but recent research would seem to undermine, rather than support his thesis, and it clearly provides no indication of a systematic correspondence between the circulation of Creole bureaucrats and the territorial definition of subsequently independent nations.[23]

The second mechanism of territorial definition suggested by Anderson is the circulation of colonial newspapers. In line with his overall emphasis on the role of the print media, Anderson asserts that colonial newspapers constituted a defining opportunity for readers to imagine themselves as part of a community that shared a concern with the particulars appearing in the paper.

23. Anderson, *Imagined Communities,* 57. See Guerra's contribution to this volume.

"The newspaper of Caracas quite naturally, even apolitically, created an imagined community among a specific assemblage of fellow readers to whom [the mentioned] ships, brides, bishops, and prices, belonged."[24] This illustrative reference to "the newspaper of Caracas" has vivid concreteness, but Anderson is not really referring to a specific paper here. Only a tiny handful of the kind of newspapers he describes existed in Spanish America before independence. This second interesting idea, like the first, rests on no specific evidence whatsoever. Literary scholars in attendance at the conference suggested an important role for reading in the development of Latin American nationalism, but not in the original territorial definition of its republics.

A better explanation of that territorial definition would claim less for the two specific mechanisms highlighted by Anderson and more for the larger phenomenon of which both are part. On the eve of independence, both bureaucrats and newspapers circulated within a general territorial framework that was not their creation, a colonial framework that was, in fact, already centuries old. The wars of independence broke the colonial viceroyalties apart, but always along existing administrative lines, into fragments that had been, themselves, units of colonial governance. The new republican map of Latin America contained almost no totally new boundaries. Disputed areas tended to be precisely those that had remained ill-defined before independence. In sum, explaining the creation of a dozen, and then twenty, Spanish American nations is largely a matter of explaining how errant provinces (also "presidencies" and "kingdoms") were able to break away from former viceregal capitals. These explanations have something to do with the Creole's social world as imagined by Anderson before independence, but also with economic, political, and military concerns arising after 1810—matters that Anderson disregards utterly. No single principle accounts for the phenomenon as a whole. Certainly, nothing in the historical literature suggests the "decisive historical role" that Anderson assigns to colonial newspapers and "pilgrim creole functionaries."[25]

In fairness, the chapter on Creole pioneers was never intended to be a complete description of Spanish American independence. *Imagined Communities* is a synthetic, interpretive work that reaches across centuries and around the globe. The book's chapter on Latin America serves to advance a bold overarching interpretation, which, in preceding chapters, focused on the historical interaction of print and linguistic diversity in Europe. In con-

24. Anderson, *Imagined Communities,* 62.
25. Ibid., 65.

trast to nation builders in Europe, Anderson's Creole pioneers were imagining nations in a colonial context, nations not set apart from others by a distinctive print language or claims of a unique common descent.[26] Anderson argues that the creation of a dozen such new "nations," all more or less at once, each with a similar set of institutions (flag, citizenship, constituent assembly, constitution, representative legislature, presidency, and so on), made the national republic a well-defined template, a soon-to-become standard model of sovereignty, "capable of being aspired to early on, rather than a slowly sharpening frame of vision."[27] From there, Anderson moves quickly on to discuss the "pirating" of this model by imperialists; its expressions in literature, maps, museums, censuses, and public monuments; and, eventually, its universal adoption throughout the postcolonial world. Nothing said at our conference, Reading and Writing the Nation in Nineteenth-Century Latin America, called that overall interpretation into question. We agreed that while other scholars had noted that nation was a social construction, rather than a primordial fact, no one had explored the nationalist imagination as provocatively as Anderson.

Anderson's remarks on Latin America per se have had little impact in Latin American studies. Reference to the chapter on Creole pioneers rarely appears in Latin Americanist citations of Anderson. Instead, Latin Americanists cite *Imagined Communities* to invoke the book's overall interpretive project and (especially among critics) draw on his theorization of the central role of the print media in imagining national communities. Almost always, Latin Americanists are pursuing something that Anderson left out of the Creole pioneers chapter altogether—not the territorial outlines but the specific content of Latin American nationalisms. Our great problem is not how Brazil or Ecuador came to be called nations, but just what *nation* meant to Brazilians and Ecuadorians of diverse social, regional, racial, and cultural descriptions. Furthermore, Latin Americanists show a special interest in the *contested* meanings of nationalism, a matter out of Anderson's purview altogether.

Each of the following chapters goes beyond *Imagined Communities* to investigate the formation of social identities in nineteenth-century Latin America. First are the historians.

François-Xavier Guerra, a specialist on the Spanish American independence period, critiques Anderson's argument on the role of circulating

26. Ibid., 46–47.
27. Ibid., 67, 81, 135.

bureaucrats and newspapers. He finds that the print capitalism that looms so large in *Imagined Communities* played only a small part in political communication before the wars of independence began in Latin America. The point is emblematic because, while correcting Anderson's chronology, Guerra also gives fresh evidence of the powerful link between print and nationalism. The independence movements themselves introduced or radically expanded the role of print throughout the region during the years after 1808. The spotlight therefore moves to the struggles of independence themselves and to their turbulent aftermath.

Tulio Halperín-Donghi argues that in the Argentine case, the new nation was imagined in partisan terms, so much so, that party upstaged nation as a primary locus of collective identity. Given the frequency of partisan civil war in nineteenth-century Latin America, this situation was fairly common. The most intense political affiliations in people's lives were often partisan rather than national. The frequency of partisan civil war in nineteenth-century Latin America charged partisan loyalties with affective power. International wars, those great engines of nationalism, on the other hand, were infrequent. More often than nations, it was political parties that asked nineteenth-century Latin Americans to kill for kith and kin. Nation defined only the arena in which the contest was waged.

Sarah C. Chambers examines the competing claims of loyalty—party, region, nation—negotiated by early nineteenth-century women, asking how engagement with large imagined communities played out in the face-to-face communities of daily experience. Abstractions like imagined communities were easily invoked by essayists, orators, and novelists, but what did they mean in the lives of ordinary people? It was the intention of the conference to ask consistently how nations were "read" as well as how they were "written." Chambers finds politically active women, women who were most assuredly readers, and also writers (especially of letters), less attuned to abstractions, more attentive to networks of kin, allies, and clients. This pattern probably held for most people, male and female, outside the narrow political elites of nineteenth-century Latin America.

Andrew Kirkendall's study of student culture at Latin America's institutions of higher education reminds us of the continuing influence after independence of a lettered elite, what Angel Rama called *The Lettered City,* social specialists in reading and writing. Kirkendall shows how the cultivation of literary culture legitimated an elite sense of privilege within Latin America's post-colonial nations. The students described by Kirkendall were the people who "wrote the nation," and their special concern was the creation of national literatures. And whatever their literary aspirations, many of these students were destined in practice to become circulating functionaries like those described in *Imagined Communities*. These, too, are post-independence developments, however.

Among the critics who contributed to our reassessment, Fernando Unzueta explores how nineteenth-century romantic novels played on the heartstrings of their relatively large, and often feminine, readership. Perhaps more than any other source of the period, such novels illustrate how the Latin American search for unifying national identities imaginatively negotiated the racial and regional diversity inherent to the region. Of all the participants in the conference, Unzueta focuses most steadily on the print media themselves, and his fine-grained examination does lend some support to Anderson's contention concerning the role of colonial newspapers. Yet the novels to which Unzueta gives primary interpretive emphasis—as well he might, since the idea of nation was central to so many—were an overwhelmingly nineteenth-century phenomenon. Once again, the main development of Latin America's imagined communities turns out to be a post-colonial story.

The other three critics all discussed materials that are not part of traditional literary canons. Interestingly, it was these critics, rather than the historians, who examined the construction of a national past. Origins are, after all, normally a crucial reference point in the construction of social identities. Latin American nations are no exceptions to this rule, as the assiduous historical, literary, and artistic elaboration of their foundational myths makes abundantly evident.

Both Sara Castro-Klarén and Gustavo Verdesio[28] explore nineteenth-century encounters with the pre-Columbian past. Castro-Klarén's chapter shows how vigorously nineteenth-century Andean texts moved to appropriate the splendors of an indigenous past for their national narratives. It certainly made sense that they do so, given the undeniable testimony to those splendors still present in Inca and pre-Inca ruins. Yet any attempt to incorporate indigenous origins into nineteenth-century nationalist imaginings was inevitably complicated by post-colonial Latin American attitudes about the superiority of everything European over everything American. Verdesio, on the other hand, suggests that when the indigenous past was less imposing, as in Uruguay, where only low mounds betrayed the former presence of Charrúa people, a viable alternative solution was to erase the past

28. Verdesio is the one contributor to this volume who was not present at the conference.

altogether. Costa Rica and, on a larger scale, Argentina, more or less follow
this pattern. Given the pervasive importance of indigenous genes in Latin
American populations, of course, total erasure was rarely an option, although partial erasure was frequent. Together, the chapters by Castro-
Klarén and Verdesio illustrate the range of possibilities.

Finally, Beatriz González-Stephan draws attention to additional mechanisms whereby national elites advanced their projects of nation building in
the second half of the nineteenth century, creating carefully styled national
pavilions for the period's numerous "universal expositions" and publishing
voluminous and richly illustrated literary histories to represent new national
cultures. Expositions offer an especially rich vein of study, both because of
their frequency in the closing decades of the century and because their national pavilions were so explicitly representations of the nation—representations prepared with a heightened awareness of the European "gaze," that
imagined audience so devastatingly influential in the collective mind of
nineteenth-century Latin American elites.

Neither ruins nor expositions are outside the limits of *Imagined Communities,* but they do not figure in its account of the emergence of Latin
American nationalism. In going beyond what Anderson says about Latin
America, the critics were often drawing on, or at least echoing, elements of
his overall interpretation. In confirming that the production and circulation
of print defined a national consciousness in important ways, the critics
showed why Anderson has been more persuasive, overall, in critical than in
historical studies of nineteenth-century Latin America.

Together, the contributions bring the nineteenth-century Latin American
enterprise of reading and writing the nation into clearer focus by indicating
the value and limitations of Benedict Anderson's interpretation for our current understanding of that enterprise. Anyone formerly tempted to cite
Imagined Communities for an authoritative description of the origins of
Latin American national identities will hopefully now banish the thought.
On the other hand, anyone inspired by the book's call to explore the imaginative and emotive dimensions of modern nationalism can benefit from the
new trails blazed by our contributors. The influence of manuscript (rather
than print) in the late colonial period; the vital formative experience of the
wars of independence themselves; the competition of other imagined communities, such as warring political parties; the enduring hegemonic sway
of an elitist "lettered city"; the intersection of imagined with immediate,
face-to-face communities; the "foundational fictions" embodied in roman-

tic novels; the thorny problem of how to integrate (or exorcise) an indigenous past; and the compulsive stock taking of late nineteenth-century exhibitions and literary histories—all invite further study. Anderson's argument about the territorial definition of Latin American nations proved only the starting point of the conference, most of which was not concerned with territorial definitions.

The Historians

1

Forms of Communication, Political Spaces, and Cultural Identities in the Creation of Spanish American Nations

François-Xavier Guerra

Before entering fully into the matter at hand, I would like to address Anderson's explanation of the creation of nations in Spanish America. My aim is not a sweeping condemnation of Anderson's work—valuable in many ways, and above all in its fortunate title, *Imagined Communities*—but only a critique of its validity regarding the formation of Spanish American nations.

Anderson puts the issue of language, along with that of the press and print capitalism, at the center of his argument. In this view, the invention of the printing press had allowed vernacular languages to upstage Latin, Europe's sacred language, in the constitution of new communities. While such a shift may help explain nationalist movements in some places, Spanish America is not one of them. To the contrary, the Spanish language, with its precocious standardization and administrative and literary development, always constituted a strength, and never a weakness, of the Spanish monarchy.

Translated from Spanish by John Charles Chasteen.

Because language did not distinguish Europe's colonizing powers from their American colonies, Anderson seeks other explanations for the formation of New World republics, a search all the more crucial because they were among the first anywhere founded, in principle, as nation-states. Anderson's thinking on "Creole pioneers" would seem applicable to all the Americas, but oddly it focuses on Spanish America only, the United States entering only to provide an analogous example. Anderson's concern is not so much the emergence of independence movements as the plural, national form of those movements. Depending, for this assessment, on a small bibliography quite traditional in its approach, Anderson asserts the existence prior to 1808 of Creole independence movements in various Spanish American regions, movements based on social and economic grievances. He tends to assume that this regionalization constitutes prima facie evidence of the emergence of nations, a risky assumption, given that medieval European history provides so many examples of territorial entities, some even called republics, that were far from being nations in the modern sense of that word.

In other words, Anderson's argument takes for granted that before 1808 Spanish America had quietly and informally divided into national communities aspiring to independence—a proposition problematical indeed. How, in this view, could one explain the paradoxes that serve as starting points for most current analyses of Spanish American independence? If Creole elites already thought in national terms before 1808, why did they not take the opportunity presented, in that year, by the Napoleonic occupation of Spain and the captivity of the Spanish king to proclaim their independence? How can one then explain the overwhelming wave of Spanish American loyalty to the imprisoned Spanish sovereign and the support—financial, and not merely theoretical—which Creole leaders provided to their Peninsular brothers? Why was the word *nation* so rarely used (except in Chile and New Spain) in the subsequent discourse of independence, while references to *América,* on the other hand, were so frequent? And how, above all, could one explain that, once independence had been gained, one of the greatest problems was defining the new nations?

Anderson sums up his proposed causes for the formation of new national identities in Latin America in the conclusion of the chapter: "It was the pilgrimages of Creole functionaries and the presses of Creole publishers that played a decisive historical role in accomplishing that task."[1]

1. Benedict Anderson, *L'imaginaire national* (Paris: La Découverte, 1996), 75.

Let us leave aside the first "cause," which is indefensible in light of what we now know about the operations of royal administration in colonial Spanish America. The careers of Creole functionaries were not limited territorially in the manner indicated by Anderson, any more than Iberian functionaries remained aloof from local involvement. This vision would seem to be a transposition to colonial Spanish America of Anderson's knowledge of colonial administration in Southeast Asia during the nineteenth and twentieth centuries. Current studies of the family networks that linked Creoles and Peninsulars—and, thanks to those links, united the various regions of the Spanish monarchy—were not available when *Imagined Communities* appeared.[2]

With the second "cause," the operations of Creole printing presses, we enter fully into the topic at hand. According to Anderson, although printing presses had existed in Spanish America since the sixteenth century, publishing did not develop significantly until the eighteenth century, when Creole printers discovered a new source of income, the newspaper. Newspapers supposedly then became the key to cultural and community life, an affirmation advanced through reference to the experience of the British colonies in North America and then projected onto Spanish America by the assertion that an "analogous" process occurred there during the second half of the eighteenth century.[3] The example of Caracas theoretically illustrates the way in which a new national "we" was imagined. In this scenario, newspapers supplied especially local news: marriages, price lists, the arrivals and departures of ships or bishops. As time passed, the Creole readers of Caracas supposedly developed an apolitical awareness of the restricted community within which these particular marriages, prices, and communications mattered. Finally, Anderson alleges that Peninsular residents of Caracas did not read the local paper, further accenting the process of differentiation between them and the Creoles.

The problem is that virtually every step of this argument is false. It is true that the number of newspapers increased in Spanish America during the second half of the eighteenth century, but there was no explosive growth of the press analogous to what occurred in the British colonies. Anderson's chosen example, Caracas, makes the contrary point with spectacular clar-

2. See, for example, Michel Bertrand, *Grandeur et misère de l'office: Les officiers de finances de Nouvelle-Espagne, XVIIe-XVIIIe siécles* (Paris: Publications de la Sorbonne, 1999), or Jean Paul Zúñiga, *Espagnols d'outre-mer. Emigration, reproduction sociale et mentalités à Santiago du Chili au XVIIe siécle* (Ph.D. diss., Institut Universitaire Européen de Florence, 1995).
3. Anderson, *L'imaginaire national,* 72.

ity. The first printing press and the first newspaper of Caracas date only from 1808, the very same year in which the crisis of the Spanish monarchy began. How then—and how rapidly—did the consciousness of a new national "we" develop? Was the resulting imagined community Caracas or Venezuela? And the case of Chile is even more challenging to Anderson's assertions. There the first press and first newspaper did not begin to operate until 1812, when a local junta had already assumed power.

In other places, where newspapers had existed for a longer period, neither their content nor their circulation matches the description given in *Imagined Communities.* The most important part of those papers was not the local news, where that figured at all. These were erudite periodicals devoted to literature, geography, science, and technology. In some respects, as with matters of local patriotism or geographic description of the "kingdom" or "province," they dealt with identity much more directly than did the local news trivia mentioned by Anderson. Almost nowhere do they seem to have been profitable business ventures. To the contrary, many of them folded precisely because of economic difficulties associated with the narrowness of the reading public. That happened, for example, to both *El Papel Periódico de Santa Fé de Bogotá* and to *El Mercurio Peruano.*[4] Only in New Spain, in the years immediately preceding the crisis of 1808 does one begin to find real newspapers (even in some regional cities such as Veracruz) that correspond, at least in part, to Anderson's description. But this is too late for such publications to have generated a sense of national identity before the impending crisis of the monarchy erupted in 1808. The real explosion of the press in the Spanish-speaking world occurred precisely during that crisis.

I do not mean to imply that local and regional identities did not exist in Spanish America by the late eighteenth century, only that periodical publications and the expansion of the print market did not create those identities and that they were not yet *national* in character. There were, in fact, a number of different sorts of overlapping territorial identities in the late colonial period, many of them mutually incompatible. Nestled inside one another like a set of Russian dolls were the jurisdictions of *pueblos,* then of principal cities (sometimes called *provincias*), and then, in some places, the ter-

---

4. On the economic difficulties faced by these publications, see Jean Pierre Clément, *El Mercurio Peruano, 1790–1795* (Frankfurt/Madrid: Vervuert-Iberoamericana, 1997); Renán Silva, *Prensa y revolución a finales del Siglo XVIII* (Bogotá: Banco de la República, 1988).

ritories of colonial "kingdoms" or *reinos,* followed by the Crown of Castile and, at the broadest level, by the Spanish monarchy as a whole. Distinct, elaborated cultural identities only partly paralleled these territorial divisions. Reinos did not exist in the Río de la Plata or Venezuela, nor in most of New Granada. In addition, there was a powerful cultural distinction (of little political content before the crisis of 1808) made between Spanish Peninsulars and people of American birth, crosscutting all of the above.[5]

Reading and Writing in a Baroque Society

The relationship between writing and identity is not a simple one. Although writing facilitates communication and, in the right circumstances, the creation of group consciousness and a common repertoire of images, it is not the only medium that can do these things. In societies without writing, or societies in which writing is a minority activity reserved for a cultural elite, other mechanisms permit the constitution and affirmation of the group. Spanish American societies lay somewhere between the two extremes. Writing was far from a universal medium, but neither was it so rare as some believe. First, in many Spanish American cities, and particularly in New Spain, the growing number of schools had spread literacy fairly widely. Secondly, even in regions such as the Andes where literacy rates were apparently lower, writing was not limited to narrow elite circles but, to the contrary, present to some extent at all social levels. On the other hand, as in other societies of baroque culture, images and rituals occupied a central place in the communication systems of late colonial Spanish America and, consequently, in any affirmation of collective images and values. Images and rituals were politically as important as writing well into the independence period, and no study of the creation of national identities can be complete without consideration of them.

Let us consider, for example, the role played in New Spain by paintings and other graphic representations, from the innumerable images of the Virgin of Guadalupe—expression and medium of diffusion of a cult central to

---

5. For further details, see François-Xavier Guerra, "La nación en América Latina: el problema de los orígenes," in *Nación y modernidad,* ed. Marcel Gauchet, Pierre Manent, y Pierre Rosanvallon (Buenos Aires: Nueva Visión, 1997), 97–121; and "Indentidad y soberanía: una relación compleja," in *Revoluciones hispánicas: independencias americanas y liberalismo español* (Madrid: Editorial Complutense, 1995), 207–238.

the identity of the reino—to images of other manifestations of the Virgin, of San Miguel, or of the patron saints of cities, provinces, and regions. And along with simple images of patron saints, one would have to include the invocations of their miracles and protection. This sacred imagery mixed strongly with secular elements in the construction of local and regional identities. Thus, the essential date of the history of Querétaro, represented by an eighteenth-century indigenous painter, was the 1531 battle won against the Chichimecas by the Otomí leader Don Nicolás de San Luis Montañés, lord of Tula and general of the "Christian army." A similar foundational act was represented by the series of historical paintings that depicted the capture of Tenochtitlán in a manner that conferred dignity, not only on Cortés and the Spaniards, but also on the lords of the defeated Mexica. Along the same lines, one could mention the series of paintings that presented the genealogy of Tlaxcaltecan chieftains.[6] New Spain as a reino, its towns and cities, its nobility and its two republics, all affirmed their identities through illustrations, whether of the patron saints that protected them, the foundational acts that brought them into being, or the noble lineages that defined their leadership. The same point can be made about Santa Rosa de Lima and images of Inca rulership in Peru, about the Virgin of Chiquiquirá in Bogotá, about the Alonso de Ercilla's celebration of the gallant Araucanos in Chile. Religious images were glossed by sermons and various sorts of prayers. Sermons, in all their forms, constituted an essential vehicle for the construction and diffusion of values and identities, a point well illustrated by the use that both royalists and patriot insurgents made of sermons during the wars of independence.[7]

Finally, civil and religious ceremonies, with their symbols and allegories, must be added to complete the panoply of important forms of social communication typical of baroque culture. The processions integral to the feasts of patron saints and to important dates on the liturgical calendar, the prayers that responded to moments of particular need such as wars, epidemics, and natural disasters—these brought the community together both figuratively and physically. Ceremonies represented society and arrayed it according to its constitutive hierarchies and corporate groups, throwing into relief its multiple patterns of communal belonging, from religious brotherhoods and

6. See *Los pinceles de la Historia: El origen del Reino de la Nueva España, 1680–1750* (Mexico City: Museo Nacional de Arte, 1999), 319 and passim.
7. See, for example, on the Río de la Plata, the documents collected in Adolfo Carranza, *El clero argentino de 1810 hasta 1830,* 2 vols. (Buenos Aires: N.p., 1907).

trade organizations to overlapping political entities. Royal ceremonies—
from coronations and military victories to regal weddings and birthdays—
played a similar role in defining people's collective belonging as loyal subjects of a monarchy conceived as a family that experienced together its
moments of elation or suffering. This "family," structured by individual
links between subjects and the person of the monarch, often gathered cere-
monially to renew those links. The importance of royal ceremonies in maintaining the Spanish monarchy across vast distances, in spite of diverse interests and plural regional and local identities, is becoming increasingly
evident.

Nor did public ceremonies lose their role in the performance of social
identities after independence. Ceremonial oaths of loyalty to Fernando VII
all over Spanish America in 1808, the oaths of loyalty to the American juntas in 1810, the celebrations around foundational acts of independence (like
the May festivals of Buenos Aires, for example, already in 1811), the celebrations of military victories, when victorious armies entered "liberated"
cities in triumph—all indicate the continued centrality of public ritual in the
political culture of the period.[8]

Thus, Latin American discourses of identity extended beyond writing,
even beyond language, to involve images and ceremonies as key elements.
These additions allow us to see how political discourses circulated throughout colonial- and independence-era societies, how they flowed from the
rulers to the ruled, how they engaged patricians and plebeians, Spaniards,
Indians, blacks, and *castas*. It is within this frame of reference that we must
view the role of print as a creator and disseminator of political identities.
We now turn directly to that question. First, we must consider what is known
about reading and writing in Latin America at the turn of the nineteenth century, although space permits no more than brief reflections on matters worthy, in themselves, of a lengthy study.

How many real or potential readers were there? Who were they? Literacy
rates remain largely unknown to us. For New Spain, however, available data
indicate unexpectedly high literacy rates.[9] The work of Tanck de Estrada, first
on Mexico City schools and more recently on village schools, indicates an

8. See, for example, George Lomné, "Les villes de Nouvelle-Grenade. Theatres et
objets des jeux conflictuels de la mémoire politique," in *Mémoire en devenir: Amérique
Latine, XVIe-Xxe siécles,* ed. François-Xavier Guerra (Bordeaux: Maison des Pays
Ibériques, 1994).

9. See also François-Xavier Guerra, *Modernidad e Independencias* (Madrid: Editorial Mapfre, 1992), chapter 18.

extraordinary expansion of the number of schools in eighteenth-century New Spain, reaching over a thousand, some of them in small indigenous villages.[10] While all students did not necessarily learn to read, and some who learned to read did not learn to write, nevertheless one can deduce a fairly wide distribution of literate people in New Spain, even in the countryside. Any village or town was likely to have its group of readers, a handful perhaps, or several dozen, depending on the size of the population. The correspondence of the wars of independence demonstrates as much. In 1811, for example, the dean of Mexico City's cathedral worried about the diffusion of "a multitude of letters, notices, and other opinions that circulate, undermining the loyalty and patriotism of Americans, especially *Indians and smallholders*" [my emphasis].[11] The importance of literacy is even more obvious for Mexico City, where a good half of the population (including elements of the lower classes) could read. Writings by castas and even slaves—also written appeals to clearly plebeian audiences—suggest the wide dissemination of reading in other Spanish American cities, as well.[12]

In addition to those who read, we must consider those who listened as others read aloud. Many texts were printed specifically for reading aloud. Among these were *bandos* (public proclamations of law), obviously, but also various sorts of broadsheets, notices, *pasquinades* (tracts/posters), and lampoons. Verse satires that circulated in writing were committed to memory and recited orally. Overall, microhistorical studies of the independence period reveal the circulation of all sorts of written documents, among all social classes in the cities, and even in the countryside, mostly in Spanish, but even on occasion in indigenous languages as well. The density of this network varied from place to place, but no place lay outside it.

Many of these writings were not printed, however, but handwritten—so we must reflect on the relationship between print and manuscript in Span-

10. Dorothy Tanck de Estrada, *La educación ilustrada (1786–1836)* (Mexico City: El Colegio de México, 1977), and *Pueblos de indios y educación en el México colonial, 1750–1821* (Mexico City: El Colegio de México, 1999).

11. "Informe sobre la libertad de prensa hechos por los venerables Deán y Capítulo de la sede vacante de México al Virrey Don Francisco J. Venegas, el 14 de junio de 1811," in *Documentos inéditos o muy raros para la Historia de México,* vol. 9, ed. Genaro García (Mexico City: Vda. de C. Bouret, 1910), 173.

12. Cf., for example, a 1790 pasquinade from Caracas that threatened whites with throat-cutting. Archivo General de Indias (hereinafter, AGI), Spain, Pasquines y Loas 4 (Indiferente 802).

ish America at the close of the eighteenth century. Documents written by hand continued to dominate the sphere of political communication, most especially among the popular classes, as written reactions to unpopular measures or the arbitrary exercise of authority often revealed. Circulating manuscripts originated and propagated rumors expressing popular dissatisfaction and the need for protest, or, perhaps, elite efforts to mobilize popular energies manipulatively in favor of one faction or another. Nor was the use of manuscript communications peculiar to the popular classes. To the contrary, colonial Spanish American elites made wide use of handwritten documents in everything from social gatherings to literary societies, not to mention bureaucratic or business settings. As a means of communication within an elite, manuscript was superior to print, not only because it more easily escaped official vigilance and control, but also because of elitist assumptions about public opinion. The only public whose opinion mattered, in this view, was the narrow group of enlightened men at the top of the social hierarchy. Reference to public opinion, *la opinión,* did not include the views of the general population, much less the "vulgar throng" at its lower reaches, whose ideas were discarded as too unenlightened and too governed by thoughtless passions.

Overall, the press occupied a dual position in the "enlightened" thinking of the late eighteenth century. It permitted wider circulation of enlightenment ideas, as well as news and useful information, among the elite. Regarding the population at large, on the other hand, the function of the press was conceived as essentially pedagogical, a tool to foster the diffusion of Enlightenment ideas and create a larger thinking public. Therefore "enlightened" elites not only accepted but also applauded Crown limitations on freedom of the press.[13] The dichotomy "enlightened elite/ignorant masses" encouraged the elite to continue using manuscripts among themselves—particularly in Spanish America where, with the exception of New Spain and Peru, "enlightened" circles were tiny. In fact, the narrowness of enlightened readership—more than legal restriction—explains the small scale and ephemeral character of the late eighteenth-century Spanish American periodical press. That is why the absence of newspapers in Venezuela until 1808 and in Chile until 1812 caused little stir. Multiple copies of manuscript

13. In this way Jovellanos justified not publishing *Lo que hay de más y menos en España.* Attributed to José del Campillo y Cossío, this work had circulated for forty-five years in multiple manuscript copies.

correspondence and literary production, even handwritten copies of gazettes were sufficient for intra-elite purposes.[14]

The majority of books, newspapers, and other printed materials read in colonial Spanish America came from Europe, especially Spain, of course, but also the Low Countries, Italy, Switzerland, and France. Printed materials originating in Spanish America encountered legal limitations and were not numerous. Mexico City and Lima had the most active presses, and their chief subjects were devotional, with a smattering of law, science, and technical materials. The inventories of the private libraries of the educated elite show books in Latin, Spanish, French, and Italian. They contain dictionaries, grammars, histories, and geographies, as well as works of a literary, scientific, theological, or philosophical character. One finds newspapers from Spanish cities, especially Madrid, and occasionally from other European cities. By means of such publications, enlightened Spanish American readers could keep abreast of cultural and scientific developments in late eighteenth-century Europe, and then with the debates surrounding the French Revolution.

Let us consider different forms of reading, a matter closely connected with different forms of writing. To begin, a number of the new forms of sociability that engaged Spanish American elites—whether formal ones such as academies and patriotic societies, or informal *tertulias* in cafés, libraries, convents, or private residences—consisted of reading aloud, followed by conversation. The scarcity of printed matter from Europe, along with the new interest in cultured conversation, extended the practice of public reading increasingly into private spaces. Also read aloud and discussed in such settings were letters and various local compositions in manuscript of the kind that also found their way into the literary periodicals that began to appear in the late eighteenth century. The private reading of individuals, long important for study and religious devotion, combined with the new interest and pleasure in contemplation of nature to encourage solitary reading in the countryside.[15]

We know less about the reading of the popular classes, except for what as already been said about various forms of reading in the street. Nonetheless, stray bits of information suggest that people without social pretensions

---

14. See the fine analysis of these practices in New Granada, in Renán Silva, "Les Éclairés de Nouvelle Grenade, 1760–1808: Généalogie d'une communauté d'interprétation" (Ph.D. diss., Universidad de Paris I, 1996).

15. See Silva, "Les Eclairés."

might have in their houses a pamphlet or two, especially of the religious kind, and certainly some of the captioned images or prayers that had been printed in great quantities since the seventeenth century. On this point, the reading of the popular classes did not differ so much from that of the elites, most especially elite women. The ephemeral printings of satire or verse that constituted the chief manifestation of popular publication did not escape the notice of more cultured readers, who clearly read and discussed them and even committed some to memory.

Therefore, we cannot draw a clear line between elite reading and popular reading. While it is true that Spanish American elites read much that the "unenlightened" did not, "popular" writings reached far beyond a "popular" audience. To some extent, as with images and ceremonies, reading involved late-colonial Spanish American societies in an enveloping sphere of communication, a circumstance crucial to the evolution of print in the coming political crisis.

The Crisis of the Monarchy Begins, 1808–1809

The independence period offers privileged opportunities to study the relationship between print and social identities. The proliferation of printing during these years reveals the variety of existing identities and their rapid evolution.

The salient characteristic of the period is an extraordinary expansion in the volume of writing. The crisis of the monarchy that began when Napoleon occupied Spain and placed his brother, Joseph Bonaparte, on the Spanish throne, provoked a profusion of all sorts of writing, manuscript as well as print, in Spain as well as Spanish America. Refusals to accept this new king and powerful expressions of loyalty to the deposed Fernando VII occurred practically everywhere not occupied by French troops. Caretaker juntas assumed power in the name of the legitimate monarch and the political rights of his subjects. These unprecedented events generated an equally unprecedented wave of public discourse, verbal and iconic, oral and written, collective and individual, impromptu and ceremonial, as subjects of the Spanish monarchy multitudinously spoke up.

The main impulse was the need to express resistance to the Napoleonic usurper and legitimate the creation of new political powers. That resistance and legitimation was expressed first in Spain itself, where the proclamations and manifestos of Spanish juntas constituted the leading edge of the explosively expanding public discourse. Almost every junta founded a gazette to publicize its patriotism, to disseminate its announcements and official documents, and to provide its own spin on political events. The publications of the juntas were quickly joined by a flock of other patriotic writings in every genre: sermons, poetry, songs, plays, and political catechisms, not to mention private letters. In Spanish America, where caretaker juntas were slower to emerge, a similar proliferation of patriotic writings, both Peninsular and American in origin, began to dominate the existing periodical press.

Most of the new political writing expressed rejection of the usurper and fidelity to the legitimate king. These writings exalted the Spanish nation, its religion, laws, and customs, and rejected the imposition of a foreign monarch. A combative tone typified the new discourse. It justified struggle, exhorted to resistance, and execrated the enemy. Reasoned discernment among competing arguments—in fact, any diversity of opinion—had little place in this discourse. Unanimity was the order of the day, corresponding to the nature of what all these publications hoped to express: the voice of a unified political community, the supremely legitimating *vox populi*.

Rhetorical unanimity expressed an important reality. The enormous quantities of independence-era writing preserved in archives and libraries display an exceptionally unified set of cultural and political references, the same repertory of images, often expressed in the very same words.[16] The unity is all the more remarkable given the diverse regional and social origins of the authors, from Spaniards to indigenous Americans. In a representative example from 1808, an indigenous community of New Spain offers "its belongings and its lives in the service of the Catholic Sovereigns, with heartfelt regret for the treacherous deception they have suffered." The document continues with a declaration of faith: "Never have the people of the God of Israel asked anything of his Divine Majesty, in order better to serve him, without his responding, sending even angels to exterminate their enemies." And divine aid was all the more certain, indicated the authors, for those enjoying the protection of Our Lady of Guadalupe.[17] The unanimity of these writings is not indicative, of course, of "public opinion" in the modern sense. But it does indicate manifestly shared beliefs, hopes, and fears, a "public" consensus in the older sense of the word.

16. For further development of this theme, see Guerra, "Imaginários y valores de 1808," *Modernidad e Independencias,* chapter 5.

17. Archivo General de la Nación (hereinafter AGN), Mexico, Santiago del Rio, Historia, t. 46, f. 454.

Because of the circumstances and manner in which it occurred, this explosive manifestation of common sentiments brought profound change. It swept away the old regime model of "publication," whereby to *publish* meant "to make known, by the voice of a town crier, or other means, something which should come to the attention of everyone."[18] Publication, in the old regime model, had been above all an attribute of authority, a matter of official initiative, or at least, subject to official control. The patriotic literature that suddenly flourished on both sides of the Atlantic during the crisis of the Spanish monarchy functioned according to a contrary model, in which initiative for publication came from civil society, or more precisely, from the body politic, with a liberty of expression previously unknown. In Spain, government censors disappeared during the first months of the crisis, along with most other agencies of royal authority, and the caretaker juntas either did not attempt, or failed, to replace them. Even where censors continued to exist, as in Spanish America, they found it hard to limit the expressions of patriotism that typified the new sort of publication.

In addition, the pervasive mood of patriotic exaltation, in which the authorities themselves were very much engaged, encouraged endless published descriptions of the many public acts that manifested that mood: oaths of loyalty to Fernando VII, religious ceremonies such as collective supplications and Te Deums, patriotic parades and allegories, sundry displays of political solidarity and military heroism, and so on. The pervasiveness of these texts further illustrates a point made earlier. The Spanish monarchy was more than a political space structured by family networks. It was also a discursive space, densely knit by networks of communication, whose inhabitants shared common concerns and responded to many of the same joys and fears. The primary political identity discernable at the moment in question, on both sides of the Atlantic, was defined by the Spanish monarchy and its associated values. In the words of a woman of Yucatán:

> Yes, my children, the Patria, the beloved Patria, is nothing more or less than the sweet brotherhood that binds one citizen to another with indissoluble links to a single country and language, their own laws, an immaculate religion, a government, a King, a body, a spirit, a faith, a hope, a charity, a baptism, and a God, the universal father of them all.[19]

18. Definition from Real Academia Española, *El diccionario de autoridades* (Madrid, 1737).

19. *Diário de México,* September 10, 1809.

Another factor giving print a new role in the agitated era of Spanish American independence struggles was the sharp growth in demand for news. The thirst for information was an immediate general response to transcendental events affecting the fate of the entire monarchy. Innumerable period sources indicate this thirst for information: the swift circulation of rumors, the anguished wait for news of distant events, the manner in which news arrived, the inevitable question of its trustworthiness, the way it was manipulated or suppressed. The expanded demand for information was irreversible, a primary cause of the proliferation of writing, from private correspondence to printed documents—above all, newspapers. A privileged place was given, in all this, to the war against Napoleon, especially victories and defeats on the Iberian Peninsula, matters of patriotic unanimity.

Beyond patriotic unanimity, however, the events of these years created ample scope for diversity of opinions. The disappearance of the monarch was an eventuality never foreseen and never before experienced. Immediately, a debate began about how to constitute authority in the monarch's absence. The great theme of the Spanish crisis of 1808–1809 was the need to establish a unified, legitimate government and to convoke the Cortes, or national assembly. Even as emissaries and correspondence among the various juntas urgently addressed the issue, a multitude of pamphlets and periodicals aired it publicly. High matters of state were no longer problems to be solved privately among statesmen. They had become matters of public debate.

Public political debate, though varying in liberty and intensity, became a permanent legacy of the crisis of the Spanish monarchy. True, the debate (unlike the effusions of patriotic unanimity) occurred within restricted circles, around the provisional governments that temporarily took the monarchy's place, and above all, among the cultural and political elites close to Spain's Junta Central. But these restricted circles produced the publications that, when read and republished in the rest of Europe and in America, broadly defined the new discourse.[20] Here, then, we are witnessing the invention of "public opinion" in its modern sense, reasoned debate expressing a (relative) diversity of opinions on matters formerly reserved for governing officials. The Enlightenment's republic of letters left the eighteenth century behind and emerged from its old regime soirées and literary salons, not driven by its internal development but because the circumstances called

20. The main such publications in this early period are *El seminario patriótico, El Espectador sevillano, y El voto de la nación española.*

it forth. Public opinion was on its way to becoming a supreme arbiter of political life, on an intimate footing with the principle of sovereignty itself.

American Writings and Debates

The emergence of modern public opinion occurred somewhat differently in Spanish America. The principal difference was that in America, aside from two ephemeral juntas in Quito and Upper Peru, the institutional rupture did not take place until 1810. During 1808–1809, royal authorities remained in place and, along with them, the old-regime pattern of social communication. Although an outburst of patriotic fervor led to the rapid multiplication of printed texts, these continued to be published by prior permission of the authorities, a circumstance that limited free public discussion of the many political issues raised by the crisis of the monarchy. These issues certainly were debated, on the other hand, in salons and literary societies attended by Spanish American elites, where manuscripts, books, newspapers, and letters were read aloud, circulated, and discussed.

Feverish commentary on the uncertain situation in Spain and of various possible responses began among colonial elites as soon as news of the crisis of the monarchy crossed the Atlantic in 1808. Handwritten manuscripts suddenly multiplied as vehicles of unpublished news and rumors, replete with hopes, fears, and proposals for action. Far from impeding the appearance of such manuscripts, traditional censorship of print constituted, to the contrary, an incentive to their production.

A notable characteristic of these writings is that discussion of any new information involved anxious questioning of its veracity. Accustomed as we are now to a rapid, regular, and continuous flow of news, we can hardly imagine the full ramifications of a situation in which news arrived slowly, unevenly, uncertainly, and discontinuously. Not only did news from Europe take months to reach America—two months for New Spain, five months for Peru—the length of the delay also varied from voyage to voyage, as did the port of embarkation, which inevitably affected the character of the information. Then, too, when news arrived, it arrived all at once in the form of letters, newspapers, and official dispatches brought by a single vessel. As a result even the most fundamental events appeared fragmented and confusing at first blush, and widely varying constructions of them might be equally persuasive. The uncertainties of the situation were aggravated by the circulation of rumors (whether representing the scarcity of information or purposeful misinformation) that could not be verified or discounted for long periods of time.

This constant assessment of incoming information clearly contributed to a new climate of critical reflection. In Chile, for example, many of the debates that divided local elites during the crisis years turned precisely on their diverging evaluations of news arriving from Spain. The first "public" debate to agitate the Chileans in the southern hemisphere winter of 1808 was sparked by the circulation of an anonymous manuscript entitled "Precautionary Warnings." The author, quickly identified as Don Ignacio Torres of Quito, a scribe at the *consulado* (merchants' guild), accuses all those repeating the bad news about the political situation in Spain of being disloyal plotters.[21] His adversaries, future founders of the Chilean junta of 1810, argue in their defense that a critical examination of information coming from the Peninsula must not be confused with a lack of patriotism, much less with treachery: "How can discussing what seems true or false in the news indicate ill will toward the monarchy? That is to mistake understanding for will and discourse for desire."[22] Such debates over information led gradually to an inversion of the function of publication characteristic of the old regime. "Public papers" (proclamations and official gazettes, above all) lost much of their former authority and became subject to critical examination as Spanish American elites began to fear, and rightly so, that such publications reflected not reality but policy, an effort to bolster patriotism by not telling the whole truth. In response, these readers began to regard published news more skeptically than information from private letters or foreign newspapers—an attitude that, if occasionally wise, was often ill advised.

Along with newly critical assessments of incoming information, public discussion of the crisis in the Peninsula evolved with the events unfolding between 1808 and 1810. At first, Spaniards and Spanish Americans alike debated the position to take toward an acephalous monarchy. For Spanish Americans, the question was whether to declare temporary independence from a mother country that had fallen under the control of Napoleon to form American juntas that would exercise sovereignty in the name of the legitimate king Fernando VII. The issue spawned a series of manuscripts, some

---

21. See *Colección de historiadores y de documentos relativos a la independencia de Chile,* vol. 8 (I) (Santiago de Chile, 1902).

22. Juan A. Ovalle, Declaraciones, 1810, in "Expediente remitido por el Presidente de Chile con motivos de envío a Lima de Juan A. Ovalle, José A. Rojas, y Bernardo Vera," in *Colección de historiadores,* 6:327–328.

of them veritable treatises, such as the famous writings of the mercenary Fray Melchor de Talamantes, which became a justification for the attempt of the Mexico City *cabildo* (town council) to convoke a national congress in New Spain.[23]

Public discussion of the matter spilled over into every kind of genre. Treatises like those by Talamantes were soon joined by "representations" of this or that Spanish American collectivity directed to authorities in Spain but also circulated to the reading public at home. A notable example of that genre is the "Memorandum of Grievances" authored by Camilo Torres, a text presented by the cabildo of Santa Fé de Bogotá to the Spanish Junta Central concerning equality of political representation between the two continents within the monarchy. The "Memorandum of Grievances" appeared in multiple manuscript copies before being printed and many times reprinted.[24] Other texts of this period are true manifestos. One circulated clandestinely in Peru in 1809 with a title that speaks for itself: *The Alarm: Discourse or Reflection made by an American Patriot to his Lethargic Brothers so that they may Shake Off the Chains of Despotism, Oppression, and Tyranny and Establish in their Stead a Wise, Free, and Independent Government Useful to All the Denizens of the State.*[25] In some texts, political discussion is disguised in the form of a political "catechism" that uses a question-and-answer format to teach Spanish Americans their rights and denounce the abuses of Peninsular Spaniards. As examples, one could mention the famous *Christian Political Catechism* of "Don José Amor de la Patria" or the *Patriotic Catechism for the Instruction of the Youth of the Kingdom of Chile,* neither of which was intended for children.[26] Yet another

23. One is a theoretical dissertation, "Representación nacional de las colonias: Discurso filsófico," and another, a more practical juridical document, "Plan de independencia," in Ernesto de la Torre Villar, *La constitución de Apatzingán y los creadores del Estado mexicano* (Mexico City: Universidad Nacional de México, 1964).

24. An example of a reprinting from Lima is the *Representación elevada a S.M. por el Cabildo de la capital de Santa Fé en el año de 1810 sobre el derecho de igualdad de la América en la soberanía nacional* (Lima: Don Manuel Peña, 1820).

25. *El Despertador: Discurso o reflexión qhe hace un Patriota Americano a sus hermanos aletargados para que sacudan las cadenas del despotismo, opresión, y tiranía y establezcan sobre sus ruynas un Govierono savio, livre, y independiente y útil para todas las clases del Estado,* AGI, Diversos 2, 1812, ramo 3, no. 1, 8.

26. The *Catecismo político cristiano* was no doubt written in Upper Peru in 1809 or 1810, and reprinted in Santiago, Chile (1975). *Catecismo patriótico para instrucción de la juventud del Reino de Chile* (Archivo Abascal, 1810 or 1811), AGI, Diversos 2, 1811, ramo 3, no. 15.

genre was the fictitious letter, such as the *Letter from Santiago Leal to Patricio Español,* also from Chile, which justifies the loyalty of Santiago Creoles toward their Peninsular compatriots despite the Creoles' recent actions against the Spanish governor.[27]

Song lyrics, too, became a vehicle of political discourse, an especially useful one, because rhyme and music facilitated memorization of the message. An especially well-known example, among many, is the "Carmañola americana" composed by two partisans of the French Revolution in Venezuela during the 1790s. Another, also surely sung to the music of the Carmagnole, is the following patriotic song heard in Lima around 1810:

> Viva Compatriotas,
> Nuestro patrio suelo
> y la heróica Junta
> De nuestro gobierno.
> Heróicos Patriotas,
> En unión cantemos
> A la Madre Patria
> Sonoros conceptos,
> Ella que nos ofrece
> Tesoros inmensos,
> Unión fraternal,
> Sol en premio.
> Viva!
> Cantemos alegres
> Himnos, pues tenemos
> La aurora feliz
> En nuestro hemisferio.
> Ya está en nuestra esfera
> El brillante Febo
> Dejando en su Ocaso
> Los selages Negros.
> Viva!
> Si ayer oprimido
> De América el suelo

---

27. The *Carta de Santiago Leal a Patricio Español* is attributed to Manuel de Salas and dated 18 August 1810. See *Colección de historiadores,* 8(5):213 ss.

Era de sus hijos
Duro cautiverio,
Hoy a todos los llama
Con reclamos tiernos
Para hacerles ver
Que libres nacieron.
Viva!
La América tiene
El mismo derecho
Que tiene la España
De elegir gobierno.
Si aquella se pierde
Por algun evento
No hemos de seguir
La fé de aquellos.
Viva![28]

Finally, many political writings of the crisis years took dialogical form. These were often half serious and half humorous, like the 1811 "Doormen's Dialogue," in which two doormen, a Chilean and a Peninsular Spaniard, provide arguments to refute those opposed to the constitution of American juntas.[29]

In sum, many forms of political writing appeared in Spanish America at the onset of the crisis of the monarchy, and their character suggests something about the audience for which they were intended. It was not an audience of anonymous, solitary readers, but rather a cultivated, gregarious audience of elite readers, interested in sober discussion of political issues, but

¿I thought most of ~ World literate?

28. The spelling of the lyrics, clearly from 1810–1811, has here been modernized. A paraphrased translation follows: "Compatriots, long live our country and the heroic Junta of our government. Heroic patriots, together we sing sonorously to the Motherland, she who offers us immense treasures, fraternal union, the sun itself as our reward. Long may she live! Let us sing joyous anthems, the happy dawn of our hemisphere before us. Brilliant Phoebus arrives, leaving black savages in his dusk. Long may he live! If yesterday the oppressed land of America could offer only captivity to its sons, today it calls them tenderly to the awareness that they were born free. Long may they live! America has the same right as Spain to choose its government. If Spain is annihilated, we have our independent course. Long may it live!" AGI, Diversos 2, 1811, ramo 3, no. 16.

29. Manuel de Salas, 15 October 1811, *Colección de historiadores,* 19 (5):169–220.

also interested in humor, gallantry, and literary flair. It would be entirely wrong to imagine that women were excluded from the discussions provoked by these various genres of political writing. Women commonly participated in the salons in which elite Spanish Americans gathered to socialize.[30] Period evidence indicates that interest in, and discussion of, political events was not limited by gender. A witness describes a political conversation in Cartagena de Indias: "Last night I accidentally entered a salon where several pretty girls were excitedly condemning a certain 'penitent' who generally passed as a great patriot. Curiosity led me to ask what this was all about and exactly what this so-called 'penitent' had written."[31]

The political identities that appeared dominant throughout the monarchy in these early crisis years were, in terms of the moral imagination, a "Spanish" identity in the largest sense and, in immediate political terms, the specific identities attached to the cities (respective capitals of territorial subdivisions of the monarchy) where the debates were taking place. An "American" identity, in direct contradistinction to a European one, quickly gained strength, however, and the central "American" demands were the right to form juntas, equality of representation in the central institutions of the Spanish monarchy, and, most importantly to the matter at hand, liberty of political expression.[32] The emergence of new collective identities in the independence era cannot be properly understood without due consideration of the social milieu described here: the salons and other gatherings, the travels of family and friends whose correspondence created long-distance networks of communication. It was this audience for which the political documents of the period were primarily written, here that they were read and discussed, here that patriotic ardor rose, and here that one finds the initiative for the formation of American juntas, championing the American identities so important in coming years.

30. It is well known that elite ladies were at the center of many of the important salons where political matters were discussed before, during, and after this period. Cf. for Cádiz, María Esther Martínez Quinteiro, *Los grupos liberales antes de los Cortes de Cádiz* (Madrid: Narcea, 1977); and for Perú, Clément, *El Mercurio.*

31. *El duende patriótico: Carta de un amigo a otro* (Cartagena de Indias: Imprenta de Diego Espinosa, 1813).

32. For further discussion of these topics, see François-Xavier Guerra, "Lógicas y ritmos de las revoluciones hispánicas," and "Identidad y soberanía: una relación compleja," in *Revoluciones hispánicas: Independencias americanas y liberalismo español,* ed. François-Xavier Guerra (Madrid: Editorial Complutense, 1995), 13–46, 207–238.

The War of Words

Beginning in April 1810, discussions of temporary self-government and proposals of equality between American and Peninsular Spaniards gave way to escalating confrontation. Across Spanish America, rival camps formed around two poles: on one hand, authorities loyal to the central monarchy; on the other, American juntas (soon to be joined, in disobedience of the authorities, by the insurgency of Bartolomé Hidalgo). Clashes between these rival camps grew into a Spanish American civil war that gradually involved all social actors, progressively dismantling and restructuring social identities throughout the hemisphere.

This new situation called forth new writings. From their first days, the Spanish American juntas produced information and propaganda. As new powers of fragile legitimacy, they had to justify their existence politically and juridically. They therefore cited the precarious military and political situation of Spain, without a legitimate central government and now on the verge of losing its independence totally to Napoleon. They appealed to the concept of devolution of powers, which could not now be exercised by the absent monarch and therefore returned to the "pueblos" from which those powers originated. They maintained their hereditary right as Spaniards to refuse obedience to illegitimate rulers. But it was not enough to rationalize matters to their own satisfaction. The new juntas also knew, or at least suspected, that many would not follow their example, that they would very probably have to face determined adversaries. Although the dimensions of the coming conflict were unforeseeable, the prospect of political persuasion by force of arms existed from the beginning. The Junta of Buenos Aires thus sent an army into the interior provinces and to Upper Peru almost immediately.

Therefore, the documents produced by the Spanish American juntas of 1810 are a mixture of authoritative command and passionate wartime propaganda. Old-regime systems of social communication were harnessed to both purposes. Official proclamations (and government gazettes, where they existed) publicized the foundational acts and manifestos of the new juntas. Because the formation of these juntas was essentially a local phenomenon, their first objective was to garner the legitimating recognition of other cities. This task was especially urgent for the juntas of Caracas, Buenos Aires, Santiago, and, to a lesser degree, Bogotá—cities that had all been capitals of colonial viceroyalties or general captaincies. Aspiring to inherit the territorial sway of former royal authorities, these juntas lost no time in sending missives and emissaries to secondary cities in their subordinate provinces.

The deeply divided sympathies of Spanish America required a larger, long-distance propaganda effort, however, mostly in the form of letters. Letters poured out of Chile, Venezuela, Nueva Granada, and the Río de la Plata, inviting cities elsewhere to follow the example of the new juntas. This correspondence throws into relief the vast communications system and network of personal relations that had functioned in colonial Spanish America. Buenos Aires directed correspondence not merely to the cabildos of its interior provinces, but also to those of Santiago, Caracas, and Veracruz, and most especially to the cabildos of Upper Peru, part of the colonial jurisdiction of Buenos Aires in the closing years of colonial rule, but now again disputed by its former viceregal capital, Lima. Bogotá wrote to Peru and Chile; Cartagena de Indias to Veracruz; Caracas, to Nueva Granada, Peru, and Chile; and so on.

These letters were often official—especially from juntas to cabildos—but many were private letters. Members or supporters of Spanish America's newly constituted powers conducted an intense political proselytization through personal correspondence. Personal letters had a better chance of evading the control of monarchist authorities. Still, we know of these currents of correspondence precisely because so many such letters were intercepted. Here are some examples that ended up in Spanish archives. José Joaquín Cortés Madariaga, one of the leaders of the Caracas junta, wrote to his cousin Joaquín López de Sotomayor in distant Chile:

> Dear Cousin: Spain is finished and the American Continent's time has come. Caracas has been the first to plan its new system, and I, as a representative of Clergy and People, had a part in promoting the felicitous independence that has reigned in this land since the nineteenth of this month. I am enclosing some printed matter that can serve as a model for you there in Chile. Long live our Religion, and may our Country prosper! To Francisco, Ramón, Capuchina, and to you, cousin, I send the heart that so esteems and desires soon to embrace you.[33]

33. José Joaquín Cortés Madariaga to Joaquín López de Sotomayor, 22 April 1810, attached to Bando de Caracas of 19 April 1810, AGI, Diversos 1, 1810, ramo 3, doc. 4.

Cortés Madariaga also wrote, in very similar terms, to his friend in Lima, high-court *oidor* José de Baquijano.[34] The propagandistic urge was so strong that, even when ties of family or friendship did not exist, exponents of the new powers tried to reactivate various other relationships in order to send a personal message, as when José de Varga, a military doctor in Cartagena de Indias, wrote to a medical colleague in Lima, reminding him that they had been classmates years before, or as when Francisco de la Cámara y Mollinedo wrote enthusiastically from Caracas to a countryman in Cuzco (not, apparently founding his appeal on a preexisting friendship) about the creation of the Caracas junta.[35] These examples reveal social networks that were not defined by the boundaries of colonial administration or future independent states. To the contrary, these networks spanned the entire area of the Spanish monarchy, and they indicated a high degree of mobility within it. The strength and pervasive reach of such networks render inadequate any attempt to analyze the process of Spanish American independence purely at the local or regional level.

The initial stage of publicity for the new political powers of Spanish America soon gave way to another stage: direct confrontation between the opposing parties. The viceroyalties of New Spain and Peru and the Captaincy General of Guatemala (comprising all of Central America) was well as various cities of Venezuela, New Granada, and the Kingdom of Quito all refused to accept the authority of the juntas and seemed ready to oppose them militarily. The result was a Spanish American civil war of continental proportions. The conflict between "royalists" and "patriots," as they were eventually designated, was fought between armies, but it was also a propaganda battle.[36]

This was not the dispassionate discourse of a modern public sphere. Each side wished, above all, to denigrate its adversaries, defend its own cause, and attract new partisans. To the sorts of arguments already mentioned, the pro-junta Spanish American "patriots" added a celebration of liberty, an exaltation of their native land, and a rejection of Peninsular "despotism." They

34. Ibid., doc. 5.
35. José de Varga to Ignacio Hurtado, 20 February 1811, AGI, Diversos 2, 1811, ramo 1, doc. 5.1; Francisco de la Cámara y Mollinedo to Antonio Ulloa, 22 April 1810, AGI, Diversos 1, 1810, ramo 3, doc. 5.
36. At the beginning of this war, it would be more accurate to describe the sides as the supporters of the Regency versus the supporters of the American juntas, because both sides still proclaimed their loyalty to Fernando VII.

paid particular attention to their unequal treatment from the government of the central monarchy, especially from bossy regency authorities in Spanish America. These were the "tyrants" against which they rose up, and not just in general, but very specifically by name: the Peruvian viceroy Abascal, the president of Charcas, Nieto, and, the Creole general Goyeneche, for example. In Mexico, they excoriated the viceroy Venegas and, above all, the regency's general Calleja. These defenders of the regency, on the other hand, employed principally the language of loyalty to the king, inseparable from loyalty to his representatives, castigating the rebels' supposed abandonment of the mother country in time of need and condemning the revolt as illegitimate in religious as well as political terms.

The two sides adopted similar communications policies, with offensive and defensive aspects. Offensively, each side elaborated and disseminated writings that justified its cause and discredited the cause of its adversaries. To advance this purpose, each side smuggled its propaganda to its partisans in the territory controlled by its adversaries, hoping to receive in return a kind of intelligence that can fairly be called espionage. Defensively, each side tried to impede similar operations by the enemy. To do so, it exercised surveillance over the flow of correspondence into its own territory, conducting checks of ports, mail carriers, roads, and inns, following the movements of suspicious persons, limiting travel (sometimes by requiring internal passports), monitoring cafés and other gathering places, and trying to identify the authors of seditious communications by analyzing their handwriting.[37] Each considered the other's propaganda extremely dangerous and misleading.

The media used in the propaganda war were diverse, indeed. Publication, in the traditional sense of "public information" provided by the authorities (through criers, official gazettes, broadsheets, and so forth) had a central role. The pro-junta leader, Juan José de Castelli, in his propaganda campaign aimed at the cabildos of Peru, denounced the published misinformation of "the Gazettes of the [pro-Regency] Government of Lima, its Proclamations and Manifestos," while at the same time declaring: "Fellow Citizens, you can be free as soon as you decide to be, the plans of the Government [of Buenos Aires] are well laid out in its public papers; its fraternity, equity, and justice cannot be denied; it will be free and will protect all who desire freedom."[38] On the other side, Viceroy Abascal described his

---

37. See, for example, AGI, Diversos 1, 1807 (1810), ramo 2, doc. 2.
38. "Manifesto que dirige a los Pueblos interiores de Virreynato del Perú el Excmo. Señor Don Juan José de Castelli, Representante del Superior Gobierno de la Capital del

own information policy: "I have worked personally to maintain an official Gazette, extracting the best materials from papers of that kind published elsewhere and from other interesting and valid reports on the state of our Armies."[39]

The period's propaganda used not only "public papers," but many other kinds of writing as well, much of it manuscript. One of the most used forms was the pasquinade, sometimes in verse, sometimes illustrated, put up secretly in a busy place, frequently the church door or the town plaza. The pasquinade mirrored the function of an official edict, or *bando,* often starting with the same words: "Notice to the Public" or "Be It Publicly Known." In its role as "anti-bando," the pasquinade refuted the proclamations and arguments of the authorities. "Yesterday's Bando was a pack of insulting, hastily concocted lies," announced one pasquinade of Upper Peru in 1810.[40] Interestingly, pasquinades were often addressed to "the public," but they were sometimes signed by "the public," too, thus opposing the delegated legitimacy of the authorities with the supreme legitimacy of "the people." More than the abstract "people" employed in modern conceptions of popular sovereignty, "the people" referred to here were the inhabitants of a particular city, the potentially menacing plebeian masses whose access to writing has already been established.

The tone of such texts is almost always extremely violent. Pasquinades aimed to intimidate the authorities and create a climate of fear. An 1810 pasquinade from Cochabamba addressed the intendant of Potosí, Francisco de Paula Sanz, in the following terms: "Look, you loud-mouthed cripple, you think we don't know that King Fernando is gone and in the tomb with the rest of the house of Bourbon? You are the ones who want to be the kings now. . . ."[41] The text goes on to name and excoriate various other local authorities. Pasquinades often contained insults and threats to persons and property, as in the following 1811 example from Oaxaca whose shaky

---

Río de la Plata sobre las axtuales ocurrencias," Oruro, 3 April 1811. The documents was sent clandestinely to the cabildo de Tarmo, which forwarded it to Abascal. AGI, Diversos 2, 1811, ramo 1, no. 11.

   39. Abascal to Pérez de Castro (in Cádiz), describing the disorders that had occurred in Upper Peru. AGI, Diversos 2, 1811, ramo 3, no. 8.

   40. Document remitted by the President of the Audiencia de Charcas, Vicente Nieto, to Viceroy Abasacal, 25 August 1810, AGI, ramo 1, no. 2, 9.

   41. Pasquinade sent to Abascal by the President of the Audiencia de Charcas, Vicente Nieto, 25 August 1810, AGI, Diversos 1, 1810, ramo 1, no. 2, 9, 1.

spelling and difficult transcription do not impede the clarity of its onerous message, "Let the sacking begin / Beat, wound, and kill":

> Toda América ha adbertido
> En esta Epoca presente
> Que Hoyendía como Prudente
> Tiene el Yugo sacudido
> Y nuestro animo esta unido
> A echar fuera los gachupines
> Sarna [?] aquestos ruines
> Sin ninguna dilacion
> Ninguno tenga perdon
> Con Lucifer sean sus fines
> Arriba tunantes [?] fuertes
> De la escuela de Asmodeo
> Comensemos al saqueo
> Golpead, heryd haced Muertes.[42]

The chaotic spelling so frequent in such documents is not a sure indication of popular origin. In fact, it may be an attempt to attribute to them a popular origin they did not in fact have. The allusion to Asmodeo in the cited example suggests a relatively well-educated author, despite the poor spelling, which functioned in part to conceal the writer's identity.

Libelos, libelous letters sent to authorities or private individuals, were much like pasquinades in their threatening tone and content, and also in that libelos sometimes circulated rather broadly. In Mexico, for example, partisans of the insurgents put the following text in Sagrario Church and underneath the doors of several European merchants: "Contumacious Europeans: American arms dominate and announce your total ruin, that of your interests and families, if you do not give visible and convincing sign of your good will and adherence to our party."[43]

One should also mention, among the various weapons of the independence-era war of words, the *cedulilla,* what today would be called a pam-

---

42. "Today all America has become aware and shakes off the yoke of tyranny. Our spirit is united to expel the Spaniards. Out they go, without delay, without forgiveness, to end their days at Lucifer's side. Rise up powerfully to begin the sack, to strike the blow, to wound and kill for our cause." From Oaxaca, 7 January 1811, AGI, México 1321, letter from Viceroy Venegas.

43. Addendum to a viceregal letter, AGI, México 132, no. 158 (N.15).

phlet, small printed texts that were distributed anonymously in public places, such as the one distributed in Mexican churches and cafés in 1809, beginning with the words "Liberty, cowardly Creoles!"[44] Cedulillas were similar to pasquinades, but whereas pasquinades were generally posted, and therefore vulnerable to removal, cedulillas were distributed in large numbers less obtrusively.

This confrontational war of words absorbed considerable energies among the political actors of the post-1810 period. Pedro Vicente Cañete, one of those actors, illustrates that fact in the following narrative:

> I found the people of Tarma seduced by the innumerable print documents that had been smuggled in, propagating anarchy for lack of opposition voices. I managed to erase their progress by means of my own quick and spirited writings. . . . In fact, I was able to disabuse the most influential inhabitants by virtue of the persuasions I published, and I managed to contain a tumultuous explosion because of the respect accorded my opinion, as Captain Gabino Barrios told me, circulating my proclamations and catechisms in Monquegua and other coastal cities to strengthen the rule of the legitimate authorities.[45]

Finally, one must add to the previously mentioned writings—urban both in origin and in destination—the writings that circulated in the countryside. Some were of the same sort as circulated in the cities, but others, such as propaganda directed to indigenous communities, were distinctively rural. We find examples in Peru during the Huanuco revolt of 1813, in Upper Peru during the Castelli period, and in insurgent Mexico.[46] It is impossible to analyze them in detail here, but worthwhile to highlight some aspects of these writings that remain, as yet, inadequately studied, such as the tone they adopt, their propagandistic use of indigenous languages,[47] the problem of

44. *Libertad, cobardes criollos!* (Mexico, 1809), AGN, Historia, vol. 415, exp. VIII.
45. Pedro Vicente Cañete (in Oruro) to Viceroy Abascal, 25 April 1813, AGI, Diversos 3, 1811, ramo 1, no. 1, 14.
46. Cf. Joïlle Chassin, "Pasquines et chansonsm version écrite, version orale de la subersion dans le P'erou colonial," *Mélanges offerts Frédéric Mauro* (Lisbon and Paris: Arquivos do Centro Cultural Caalouste Gulbenkian, 1995), 715–855.
47. Both royalists and insurgents published their principal texts in translation. See, for New Spain, the 5 October 1810 bando of Viceroy Venegas concerning Indian tribute (AGN, Bandos, vol. 25). For the Río de la Plata, see the 1 September 1811 bilingual document of the Junta de Buenos Aires on the abolition of Indian tribute or the 1816 Acta

translating modern political terminology into those languages (and the related question of how such usually untranslated terms were interpreted by
the target audience), and the indigenous communities' surprisingly good
knowledge of distant events.[48] The discourse of such documents is quite revealing of the worldview of writers and readers alike, as illustrated by the
following letter from José Eduardo Cabadas, a lieutenant of Morelos:

> My Well Beloved: Things have reached the point that Your Worthies, who
> are the most loyal to the Nation, lovers of your Country, and defenders
> of the sacred Religion must kindly gather the sons and Fathers of that
> Pueblo, as soon as you receive this letter, with all the arms you have, and
> come with me, leaving only those necessary to protect the Pueblo.
> Though I love you dearly, this is the way it must be. I am enclosing the
> Letter that the Reverend Curate [Morelos] sends to you. May our Lord
> God keep you safe all the years desired by me, your loving and affec-
> tionate Captain, José Eduardo de las Cabadas.[49]

Thus did the process of political mobilization bring to light the language,
images, and modes of communication specific to independence-era Spanish America's variegated cast of social actors.

Conclusion

Thesis

In sum, it was after 1810, and not before, that the print media expanded and
took on salient political importance in Spanish America. As in Spain in
1808, this process of expansion was at first a response to the needs of new
political powers to legitimate their existence, publicize their official documents, and combat enemy propaganda. The resulting printed documents
were therefore a curious mix of the manuscript genres that preceded (and
overlapped with) them: polemics, letters, decrees, manifestos, proclamations, and always, news of distant events crucial to the unfolding conflict.

---

de Independencia of the United Provinces, appearing in Spanish, Quechua, and Aymara;
reprinted in the *Boletín del Instituto de Investigaciones Históricas* [Buenos Aires] 25
(1940–41).

48. For example, the evidence suggests that they knew of various European countries and understood major monarchical institutions such as the Cortes and the Regency.

49. José Eduardo Cabadas to "Señor Alcalde D. Juan Manuel y demás común de
República de San Marcos, 17 Jan. 1811," AGI, Mexico 1321, attached to a letter of
Viceroy Venegas, no. 142 (N. 13).

Examination of these materials shows the territories of the Spanish monarchy to have remained a vast sphere of communication even as it began to fall apart. The political debates of the period were carried on across long distances, back and forth between insurgent capitals like Caracas, Bogotá, and Santiago, and royalist holdouts like Lima and Mexico City, back and forth between all of these and Cádiz. Furthermore, all sides—Peninsulars and Americans, partisans of independence and of unity under the monarchy—also debated in London, the place of publication of Blanco White's periodical *El Español,* which achieved enormous distribution on both sides of the Atlantic during these years. The geographic reach of modern public opinion, emerging as a result of the crisis itself, was continental, or rather, bi-continental, a phenomenon that logically coincided with the cultural homogeneity of the monarchy, with its broad networks of communication, and with the still mostly undefined status of future American national identities.[50]

The proliferation of writing accompanied and expressed the evolution of political imagery, values, and identities. But these writings illustrate the disintegration of old identities more than the creation of new ones. Two sorts of political identities, formerly subordinate within the identity pyramid of the Spanish monarchy, rose in importance during the post-1808 crisis: the overall American identity, on the one hand, and the identity called "*patria,*" on the other. In both cases, the process was essentially political.

The rise of the general American identity was the direct result of confrontation, as the old term "American Spaniards" came to seem an impossible coupling of antagonistic opposites. The American identity had been gaining strength during the second half of the eighteenth century because of rivalry between Peninsulares and Creoles and the ongoing dispute in which polemicists asserted or denied the inherent superiority of the Old World over the New.[51] After 1808, new political debates widened and deepened the already existing divide. In addition, the term "Americans" accomplished a feat highly advantageous to the insurgents, rhetorically uniting diverse social groups under a common political identity. Americanist discourse was essentially tactical and anti-Peninsular. For American elites, it

50. *El español* was published in runs of about 1,500 copies per issue, like the principal newspaper of Cádiz, but multiple reprintings make it possible that for the period 1810–1811, circulation was closer to 25,000. See André Pons, "Blanco White et la crise du Monde hispanique, 1808–1814" (Ph.D. diss., Université de Paris III, 1990).

51. See Antonello Gerbi, *La disputa del Nuevo Mundo* (Mexico City: Fondo de Cultura Económica, 1960).

meant a struggle against despotism; for most others, a fight against "bad government" and its social consequences. An effective rhetorical tool of civil war, invocation of an American identity was of little political use after independence, when invocation of the patria came to the fore.

At first, "Patria" designated a political identity with multiple ambiguities. During the wars of independence, "Patria" sometimes referred to America as a whole, but more often to local identities complicated by the pyramid organization of Spanish American urban centers. The "pueblos" (of various ranks in the pyramid hierarchy) that had assumed sovereignty beginning in 1810 long remained the principal actors and the primary focus of patriotic feeling. Local patriotism was at the same time a strength and a weakness: a strength in its capacity for political mobilization, and a weakness in its fragmentation of the sovereignty claimed by new nations.

Therefore, except for the few cases where unified, distinct reinos had already been constituted under centuries of colonial administration, nation-building efforts faced two major difficulties. First, it was hard to know exactly which local patrias would belong to which future nation, and second, it was then hard to invent a distinctive cultural content for that administrative space. If, at the end of the wars of independence the new states of Spanish America may be considered nations in the sense of sovereign collectivities, they were very far from possessing other essential imaginative attributes of a modern nation: a history and ancestral territory, common heroes and ancestors, and a national character and destiny. Spanish American elites dedicated themselves to creating that discursive infrastructure of nationhood only after independence was won. The print media played an ever increasing role in that process of creation and political socialization, but never an exclusive one.

2

Argentine Counterpoint: Rise of the Nation, Rise of the State

Tulio Halperín Donghi

Like Barrington Moore's *Social Origins of Dictatorship and Democracy,* Benedict Anderson's *Imagined Communities* is the kind of book that by actually putting to work the systematically comparative approach to history that is more frequently recommended than practiced, makes a contribution to its subject that is quite independent of the validity of its specific conclusions. It should not then be a surprise to find so many among Anderson's admiring and grateful readers regretfully acknowledging that in the area of their own expertise he got almost everything wrong. Their reaction is less paradoxical than it would appear: in history, as in any other discipline, finding the right questions is no less important than reaching the right answers.

Anderson has indeed found a novel way of posing the basic questions on nation and nationalism. By looking at the nation as a species of the genus "imagined community," he makes its rise a moment in the history of that genus, one in which the nation supersedes the two previously dominant "imagined communities"—namely the religious community and the dynastic kingdom—availing itself of the instruments fashioned in a parallel development by the triumph of "print capitalism."

I do not intend to discuss here Anderson's core insight, nor its applicability to Spanish America—an area that, together with the rest of the Americas, and much to his surprise, had been neglected by previous students of nationalism. Perhaps he should not have been so surprised. Such neglect, as Anderson is quick to recognize, is in part a response to the absence in the Americas of features that in the Old World are usually (but not always—Germany and Italy immediately come to mind as exceptions) present in the processes that give rise to nation-states and nationalisms. An example of these features is the introduction of an increasingly conflictive dimension in the coexistence of an administrative language of the state and the ones used in day-to-day life by the diverse populations it rules, due not only to the impact of democratization that enhances the social and political assertiveness of the popular masses, but even more directly, to the progress of literacy, which opens a common ground on which the rival languages can wage battle.

It would appear that the absence of such features in Spanish America should make it possible for him to apply to the region the conclusions that he reached vis-à-vis certain Eastern European regions or Indonesia, where these features were not taken into account. But this is not quite the case; when we look more carefully at Anderson's argument, we discover that these features are taken for granted, rather than ignored. What he offers is indeed closer to an addition than to a correction to the views on the rise of nations and nationalism that he criticizes. In his own view, the triumph of "print capitalism" is less an aspect of the processes in which nations and nationalism were born than a precondition for them that he then describes in terms very similar to those of his predecessors.

It should not then be a cause for surprise to discover that there is very little in Anderson's analytic framework that can be usefully applied to Spanish America beyond his characterization of nations as "imagined communities." In this respect he has become the victim of his own success, so much so that many current readers will probably (and wrongly) be tempted to conclude that in arguing the point so insistently he has been belaboring the obvious. Anderson himself is aware of the anomalous features in the rise of the Spanish American nations, and so, more than stressing the role of "print capitalism," he invites his readers to recognize in the paths followed by Creole bureaucrats in peripatetic career paths that supposedly anticipated the territorial contours of the new nations.

Here we see reflected one of Anderson's most attractive qualities. Notwithstanding the apodictic tone he uses when he argues his main thesis, he is always ready to explore other approaches that promise to be more germane to the specific example under his eyes. Thanks to this openness to alternative perspectives, even when the distance between the model embedded in his main thesis and the example under consideration is too great for the connections with the rise of "print capitalism" to retain much explanatory value, he is able to offer a wealth of suggestions and insights that, while not claiming to provide a universal key to the rise of nations and nationalisms, can nevertheless be extremely helpful for understanding the specific processes under examination.

For these reasons, students of Latin America will find in *Imagined Communities* a constant source of intellectual excitement and stimulation, even if these will sometimes be accompanied by some perplexity. And they will probably find the first occasion for perplexity at the very beginning of Anderson's argument. There, by conflating the birth of the nation as an "imagined community" and the rise of nationalism, he concludes that "it would, I think, make things easier if one treated [nationalism] as if it belonged with 'kinship' and 'religion', rather than with 'liberalism' or 'fascism'."[1]

I am not sure that such conflation is valid even for the "historic" countries of Western Europe. For instance, the German national anthem, dating from the mid-nineteenth century, contains, like a fly captured in amber, a couple of lines in praise of German wine and women, both proclaimed the best in the world, which were borrowed from the late medieval verse of Walter von der Vogelweide. This incongruous nonmartial element in the middle of a fierce call to win or die for the fatherland reminds us that, centuries before becoming the nation imagined by nationalism, Germany had existed as an "imagined community" of a quite different kind.

When considering Spanish America in particular, it is a matter not of debate but of record that the rise of the nation as an imagined community and that of nationalism are two discrete phenomena whose separate starting points in time can be dated with some precision. What came first was the discovery, not exactly of the nation (its existence had never been doubted, even if it had not attracted much attention) but of its availability as a credible substitute for monarchy as a font of political legitimacy. The occasion for such a discovery was the change of the reigning dynasty in Spain, imposed by Napoleon when he placed on the Spanish throne his brother Joseph, whom he had previously made King of Naples to the apparent satisfaction of the Neapolitans.

1. Benedict Anderson, *Imagined Communities,* rev. ed. (London: Verso, 1991), 5.

Same as *guerra.*

What followed was an insurrection launched in the name of the Bourbon king Ferdinand VII, and it was in the course of this insurrection that Spain had to tackle, both at the theoretical and the practical level, the problems that an absolute monarchy faces when having to wage a desperate war for survival without that essential linchpin in its structure, the king. The result was a sort of revolution, not a rebellion against the absolute monarchy but a response to the need to fill the void created by its demise. This void was vaster, both in reality and in collective imagination, than we are retrospectively inclined to recognize. Already in the sixteenth century, Francisco de Vitoria (frequently denounced as an inspiration to tyrannicides) had concluded that a republic in which power had been illegitimately captured by a tyrant had no alternative but to obey that same tyrant, because "if it did not obey the tyrant, the Republic itself would perish."[2]

It can be said, then, that while elsewhere national awareness originated in nations that claimed a right to a state of their own, the birth of national awareness in Spain reflected the need of an existing state, one already embattled in a war for national independence, to find a new source of theoretical legitimacy in the community of its subjects. The search for legitimacy in that problematic source was preceded by the attempt to find it in certain royal officials already designated by law in prevision of a temporary vacancy of the throne. But most of these were too interested in maintaining their positions under the new dynasty to accept the heroic role of patriotic rebels against Joseph Bonaparte. It was only after this disappointing reaction that rebellious leaders who rose from the ranks of combatants placed themselves outside the pale of monarchical legitimacy, which these initially reluctant revolutionaries, gradually and revealingly, began to call the "old regime."

It was in these circumstances that notions discussed by legal and political thinkers for centuries (without much influence on the administration of absolute monarchies then on the rise) acquired an immediate relevance they had lacked in the past. In the proclamation to the overseas domains of the captive Bourbon king Fernando, the new Regency Council created in Cadiz in 1810 did not address them in the name of the king but of the *patria*.[3]

---

2. "Quia cum Respublica oprimatur a tyranno et non sit sui juris, nec possit ipse ferre leges nec iam ante datas exequi, si non preret tyranno, iam Respublica interiret." Francisco de Vitoria, "De potestate civili," in *Reverendi Patris F. Fracisci de Vitoria Relectiones Theologicae XII*, vol. 1 (Lyon: Boyer, 1607), 134.

3. Proclamation in *La Gaceta de Buenos Aires*, June 7, 1810, p. 1, in facsimile reprinting, vol. 1 (Buenos Aires: Junta Argentina de Historia y Numismática, 1911), 15.

The adoption of the new term was made easier by the increasing recognition that the war Spain was waging was one of national liberation. Thus, Melchor Gaspar de Jovellanos, responding to the *afrancesado* Francisco de Cabarrús, who accused him of defending an anachronistic dynastic legitimacy, claimed that "Spain does not wage war on behalf of the Bourbons or of Fernando, but in defense of its original, sacred, inalienable [*imprescriptible*] rights, superior to and independent from any family of dynasty. Spain struggles for its religion, its Constitution, its customs, its usages, in a word, for its freedom."[4]

As Jovellanos's impassioned defense of the Spanish cause suggests, many future nationalist themes were here making a clear, although still discreet, appearance. Jovellanos's definition of the war's objectives owes much to Francisco Martínez Marina's search of Spanish roots for the constitutional monarchy that both men wished to see adopted in their native country. And Martínez Marina's development of Montesquieu's dictum that in Spain freedom is old and despotism is new can be understood as part of a larger effort to find a via media between monarchic absolutism and republican revolution. The search for such a via media inspired thinkers from the most unexpected corners of Europe to call for the restoration of the kind of historically embedded freedoms that Edmund Burke thought the distinctive and fortunate hallmark of English history.

But quests for distinctive roots had little to do with the emergence of nationalism in the Río de la Plata. The revolution launched in Buenos Aires on May 25, 1810, had exact counterparts in Quito, Caracas, Bogotá, and Santiago de Chile. All strove to push the whole of Spanish America into a new and still open-ended course, one that could lead to the radical restructuring or the total destruction of the Spanish imperial system. These pan-Spanish American ambitions were natural to a movement that started, as Anderson quite rightly reminds us, by the Creole sectors of the colonial elite. But could such ambitions be transferred to the rest of the American-born populations, whose support was indispensable for the success of the revolution? Some tantalizingly limited glimpses suggest that, at least at the start, and at least for the Río de la Plata, this would not have been a totally impossible

---

4. In Melchor Gaspar de Jovellanos, *Obras,* vol. 4 (Madrid: Biblioteca de Autores Españoles, 1858), 343. Admittedly, the Regency Council's claim to speak for the king would have been extremely problematical, since it had been improvised in the most irregular way under mob pressure and amid the panic created by the imminent loss of Andalusia to the French invaders.

task. According to the *La Gaceta de Buenos Aires* of 15 November 1810, the whole population of Salta, gathered to welcome the revolutionary expedition sent from Buenos Aires, tirelessly repeated choruses of a ditty that went "to us belongs dominion, of everything within la indiana nación."

But when the revolutionary pronouncements launched in 1810 collided with unexpectedly vigorous resistance from the partisans of the old regime, the word "patria" began to denote less a historic or imaginary national community than a political regime. Thus, Chile and Nueva Granada had a patria *vieja* (as it was later called) until its destruction by the royalist counteroffensive of the mid-1810s, and Venezuela had a patria *boba* that suffered the same fate. Salta, a province of the almost virtual country that was later to be called Argentina, had its own a patria vieja and patria *nueva:* the first made up by the circle of the great caudillo Martín Güemes; the second, by the circle of his enemies within the Salta oligarchy who seized the provincial government after the caudillo's death.

Each nascent patria made some sort of territorial claims. Venezuela declared itself an independent republic in 1811, and in Mexico the Morelos movement struggled for a Republic of Anahuac. But the claim to a specific territorial base posed more complex and delicate problems for Buenos Aires than for the independence movements in most Spanish American sections.

"Sections" was, in fact, a term frequently used to denote the separate political units that emerged from the remains of the Spanish Empire. The term reflected a reluctance to recognize such sections as full-fledged nations that was nowhere better justified than in the Río de la Plata area. The Buenos Aires revolution was the only one of those launched in 1810 that royalist reaction could not suppress even temporarily thereafter. Buenos Aires had been the capital of a viceroyalty that reached Lake Titicaca and the Pacific Ocean. In 1820, when that revolution concluded, Buenos Aires emerged as the capital of one of the thirteen provinces resulting from fragmentation of the rump of the viceregal territory still under control of the revolutionary regime at the moment of its dissolution, after it had failed to impose authority over territories that were eventually organized as the republics of Bolivia, Uruguay, and Paraguay.

The issue of the territorial reach of the Buenos Aires revolution was never far from the minds of the revolutionary elite. The conventional view, first argued by Bartolomé Mitre, is that the defining moment came after the third attempt to extend the revolution to Upper Peru (modern Bolivia) ended in an even more costly failure than had the two previous ones. It was then that José de San Martín put the revolution on its way to final victory by leading it to the liberation of Lima by way of Chilean liberation. But Mitre's readiness to accept the separation of Upper Peru suggests that he never envisioned it as part of the Argentine nation. Revealingly, his reaction to the secession of Paraguay, and especially Uruguay, was to be much more nuanced.

And indeed the notion that the future Bolivia had very little in common with the rest of the viceroyalty of the Río de la Plata can be already detected in the writings on economic matters that flourished in viceregal Buenos Aires. Their authors, who divide their attention between the issues of imperial trade and the problems and promises of the nascent agropastoral economies of the pampas, can only for that reason have neglected to discuss the mining economy of Upper Peru, which supplied more than 80 percent of the viceroyalty's exports.

Little interest in Bolivia, certainly, can be detected in the implicit definition of the territorial objectives of the revolution as rendered in the lyrics of the Argentine *canción patria* (national anthem), composed in 1813 by command of the Sovereign Constituent Assembly. The author was Vicente López y Planes, who had already produced a versified celebration of Buenos Aires's victorious resistance to the British invasions of 1806 and 1807. Taking the Marseillaise as his model, López y Planes composed the canción patria as a battle cry against an enemy that threatened to trample the sacred soil of the fatherland. But, while the author of his French model had not needed to define what territory he had in mind (after all, France had been invented centuries earlier), López had to devote several verses to the task. He began by reminding his compatriots of the horrors visited on the unfortunate regions already reconquered by the royalists ("See them hurl themselves, cruel and tenacious, on Mexico and Quito . . . See them spread death and mourning on unhappy Caracas"[5]), among which he revealingly included Upper Peru ("See Potosí, Cochabamba, and La Paz wailing, bathed in blood"[6]). It is only after having wasted these martyred Upper Peruvian cities that the tyrants become invaders by daring to defy the Argentines in their own territory. They should have known better. That territory is girded by a belt of victories ("San José, San Lorenzo, Suipacha, Piedras, Salta, and Tucumán"), poetic reminders that, on Argentine soil, the ferocious oppressor of the fatherland has been forced once and again to bow his proud head.

5. "No los veis sobre México y Quito/ arrojarse con saña tenaz [. . .] no los veis sobre el triste Caracas/ luto, sangre y muerte esparcir"?
6. "No veis cual lloran bañados en sangre / Potosí, Cochabamba y La Paz"?

The lyrics go on to proclaim that "the world's free peoples" already celebrate the emergence of a "new and glorious nation."

The lasting success of the canción patria owes much to its prescient view of Argentina's place in the world, which was to mature only after the cycle of civil strife and connected international wars ended in 1870. That view, while not free from arrogance, was also characterized by a remarkable reluctance to impose Argentina's claims on neighboring countries in a period rife with border disputes. While many decried such reluctance as a sign that Argentines were not committed enough to the defense of their national interests and national honor, the two major military and political leaders of the era (generals Mitre and Julio Roca) used their enormous prestige against the intermittent bouts of bellicosity of their compatriots, thus averting the danger of war first with Brazil and then with Chile. Both men remembered these bloodless victories of common sense more fondly than those they had won in the battlefield. It was, in fact, under the auspices of these two martial figures that Argentina became the country that championed the idea that "victory does not create rights" and boasted of having two teachers for each soldier.

In 1813, all this remained far in the future. The wars of independence would end only with the elimination of the last redoubts of Spanish power in the New World, an objective much more ambitious than the one implicitly delineated in the canción patria, one that went much beyond the capabilities of the Buenos Aires revolution. The author of the canción patria offered an oblique homage to that more ambitious goal when he presented the rise of the "new and glorious nation" as the resurrection of the Inca empire after a three-centuries—long eclipse imposed by the Spanish conquest.

But if the masses courted by the leaders of the Buenos Aires revolution kept an unshakeable faith in the notion that the total liberation of Spanish America was an achievable goal, it was not because they had been seduced by the verse of López y Planes or by the eloquence of revolutionary rabble-rousers. The very circumstances ensuring that the Buenos Aires revolution would be the only one impervious royalist reaction also created a relationship between revolutionary elite and Creole populace different from what one found in any other revolutionary center. Elsewhere, the task of the elite was to awaken the revolutionary enthusiasm of the general population. But the Buenos Aires revolution was made by an urban population already mobilized politically and militarily by the events of 1806 and 1807. In 1806, a small British expedition easily defeated a garrison that was on paper one of the most formidable in all of Spanish America, only to be expelled by local forces improvised and led by Santiago [Jacques] de Liniers, a French-born officer in the Spanish Navy. In 1807, a second, and this time truly formidable, British expedition, after having defeated the regular army organized by Liniers, was forced to surrender by the desperate resistance of municipal militias and the population at large. The image of the city's ladies pouring cauldrons of boiling oil on the British soldiers engaged in bloody skirmishes in the streets below was to remain forever engraved in Argentine patriotic mythology. These militias were the decisive factor in the total victory of the revolutionary movement, and even after they were gradually disbanded by the regime they had brought to power, their exploits survived in collective memory. In 1813 both Liniers and Martín de Alzaga (who had done more than anybody else to organize the victorious militia of 1807) had been executed as counter-revolutionaries, but their victories retained a subliminal presence in the canción patria. As for the vanquished "proud Iberian lion" lying at the feet of the "new and glorious nation," that was a poetic substitution. The Buenos Aires revolution could as yet hardly claim victory over the lion of Castile; the vanquished beast lying symbolically at the feet of the new nation in 1813 was really the English lion.

A Spanish proverb, born of long and sad experience, advises "con todo el mundo en guerra / y en paz con Inglaterra ("war with all the world / but peace with England"). Buenos Aires, a colonial backwater raised to the status of viceregal capital only three decades earlier, had been suddenly thrown into battle against England, and had won. The memory of that victory was to be crucial to the self-image of a revolution that, while continental in its ambitions, could not be more local in its roots. When Buenos Aires still did not know of what nation, if any, it was destined to become the capital, it already knew that its glory outshone that of much more famous cities.

While the diffusion of the revolutionary message among the Río de la Plata masses was perhaps easier in that it addressed an already mobilized public, this circumstance did not make that diffusion any less necessary. And the revolutionary authorities immediately went to the task, at first with controversial initiatives such as the publication of a Spanish translation of Rousseau's *Social Contract* to be used as a primer in elementary schools (for which purpose it was thoughtfully decided to remove the passages in which Rousseau proclaimed in no uncertain terms his hostility to all organized religions, Christianity included).

This initiative did not, however, reach the masses for whom Rousseau was as inaccessible as the *Gaceta de Buenos Aires,* the biweekly publication created as a mouthpiece for the May revolution. Although the literacy of the urban population of Buenos Aires surprised foreign visitors, it was vital for the new regime to reach the much larger numbers of those still illiterate. In this respect it was to prove more imitative than creative. It simply turned to new uses the instruments developed for that purpose by the old regime. It commanded the parish priests to read editorials of the *Gaceta* from the pulpit and to display in their comments the proper enthusiasm for the recently won freedom if they wished to avoid the punishments the revolutionary regime reserved for its enemies.

But this provided only a spoken extension of the written word. The old regime had inculcated its political messages by symbol and action, and the new regime did the same. It began by taking over the religious and civic ceremonies—from the annual celebration of the city's patron saint to the proclamation of a new monarch—long enjoyed by the urban populace, that endured no shortage of fireworks, greased-pole climbing competitions, or coins thrown to festive crowds in the years after 1810.

When using images and symbols, the Revolution was, of course, ready to innovate, as well, and here its predicament became clear. These images and symbols fortified the popular view of a continental revolution within reach of Buenos Aires, a city whose proclaimed invincibility was supposedly founded on historical precedent. So, when the revolution celebrated its first anniversary with the inauguration of a commemorative pyramid erected in the main square (named Victory Plaza in memory of 1807), the four sides of the modest monument were decorated with verses about "the exploits and victories of the courageous troops of this immortal city." One year later, during the public celebrations that followed the discovery and prompt execution of the conspirators led by Alzaga, the revolution represented its notional pre-Hispanic roots in the figure of four boys "who sang dressed in Indian garb" and in the names of two indigenous heroes, Tupac Amaru and Mangoré (a legendary local cacique from conquest times), with which it baptized two artillery pieces. The revolutionary leadership obviously sensed the overconfidence of the "immortal city," but it could not afford to encourage a more realistic tone because its war aimed at the total destruction of Spanish power in South America. Therefore, when defeats and stalemates began to accumulate, the urban populace found an easy explanation for them: the pusillanimity, or perhaps even the treacherousness, of the revolutionary leadership. These suspicions were soon justified when, against what everybody had expected in 1810, Fernando was restored to the Spanish throne and made clear that he did not look kindly on those who, while ruling in his name, had proclaimed themselves leaders of nations (even if, mixing caution with audacity, they had avoided formal declarations of independence). The same revolutionary faction that in 1813 had instituted a national anthem, national badge, national flag, and national currency, declared itself ready to lead Buenos Aires back into the Spanish fold if only the monarch would grant its members a universal pardon. Only the king's arrogant stubbornness prevented this humiliating end to the May revolution.

The May revolution had more to fear from its local opponents than from the Spanish menace. Spanish forces presented little threat after royalist Montevideo, an important naval base, surrendered after a long siege by Buenos Aires troops, a siege that had been intermittently supported by local ones led by José Artigas. Artigas, caudillo of the Banda Oriental (as Uruguay was then called), organized several northeastern provinces into a League of the Free Peoples determined to resist domination by Buenos Aires. It was this threat that indirectly brought about the fall in 1815 of the faction dominant until then in revolutionary Buenos Aires. The more prudent and steadfast leadership that replaced it in power, while courageous enough to declare independence, was also aware that the political mood now reigning in the Europe under the aegis of the Holy Alliance made moderation advisable. Some among the new leadership even hoped to undermine support for Fernando's reasserted New World claims by attracting a European princeling to an improvised throne in Buenos Aires.

At the same time, the new leaders could not—any more than their predecessors—discard the myths of invincibility, which were needed more than ever to mobilize the sagging enthusiasm of the populace for a war entering its decisive stage under the more competent leadership of San Martín. From 1816 to 1819 the revolutionary treasury bled itself white, and leaned heavily on the rich even more than on the poor to fund the campaign that was to liberate Chile. In order to husband all its resources and flagging revolutionary energies toward that goal, the new leadership purposely avoided frontal confrontations with Artigas, while making clear in Rio de Janeiro that it would offer no resistance to a Portuguese military occupation of his power base in the Banda Oriental. While in retrospect, it can be argued that these honorable men had made the best possible use of their very limited resources, thus saving the Buenos Aires revolution from total defeat, this view would have been far from popular in the revolutionary capital, convinced that only traitors could yield to the laughable threats coming from the notoriously cowardly Portuguese. The attempt to placate the opposition by mendaciously denying any previous understanding with the Portuguese invaders, who in 1819 eliminated Artigas's last strongholds, only made things worse. Finally, in 1820, leaders aligned with Artigas conquered Buenos Aires itself. After ten years of revolution and war, the central state literally fell to pieces, and the provinces that inherited its authority gave up on the war for independence—except for Salta, which intermittently reassumed combat with royalist Upper Peru. There was general agreement that this was still a victorious outcome to the revolutionary enterprise launched in 1810, and it is true that numerous Argentine forces were still to participate in San Martín's liberation of Lima. But this was not the kind of outcome that the proud denizens of "immortal Buenos Aires" had looked forward to, and, more importantly, it did not compensate for the humiliating defeat symbolized in another image that was to remain equally engraved in collective memory: that of the victorious invaders tying their horses to the iron grate around the monument commemorating the past victories of Buenos Aires.

The fractured political elites that now strove to find ways of achieving an approximately peaceful coexistence among the now de facto independent provinces had to do so under the zealous watch of urban and rural masses that the revolutionary leadership had successfully brought into the public arena. These groups had appropriated a rich and complex political imagination, in which the image of the nation, while not completely ignored, had a more peripheral place than could perhaps be expected. The revolution had been waged in the name of the patria, but, while the term denoted both a nation and a political cause, it was the second that had resonated more strongly among the masses. The state that went under the name of United Provinces entered the 1820s without a well-defined territorial base, a situation acknowledged in the stillborn constitution passed in 1819 by a second constituent congress that kept all options open by endowing it with the official name of Provincias Unidas en Sudamérica. And while the revolutionary leadership worked hard to create a sense of national allegiance among the masses, that allegiance went mostly to a political ideology. Revealingly, the United Provinces coat of arms, created in 1813, had at their center the Phrygian cap of the French revolution, and, for a few months wearing that cap (together with the white and sky-blue national badge) became de rigueur in Buenos Aires. Soon the Phrygian cap was discarded and the badge alone was considered a sufficient sign of patriotism, but it did not denote allegiance to a community whose rulers enjoyed the unanimous support of the ruled. The vast majority of European-born Spaniards, who had not been deemed worthy of receiving the citizenship of the United Provinces, were forbidden to wear the national badge, and a foreign visitor found something

Jewish about the bitter expression and shabby attire of these outcasts designated as such not by a special mark, but by the absence of it. In the view of the masses, beyond these recognizable enemies of the patria there lurked others, more dangerous perhaps because only too frequently they occupied the seats of power.

Thus, if revolutionary patriotism can be considered at all a precursor of nationalism, it would be not of the kind studied by Anderson. Rather, this was the sort of *nationalisme* that was to flourish in France under—and against—the regime of the Third Republic, which also identified the cause of the nation with that of a political faction, and thus implicitly excluded all others from the national community. This kind of patriotism, still very much alive after 1820, deepened divisions within the nation and decisively contributed in 1824–1827 to a political crisis more violent than all previous ones, when the United Provinces faced simultaneously the challenges of rebuilding the central state and making war with Brazil over the Banda Oriental. The hardships created by the war (the United Provinces were unable to break the Brazilian blockade that paralyzed their now-thriving pastoral export economy, and the war effort had to be financed through massive injections of paper money) aggravated the provinces' opposition to the centralist tendencies dominant in the constituent congress, so much so that the cycle of civil wars opened by the promulgation of the constitution of 1826 was to be much longer and more bloody than the one that reacted to the constitution of 1819.

These repeated experiences proved that, while the absence of a central administration created very real problems for the United Provinces (as proved by the fact that they convened the 1824 constituent congress under the not quite gentle prodding of British agents, who, while ready to recognize these provinces as an independent state, demanded to negotiate that recognition with a credible national authority), all attempts to solve these problems by bringing the central state back to life ended in catastrophe. Juan Manuel de Rosas's readiness to recognize these unpleasant facts, that the revolutionary and post-revolutionary political class had for too long ignored at its own risk, was one of the reasons for his gradual ascent to absolute power over the United Provinces.

More importantly, Rosas recognized in the presence of politically mobilized popular classes in the city of Buenos Aires and in the rural districts of Buenos Aires province an unpleasant but inevitable new fact of life; subsequently he took upon himself the task of channeling these people's dangerous energies into comparatively harmless directions, for which purpose he made tenacious efforts to win their total confidence. More than anything tried in the revolutionary years, Rosas's accurate diagnostic of the political predicament inspired systematic efforts to implant an "imagined community" in the collective consciousness of the masses, except that this time the community was not to be the patria but the party.

Admittedly, the presence of a clearly partisan element in the identification with the patria facilitated the transfer of popular loyalties to the new "imagined community," but its success owed even more to the tenacity that Rosas invested in achieving it. In his late writings on Joseph de Maistre, Sir Isaiah Berlin argued that, rather than an ideologue of legitimism, the Savoyard diplomat was a proto-fascist, and when looking at the Rosas regime it is equally difficult to miss many features that anticipate twentieth-century totalitarianism. Certainly the analogy should not be pushed too far. Rosas's political project was only fully implemented in the province of Buenos Aires (for the rest of the provinces he used instead, as brutally as the circumstances made necessary, the overwhelming military superiority that Buenos Aires had regained under his stewardship), and a population of less than two hundred thousand is a rather meager human base for a totalitarian experiment. In this respect José María Ramos Mejía's characterization of Rosas as "a neighborhood tyrant" is not totally off the mark.

At the same time, it should not be ignored that his rule had nothing neighborly about it, supported as it was by the imposition of political rituals that constantly reminded his subjects of the duties imposed on them by the extreme political polarization that Rosas strove to keep alive. Every hour, the night watchmen in the streets of Buenos Aires preceded the announcement of the time and the weather with the obligatory cries, "Long live Holy Federation, Death to the savage, unclean, loathsome Unitarians," and the same mottoes were mandatory at the top of all public and private documents, down to milliners' bills. The sky-blue color favored by the Unitarians was ruthlessly suppressed. When General José María Paz, after years of confinement in Buenos Aires, managed to escape to Colonia, on his first stroll in the streets of that Uruguayan town he was invaded by the unreasoned feeling that something about what he saw was deeply wrong, and it took some time for him to discover that the cause for his malaise were a few girls dressed in light-blue skirts. The crusade against the color of the enemy did not even respect the national flag, that had its two sky-blue stripes replaced with two slate-blue ones. Red was enthusiastically promoted as the color of Federalism. On the death of Rosas's wife in 1838, the mandatory black sign of mourning was complemented with the red party badge, until then only required from government employees. The same badge continued to be in universal use after Rosas decreed the end of the period of mourning. Quite fittingly, Prilidiano Pueyrredón's charming portrait of Rosas's daughter Manuelita in her thirties is a symphony in red: red dress, a red fan in her hand, red wallpaper in the background, and even a not very complimentary reddish hue to her face.

Rosas was equally committed to imprinting the party seal on institutional life. While never sharing the interest of many fellow Federalists in a formal constitution for the province of Buenos Aires, he continued to implement the norms of the quasi-constitutional *leyes fundamentales* introduced by the proto-Unitarian faction in 1821 (and modified only by the extension in 1835 of his governor's mandate from three to five years) with his usual pedantic literalness; elections for members of the legislature were held every year, and after 1835 his own election and reelection by that legislative body took place every five years with perfect regularity. The yearly elections of a single list of candidates to the legislature previously approved by Rosas were quasi-plebiscite occasions in which the citizenry confirmed its identification with the Federalist cause, and the legislature itself became an inexhaustible source of Federalist eloquence. Even the governor's Message on the State of the Province that opened annual legislative sessions, originally a token of the recognition on the part of the executive power of the legitimacy of legislative scrutiny over its performance, became a Federalist occasion that reminded the faithful of who was now the fountainhead of all powers. In the heyday of the Rosas regime, reading the Message took several days, a public holiday during which the role of the legislators was to listen in respectful silence.

And Rosas was no less attentive to the potential uses of the press. The press of Buenos Aires was gradually reduced to a single daily in Spanish, *La Gaceta Mercantil,* and one in English aimed at the cosmopolitan merchant community of the city, the *British Packet.* Both were considered, quite accurately, unofficial mouthpieces of the Rosas administration. They did not, however, read like the production of journalists who went through the motions of repeating every day the same tired arguments. Rosas wanted to make of them effective instruments of propaganda, and not only did he take charge of the supervision of the materials they published, but was ready to invest vast sums in order to enhance their effectiveness. Thus, an expensive top-of-the-line printing press was imported from Britain. Among other advantages, the new technology made it easier to have the Message printed in proper Federalist red.

A regime of political unanimity required constant vigilance, complemented by repression as frequently and as intensely as it might prove necessary. In this respect, Rosas soon acquired an unenviable and not totally
undeserved reputation as a more ruthless caudillo than most of his colleagues. But more than his conviction that in matters of repression a surfeit
was preferable to insufficiency, it was his readiness to invest enormous
amounts of time and effort to create a system of vigilance that differentiated
him from most other Spanish American caudillos who, while on occasion
no less brutal than Rosas, had a less obsessive commitment to the achievement of total control.

This commitment was best revealed in the *clasificaciones de Rosas,* a
projected census of the entire adult male population of the province, that
was to register the physical and ethnic characteristics of each inhabitant, as
well as their garments and all available information about their past criminal or political activities. Only fragments have survived, but they are an
awesome monument in their own right. From them we can learn, for instance, how much the use of footwear had advanced in the countryside, or
get a sense of the market share claimed by British-made industrial ponchos
compared with those woven in the interior provinces and those imported
from Indian territory. Of course, it was not this information (introduced only
for identification purposes) that interested Rosas. What he had in mind was
a political map of the province of Buenos Aires so detailed that (like the geographic one imagined by José Luis Borges) it could only be displayed by
covering the whole territory it represented. How successful was Rosas in
converting the Río de la Plata provinces to his invigorating political credo?
The aftermath of the recent fall of totalitarian regimes recalls what tran-
spired after the fall of their proto-totalitarian Río de la Plata precursor.
Mitre's accurate remark that Rosismo died on the day of Rosas's final defeat in Caseros says all that needs to be said on this point.

The inability of Rosismo to survive the loss of power suggests that direct
coercion was, as its enemies had always proclaimed, more significant than
the consensus that Rosas had worked so hard to impose. However, even if
this is the case, as long as he remained in power he was successful enough
at freeing elites from the pressures of the mobilized masses, now politically
committed to the party rather than to the patria. Of course, such success was
much to the advantage of the province of Buenos Aires, whose de facto
dominance was only reinforced by the continuation of existing conditions,
and more proactive alternatives would necessarily have required popular
mobilization.

Despite the temporary eclipse of a clear national idea in popular consciousness, the elite still saw a problem in the absence of an overarching state organization for the provinces constituting the rump of the Río de la Plata viceroyalty. A universal consensus existed on the problem, and not even Rosas, who probably saw in it a blessing in disguise, denied that it needed to be tackled, arguing instead that tackling it was not yet practical. To restate the problem here, however, is not to belabor the obvious because of the deservedly influential rejection on the part of José Carlos Chiaramonte of the historiographical tradition that presents the rise of the Argentine nation-state as the culmination of a process of nation building that started when the first Spaniards settled on the shores of the Río de la Plata. Chiaramonte's insight has inspired an increasing reluctance to recognize in the dilemmas posed by the absence of an overarching state structure for the United Provinces the political significance that the contemporaries unanimously assigned to them. Comments such as that of Noemí Goldman, when she approvingly refers to Chiaramonte's refusal to view "the provinces that emerged in the Río de la Plata after 1820 as parts of a preexisting Argentine national state"[7] shows the beginning of a revision that can easily slip too far, although Goldman herself is too astute to make that error. A refusal to recognize in the history of the revolutionary state created in 1810 the formation of the Argentine national state is totally justified. It does not follow, however, that the state that waged ten years of war in Argentina, Paraguay, Bolivia, Uruguay, and Chile was merely a figment of the imagination of liberal nationalist historians of a later age, nor that the political elites of the disunited United Provinces might not yearn for a stronger overarching state authority.

While under Rosas the patria had ceased to be the "imagined community" to which the masses owed a loyalty that went before any other; it still had an important place in their imagination. The nation's profile remained, however, as imprecise as during the revolution. The Rosista regime claimed very much to be heir to the May revolution; its most solemn public documents were dated according to three political calendars, starting respectively from the conquest of liberty in 1810, of independence in 1816, and of federation in 1831. Because the United Provinces were so insubstantial a state, America was an even more attractive object of patriotic loyalties than in the past. Rosismo, which favored the institutional status quo, did what it

7. Noemí Goldman, "Los orígenes del federalismo ríoplatense (1820–1831)," in *Nueva Historia Argentina,* vol. 3 (Buenos Aires: Sudamericana, 1998), 109.

could to intensify pan-American patriotism, designating the month of May, during which the 1810 revolution had taken place, as the *mes de América*. Furthermore, the *sol de mayo* (the sun of May, and of the Incas) that since 1813 crowned the United Provinces coat of arms was now routinely invoked in official allocutions as the *astro de América*.

While successfully diverting popular passions towards these comparatively harmless objectives, Rosismo strove with less complete success to impose a moratorium on the political elites' discussions on the structure of the central state. The alternatives faced in these discussions had been defined in the constituent congress of 1824–1827, when they had brought to life the Federalist and the Unitarian parties and unleashed a cycle of savage civil wars that not even Rosas had been able to completely end. Even so, as far as the Federalists were concerned, their irreversible if incomplete victory over Unitarian perfidy had forever eliminated the centralist alternative from the realm of possibility, and it only remained for them to choose the right moment to organize the United Provinces as a single state under a Federalist constitution.

Rosas was, however, firmly determined not to allow this last issue to enter the political agenda. The Federalist leaders who reminded him of Buenos Aires' solemn commitment to support the introduction of a Federalist constitution, a commitment inscribed in the Federal Pact of 1831, were to discover that such unwelcome reminders were becoming increasingly dangerous. By the late 1830s, Rosas felt strong enough to put an end to such reminders, warning his fellow Federalists that the so-called "*organizadores*" (partisans of the immediate organization of the United Provinces as a constitutional Federalist state) among them were no better than Unitarian intriguers in his eyes. While these threats forced the Federalist ruling elite to renounce any discussion of the subject that many by then unselfconsciously placed under the label of "organizing the nation," that same subject was central to the preoccupations of the members of the lettered elites who remained on the margins of the Rosista system, up to 1838 in the United Provinces themselves and, afterward, in the exile Unitarian communities of Montevideo and Chile.

It was among these opposition figures that what would later be called "the national question" finally found a place in discussions of the future constitutional state. In effect, by assuming that an Argentine nation already existed, Rosas's enemies recognized his role in the process of nation building. In their view, one echoed by the conventional wisdom of Argentine historiography, Rosas's contribution had consisted in the regeneration, under the

Federalist flag, of the center of national power that the Unitarian centralists had never been able to impose under their banner. But Rosas's strategy—based on concentrating under his authority all the resources of the province of Buenos Aires in order to impose its hegemony over the remaining United Provinces—ended in failure. He was ousted in 1852 by the governor of Entre Ríos, after it became clear that he intended to force this powerful ally to accept the same subordinate position that he had already imposed on all other governors. After the fall of Rosas, it would take ten additional years for Argentina to achieve national unification under a constitution that established a "republican, representative and federal regime."

In fact, Rosas's contribution to the maturation of the Argentine nation was of a different order. He achieved a unification of sorts for the territory that was later to be organized as a nation-state by reducing it to a single arena for civil war. Not surprisingly, the problematic that a new generation (not identified with either of the historical factions) developed in this context stressed the dichotomies that made national reconciliation so difficult. The "Creed of the Argentine Younger Generation" (written by Esteban Echeverría in 1838 with the partial cooperation of Juan Bautista Alberdi as the manifesto of a group of young thinkers and intellectuals hoping to influence the notoriously nonintellectual Federalist political elite) echoed an insight developed in Mexico by José María Luis Mora, and in Chile by José Victorino Lastarria and Andrés Bello. In this view, the revolution unleashed in 1810 had been only partially successful, ending political submission to Spain while leaving intact the burden of the colonial past that still weighted heavily on the social and cultural life of the new nations. To Echeverría, this was the root of all that afflicted the United Provinces. The provinces were the theater of a battle to the death between two opposite principles: that of progress, that the May revolution had not been able to bring to total victory; and that of reaction, which was prepared to use the victory of Federalism to restore prerevolutionary conditions in the political realm.

This rather abstract and uninspiring presentation of the Argentine predicament was to be completely superseded by the one displayed in Domingo Faustino Sarmiento's masterwork, *Civilización y Barbarie,* published in Chile in 1845. Sarmiento blended powerful historical and political insights with powerful literary renderings of all aspects of life in the Río de la Plata provinces to draw a totally convincing portrait of a country at war with itself. The forces in play were an urban society that, while originally cast in the mold of old Spain, had avidly opened itself since the Revolution to the advances of nineteenth-century civilization, and a rural one, in which survived all the barbarity of the twelfth century. In bringing to life so convincingly this image of an irretrievably fractured society, Sarmiento could then hardly persuade his readers that Argentina could aspire to a different future. Indeed the final section of the book, in which the author argues that the post-Rosas governments could eliminate with comparative ease all the ills described in the previous sections, cannot help but to be read as an anticlimax.

The optimistic predictions at the end of *Civilización y barbarie* were eventually more completely fulfilled than Sarmiento had probably believed possible in 1845, and his book could only be read, as Mary Peabody Mann, his translator into English, had it, as a quaint tableau of "Life in the Argentine Republic in the Age of the Tyrants," an age that mercifully had been closed forever. The very different image of Argentina that accompanied the belated birth of its nation-state was instead to be most appropriately drawn by the man whose victory had opened the way for the state's installation. General Bartolomé Mitre's credentials as the father of modern Argentine historiography are even more solid than those that may be invoked to claim for him the title of father of modern Argentina.

It took three decades and three editions of what had started in the 1850s as a modest biography of General Manuel Belgrano to develop into a master narrative that presented the birth of the Argentine nation as the felicitous and predictable result of the peculiarities of the land and of the pre-Hispanic populations that greeted those whom Mitre refused to call conquerors. (They were instead, he argued, the first European immigrants into the New World, recruited in cities that had reached the most advanced level of civilization in the Iberian Peninsula, having nothing in common with blood-thirsty illiterates such as Francisco Pizarro.) Because the warlike natives refused to play the servile role of their colonial Andean and Mexican brethren, Argentina did not develop "feudal" divisions between rulers and ruled. To the contrary, Argentina's lack of attractions for greedy new immigrants left it with too small a population of European origin to monopolize positions of power and influence. Soon the magistrates in the new towns, as well as the men of law and of letters, were mestizos in whom the two races (that in less fortunate regions served as the human base for a dual society) were harmoniously fused into one. Thus, colonial poverty proved a blessing in disguise, creating a rough social equality that instilled powerful democratic instincts in the new society.

The happy consequence was that, while Argentina's unfortunate Spanish American sisters could only join the liberal and capitalist civilization of the nineteenth century by repudiating their entire past, Argentina needed only to continue building on her past. And this it had done as soon as it had entered the revolutionary path, using the state structure inherited from the ancien régime to impose the new order. Then, in 1820, a social revolution that complemented the political one of 1810 put an end to this anomaly. The eruption of the masses led by the victorious caudillos explicitly realized a democratic mandate implicit in the nation's colonial prehistory. While Rosas had deplored his country's democratic vocation, Mitre unreservedly celebrated it. Admittedly, the democracy triumphant in 1820 was still "inorganic," and hence prone to find aberrant political outlets such as Rosismo, but this was no reason to repudiate it. Mitre believed that redirecting Argentina's democratic energies was precisely the task of his generation.

But Mitre was to be more successful as the writer of the nation than as its leader. From the end of his presidential period in 1868 until his death in 1906, he survived in public life by converting larger and larger portions of his dwindling political capital into symbolic capital. His jubilee in 1902 could be compared with the deification of a Roman emperor, while his political influence was by then almost impossible to detect. Meanwhile, both the friends and enemies of this increasingly marginal politician continued to see Argentina through his eyes. Only after the 1929 crisis was Mitre's vision suddenly to lose its luster, and then not so much because of the end of the constitutional regime that Mitre had inaugurated in 1862 by the military coup of 1930, as in reaction to the worldwide breakdown of the liberal capitalist civilization in which Mitre had recognized the highest achievement of humankind.

3

Letters and Salons:
Women Reading and Writing the Nation

Sarah C. Chambers

"Of course," goaded Don Fidel, delighted to employ another syllogism, "it is what every good patriot should do. The country is represented by the Government. Therefore, to show your support is to show your patriotism."

"But child," said Doña Francisca, "your syllogism is false because . . ."

"Tisk, tisk, tisk," interrupted Don Fidel. "Politics are beyond a woman's comprehension. Isn't that the case, young man?" he asked Martín, who happened to be standing closest to him.

"I am not of that opinion, sir," answered Rivas modestly.

—Alberto Blest Gana, *Martín Rivas*[1]

I would like thank John Chasteen, in particular, for his encouragement and suggestions, as well as the other authors in this collection for their comments during the conference "Reading and Writing the Nation in Nineteenth-Century Latin America," held in April 2000 at the Woodrow Wilson International Center for Scholars in Washington, D.C.

    1. Alberto Blest Gana, *Martín Rivas,* trans. Tess O'Dwyer ([1862] Oxford and New York: Oxford University Press, 2000), 56.

Just as Don Fidel silenced his wife, few of the ideas of Spanish American women from the early national period have survived in the historical record. Certainly, we have stories about the heroines of the independence wars: women who acted as spies, smugglers, financial backers, and camp followers.[2] But we know much less about what women thought, because their writings were less public than their actions and have been largely excluded from national literary canons.

Yet we should not assume that women's opinions were ignored in their own time. Like the fictional Martín Rivas, many politicians and intellectuals enjoyed the company of literate women at evening *tertulias* (salons). In his instructions for the education of his nephew, Simón Bolívar emphasized: "Above all, I recommend that you instill in him the love of cultivated society, where the fair sex exerts its benign influence."[3] Female sociability, therefore, was a cornerstone in the construction of national communities in Latin America. Although such conversations were ephemeral, some dialogues continued on paper through correspondence. Bolívar, for example, exchanged numerous letters with his sister María Antonia and relied upon her astute political and financial advice.[4] This essay will draw upon the letters of three important Spanish American women—Manuela Sáenz of Gran Colombia, Mariquita Sánchez of Argentina, and Carmen Arriagada of

---

2. See, for a few examples, José Dolores Monsalve, *Mujeres de la independencia* (Bogotá: Imprenta Nacional, 1926); Carmen Clemente Travieso, *Mujeres de la independencia: Seis biografías de mujeres venezolanas* (Mexico: Talleres Gráficos de México, 1964); Elvia Gutiérrez Isaza, *Historia heróica de las mujeres próceres de Colombia* (Medellin: N.p., 1972); Judith Prieto de Zegarra, *Mujer, Poder y Desarrollo en el Perú*, vol. 2 (Callao: Editorial DORHCA Representaciones, 1980); Armila Troconis de Veracoechea, *Indias, esclavas, mantuanas y primeras damas* (Caracas: Academia Nacional de la Historia, Alfadil Ediciones, 1990), 132–152; and Carmen Perdomo Escalona, *Heroínas y mártires venezolanas* (Caracas: Ediciones Librería Destino, 1994). For analyses of the role of women in the independence wars, see Evelyn Cherpak, "Women and the Independence of Gran Colombia, 1780–1830" (Ph.D. diss., University of North Carolina at Chapel Hill, 1973); Cherpak, "The Participation of Women in the Independence Movement in Gran Colombia, 1780–1830," in *Latin American Women: Historical Perspectives,* ed. Asunción Lavrin (Westport, CT: Greenwood Press, 1978), 219–234; and Silvia M. Arrom, *The Women of Mexico City, 1790–1857* (Stanford: Stanford University Press, 1985), 14–52.

3. On the education of Fernando Bolívar, 1822, *Selected Writings of Bolívar,* vol. 1, ed. Harold A. Bierck (New York: Colonial Press), 310.

4. For her letters, see Aníbal Noguera Mendoza, ed., *Epistolarios: Bolívar y las damas, las damas y Bolívar* (Caracas: Ediciones de la Presidencia de la República, 1983), 15–90.

Chile—in order to reflect upon the role of women in reading and especially writing their visions of the nation in early nineteenth-century South America. This analysis will show that friendships, maintained in part through correspondence, both influenced their varying degrees of national identity and allowed them to argue that women could play an important role as mediators in early republican politics.

Benedict Anderson creatively sketched out the means, particularly print media, by which citizens of a nation could form a sense of common identity with compatriots whom they had never met. Like Jürgen Habermas, however, he frequently takes as a given the abstract, political sphere as imagined by male philosophers in the eighteenth and nineteenth centuries.[5] Just as feminist critics have pushed out the analytical boundaries of the public sphere, taking gender into consideration can yield new insights into the formation of national identities.[6] Women, who were excluded from military service and whose writing remained unpublished until the second half of the nineteenth century, had to find other means of connecting themselves to a national community. For Latin America, including the perspective of women reveals that concrete social relationships remained important even as more abstract imaginings of nation and republic were emerging in the early nineteenth century. Although women were excluded from formal politics and the press, they were active in intermediary social spaces between the public and domestic spheres, where philosophies were discussed, plots hatched, and alliances formed. This essay will analyze how that intermediary position affected women's perceptions of the nation. The quality of their social connections determined the degree to which various literate women identified with their emerging nations. Their mediated relationship to the state, moreover, allowed women to claim that they worked for national unity

5. Jürgen Habermas, *The Structural Transformation of the Public Sphere,* trans. Thomas Burger (Cambridge: MIT Press, 1989).

6. Dena Goodman, "Public Sphere and Private Life: Toward a Synthesis of Current Historiographical Approaches to the Old Regime," *History & Theory* 31:1 (1992): 1–20; Mary Ryan, "Gender and Public Access: Women's Politics in Nineteenth-Century America," in *Habermas and the Public Sphere,* ed. Craig Calhoun (Cambridge: MIT Press, 1992), 264; Seyla Benhabib, "Models of Public Space: Hannah Arendt, the Liberal Tradition, and Jürgen Habermas," in *Habermas and the Public Sphere,* 73–98, and Nancy Fraser, "Rethinking the Public Sphere: Models and Boundaries," in *Habermas and the Public Sphere,* 109–142; and Carole Pateman, "Feminist Critiques of the Public/Private Dichotomy," in *Public and Private in Social Life,* ed. S. I. Benn and G. F. Gaus (London: Croom Helm, 1983): 281–303.

as opposed to particular political parties and occasionally to criticize the sacrifice of lives "for the nation," when in their view it instead furthered partisan interests.

This essay focuses specifically on women, but the findings have implications for male politicians as well. The precursors to political parties in Latin America were often built upon networks of extended kinship and personal patronage.[7] And although men could reach out to a wider audience by publishing in newspapers and pamphlets, the use of the manuscript letter remained widespread and crucial. The nation as imagined in print culture, therefore, remained intertwined with the conversations among communities of friends.

Female readers of national literature in early nineteenth-century South America would have found limited roles to emulate. In most published writing of the early republics, women, if they appear at all, are either the objects of male authors or allegorical symbols of the nation.[8] Although no prominent officials or intellectuals considered granting women citizenship, their attitudes ranged from harshly criticizing politically active women to praising those who fostered domestic virtues. In the years following independence, theater depicted home as the proper place for women. Plays, such as *Las convulsiones* by Luis Vargas Tejada (Colombia, 1828) and *Frutos de la educación* by Felipe Pardo y Aliaga (Peru, 1829), ridiculed intellectual women and dramatized the dangers posed to and by women in the public sphere.[9] A more positive ideology, influenced by the European Enlighten-

---

7. Mary Lowenthal Felstiner, "Kinship Politics in the Chilean Independence Movement," *Hispanic American Historical Review* 56:1 (1976): 58–80; and Linda Lewin, *Politics and Parentela in Paraiba: A Case Study of Family-Based Oligarchy in Brazil* (Princeton: Princeton University Press, 1987).

8. Jean Franco, *Plotting Women: Gender and Representation in Mexico* (New York: Columbia University Press, 1989), 79–101; Doris Sommer, *Foundational Fictions: The National Romances of Latin America* (Berkeley, Los Angeles, and Oxford: University of California Press, 1991); Francine Masiello, *Between Civilization and Barbarism: Women, Nation, and Literary Culture in Modern Argentina* (Lincoln: University of Nebraska Press, 1992); María Inés de Torres Carballal, "Ideología estatal, ideología patriarcal y mitos fundacionales: la construcción de la imagen de la mujer en el sistema lírico del Uruguay del siglo XIX," in *Voces femeninas y construcciones de identitad,* ed. Marcia Rivera (Buenos Aires: CLACSO, 1995), 61–132; and Rebecca Earle, "Rape and the Anxious Republic: Revolutionary Colombia, 1810–1830," in *Hidden Histories of Gender and the State in Latin America,* ed. Elizabeth Dore and Maxine Molyneux (Durham and London: Duke University Press, 2000): 127–146.

9. Susan Isabel Stein, "A Woman's Place: Nineteenth-Century Bourgeois Morality and the Spanish American Domestic Comedy," *Latin American Theatre Review* 26, no.1 (Fall, 1992): 79–90.

ment but also rooted in the Spanish American experience, asserted that even within the home women played an important role by raising loyal and virtuous citizens.[10] Domingo Faustino Sarmiento of Argentina was one of the most prominent and active advocates of education for women, asking rhetorically in 1843, "Might one doubt that a woman ought to be educated so that she in turn can educate her children well?"[11] Emphasizing the benefits for the nation as much as for the women themselves, the schools he established aimed not to graduate female intellectuals but "tender and tolerant wives, enlightened and moral mothers, diligent and thrifty heads of household."[12]

These domestic roles were the dominant identity even for the first female authors who began to comment on the role of women in the feminine periodicals that appeared around the middle of the nineteenth century.[13] Nancy Saporta Sternbach highlights the contradictory position of two such female journalists in Argentina: "Both of them struggled incessantly for women's rights through their activism and their writing while simultaneously insisting that women not make a profession of writing."[14] Although the ability of women to publish their work was an important advance, these writers were limited to presumably feminine topics, such as education and child rearing, and rarely published outside ladies' journals.[15] In more private fora, such

10. Arrom, *The Women of Mexico City,* 15–26, and Sarah C. Chambers, *From Subjects to Citizens: Honor, Gender, and Politics in Arequipa, Peru, 1780–1854* (University Park: Pennsylvania State University Press, 1999).

11. Quoted in Elizabeth Garrels, "Sarmiento and the Woman Question: From 1839 to the *Facundo,"* in *Sarmiento: Author of a Nation,* ed. Tulio Halperín-Donghi, Iván Jaksiæ, Gwen Kirkpatrick, and Francine Masiello (Berkeley: University of California Press, 1994), 286.

12. Garrels, "Sarmiento," 272; see also Elizabeth Garrels, "La Nueva Eloisa en América, o el ideal de la mujer de la generación de 1837," *Nuevo Texto Crítico* 2, no. 4 (1989): 27–38.

13. For reprints from the feminine press in Argentina, see Francine Masiello, ed., *La mujer y el espacio público: el periodismo femenino en la Argentina del siglo XIX* (Buenos Aires: Feminaria Editora, 1994). For analyses, see Nestor Tomás Auza, *Periodismo y feminismo en la Argentina, 1830–1930* (Buenos Aires: Emecé Editores, 1988), and June Hahner, *Emancipating the Female Sex: The Struggle for Women's Rights in Brazil, 1850–1940* (Durham, NC: Duke University Press, 1990).

14. Nancy Saporta Sternbach, "A mejorar la condición de mi secso: The Essays of Rosa Guerra," in *Reinterpreting the Spanish American Essay,* ed. Doris Meyer (Austin: University of Texas Press, 1995), 47.

15. Meyer, ed., *Reinterpreting the Spanish American Essay;* Montserrat Ordóñez, "Soledad Acosta de Samper: una nueva lectura, *Nuevo Texto Crítico* 2, no. 4 (1989):

as letters, some middle-class and elite women lamented the strictures of such a rigid morality.[16]

To recover the voice of literate Spanish American women from the first half of the nineteenth century, before the emergence of feminine periodicals, we need to turn from newspapers and books to unpublished works.[17] Although there are few extant women's diaries from this period, many middle and upper-class women were prolific correspondents. The genre of the letter, moreover, falls into a middle ground between the public and private spheres, calling into question a strictly gendered division between political and domestic. Letters frequently both grew out of and provided material for the discussion in salons, as well as serving as a model for epistolary novels and travel writing. As Dena Goodman asserts for France, "Letters, which were the dominant form of writing in the eighteenth century, were increasingly and creatively used by the philosophes to bridge the gap between the private circles in which they gathered and the public arena that they sought to shape and conquer."[18] Letters had long played a central role in Spanish American society, where the educated elite (*letrados*) governed and attempted to assert cultural hegemony over first colonies and then nations

---

49–55, and essays in Lea Fletcher, ed., *Mujeres y cultura en la Argentina del siglo XIX* (Buenos Aires: Feminaria Editora, 1994). For both the openings for female writers created by the Romantic movement and the constraints placed upon them in Peru and Spain, see Francisca Denegri, *El Abanico y la cigarrera: La primera generación de mujeres ilustradas en el Perú* (Lima: Instituto de Estudios Peruanos, 1996), 120–149; and Susan Kirkpatrick, *Las Románticas: Women Writers and Subjectivity in Spain, 1835–1850* (Berkeley and Los Angeles: University of California Press, 1989), 62–96. June Hahner argues that some female writers in nineteenth-century Brazil were in fact relatively radical; see *Emancipating the Female Sex,* 42–76. Later, Spanish American feminists would use the ideology of their moral superiority to push for a greater role in the public sphere; Asunción Lavrin, *Women, Feminism, and Social Change in Argentina, Chile, and Uruguay, 1890–1940* (Lincoln: University of Nebraska Press, 1995).

16. Because this essay addresses women writers, it will leave out the experiences of nonelite women; for their experiences in Peru, see Chambers, *From Subjects to Citizens.*

17. See introduction to Sara Castro-Klarén, Sylvia Molloy, and Beatriz Sarlo, *Women's Writing in Latin America: An Introduction* (Boulder, CO: Westview Press, 1991); and Stacey Schlau, *Spanish American Women's Use of the Word: Colonial through Contemporary Narratives* (Tucson: University of Arizona Press, 2001).

18. Dena Goodman, "Enlightenment Salons: the Convergence of Female and Philosophic Ambitions," *Eighteenth-Century Studies* 22, no. 3 (Spring 1989): 340. For the role of the letter in the United States during the same period, see David Shields, *Civil Tongues and Polite Letters in British America* (Chapel Hill: University of North Carolina Press, 1997), 317.

through copious manuscript correspondence.[19] During the wars of independence, male military and political leaders debated politics and plotted strategies in thousands of letters, later published in volumes that filled the shelves of national libraries.[20] Finally, in the nineteenth century, letters came to play a crucial role in the plots of Spanish American novels such as *Martín Rivas.*[21]

Conversation and correspondence integrated women into the emerging national communities of Europe and the Americas during the late eighteenth and early nineteenth centuries and offered them a way of acting politically. Feminist scholars have countered Rousseau's negative depiction of salon women in France as aristocratic *précieuses* whose feminizing influence on male philosophers was akin to the role of "power behind the throne in court politics." Goodman asserts that female sociability within Enlightenment salons was helping to construct a new "Republic of Letters."[22] After the French Revolution, such spaces were undeniably politicized. Writing of female novelists in nineteenth-century France, Whitney Walton asserts, "Politics and writing were basically inseparable for them all; indeed to some extent writing was a substitute for political activism or at least the only means (along with sociability and conversation) for these women to be involved in political affairs."[23] Although less researched, tertulias involving both sexes were also common in Spanish America and became increasingly politicized in the years before and after independence. Indeed, I would propose that emerging concepts of the nation as "imagined communities," for women and men alike, were rooted in the social interactions of these smaller but more tangible communities of writers, readers, conversationalists, and political conspirators. Correspondence could both maintain the ties among

19. Angel Rama, *The Lettered City,* trans. and ed. John Charles Chasteen (Durham, NC: Duke University Press, 1996).

20. Benedict Anderson, *Imagined Communities: Reflections on the Origins and Spread of Nationalism* (London: Verso, 1983), 62. See also the chapter by François-Xavier Guerra in this collection.

21. For the role of the letter in *Sab,* see the chapter by Fernando Unzueta in this collection.

22. Goodman, "Enlightenment Salons," 329–350. See also Janet Gurkin Altman, "Women's Letters in the Public Sphere," in *Going Public: Women and Publishing in Early Modern France,* ed. Elizabeth C. Goldsmith and Dena Goodman (Ithaca: Cornell University Press, 1995), 99–115.

23. Whitney Walton, "Writing the 1848 Revolution: Politics, Gender, and Feminism in the Works of French Women of Letters," *French Historical Studies* 18, no. 4 (Fall 1994): 1007.

such compatriots as politics and war sent them on journeys or into exile, and extend the membership of such communities to those, especially in the provinces, who were unable to attend salons regularly if at all. Women, moreover, played an especially crucial role as the social glue holding together these groups.[24] Appealing to their nonpartisanship, a credible if not always completely accurate claim, female salonierres and correspondents offered themselves as potential mediators in the increasingly fractionalized politics of the early republics in South America.

Sadly, female correspondence was not collected and protected by early archivists and most is not only lost but likely destroyed. Yet fortunately the letters of Manuela Sáenz, Mariquita Sánchez, and Carmen Arriagada survived and were published in the twentieth century.[25] Even these published letters were only a fraction of those penned by these three prolific writers. Some of the correspondence of Sáenz to key male political figures, such as Simón Bolívar and Ecuadorian President Juan José Flores, survived as part of their own official collections, but she refers to many more letters sent to political figures across South America that have yet to be located.[26] A greater range of the correspondence of Sánchez, who asserted in one letter that "[t]here is no one who writes more than I,"[27] was preserved by the recipients as well as members of her family, perhaps because she was so widely respected in her own lifetime. Finally, the letters sent by Arriagada to her Austrian lover, painter Juan Mauricio Rugendas, in almost every bimonthly post for ten years and less frequently for another five, were saved by him despite her warnings to destroy them in order to protect her reputation. But those that she wrote to her many other friends have not yet come to light.

The majority of the letters penned by these three women cannot be considered private in the strictest sense of the word. None of these writers could be sure of postal security, and at various times developed networks of

24. Shields makes a similar claim for women in the United States; Shields, *Civil Tongues and Polite Letters,* 319.

25. Manuela Sáenz, *Epistolario,* ed. Jorge Villalba (Quito: Banco Central del Ecuador, 1986); Clara Vilaseca, ed., *Cartas de Mariquita Sánchez* (Buenos Aires: Ediciones Peuser, 1952); and Oscar Pinochet de la Barra, ed., *Carmen Arriagada: cartas de una mujer apasionada* (Santiago: Editorial Universitaria, 1990).

26. January 30 and November 28, 1843, in Sáenz, *Epistolario,* 126 and 149.

27. Vilaseca, *Cartas de Mariquita Sánchez,* 312. In another letter, she wrote: "I write so much, daughter, with such frequency, to everyone, that my back aches. Hardly a day goes by that I do not write" (130).

friends who could personally deliver correspondence to keep it from falling into the wrong hands. Sánchez, moreover, apparently intended most of her letters to be circulated among friends and family, only occasionally noting that a particular letter was for the recipient's eyes only.[28] Sáenz urged Flores to destroy the letters she sent to him, in which she provided him information on his political opponents exiled in Peru, but their content was explicitly political rather than personal. The letters of Arriagada to Rugendas fall at the most intimate end of the scale, particularly those which she managed to have delivered secretly and in which she openly discussed their love. The letters she sent through the regular post, however, discussed literature and politics, as well as personal news, and included greetings for their shared acquaintances; she likely expected, therefore, that he would at least discuss their contents, and perhaps also circulate them, among these friends.

From the range of issues these women discussed in their letters, this essay focuses on their conceptions of the emerging nations. In this formative period, however, the boundaries between membership in a specific nation as territorially defined and the broader concept of adherence to a post-colonial political republic were not always clearly demarcated. The first section concentrates more on the former and highlights the varying degrees to which Sáenz, Sánchez, and Arriagada felt connected to the emerging national identities of Ecuador, Argentina, and Chile, respectively. Despite their differences, however, for all three women their sense of nation was rooted less in abstract concepts than in concrete relationships to friends and family that they maintained through both face-to-face sociability and correspondence. In terms of the role they believed women should play in the new republics—the political rather than territorial definition of nation—the similarities among the three are striking. None conformed to the increasingly narrow definition of the ideal woman as "republican mother," nor did they confine their writing to women's issues alone. They did not claim the right to play an active and direct role in the political sphere, but rather turned their exclusion from formal politics and their social connectedness into a rationale for their influence as mediators in the increasingly partisan conflicts that threatened national unity.

---

28. For example, a letter in 1856 to Alberdi in which she asks him not to read it to others because they would think she was a partisan of Urquiza; Vilaseca, *Cartas de Mariquita Sánchez*, 351.

Women Writing the Nation

The generation born in the late colonial period lived through an era of only incipient nation building. Of the three women under investigation, Manuela Sáenz had the most complicated national identity. Born in Quito in 1797, as an adult she moved back and forth across the shifting borders of what would become the nations of Peru, Ecuador, and Colombia. The illegitimate daughter of a Spanish military officer and a woman from one of the city's moderately wealthy families, Sáenz was a rebel in her personal as well as political life. In her youth she escaped, according to some accounts, from the convent in which she was educated in an attempt to elope with a lover. In 1819, however, her father arranged her marriage to an English merchant, with whom she moved to Lima, Peru. It was there that she joined the conspiracies against Spanish rule.[29] When Argentine General José de San Martín arrived to aid the relatively small Peruvian patriot movement, he recognized the participation of Sáenz and other women by establishing a Society of Patriotic Ladies and decorating the members with a special medal inscribed with the slogan "To the patriotism of the most sensitive."[30] In 1822, Sáenz left on a trip to Quito, where she met and became the lover of Simón Bolívar, the leader of independence in the former viceroyalty of New Granada. She returned to Peru by his side, never to reunite with her husband, and hosted political salons as Bolívar continued his military campaigns.

After the final victory over royalist troops, Sáenz set up her residence in Bogotá, the capital of (what in retrospect came to be called) "Gran Colombia," where Bolívar was president. She also came to share his vision of

---

29. For biographies of Sáenz, see Alfonso Rumazo González, *Manuela Sáenz: La Libertadora del Libertador,* 3rd ed. (Bogotá: Ediciones Mundial Bogotá, 1944); Alberto Miramon, *La Vida ardiente de Manuela Sáenz,* 3rd ed. (Bogotá: Librería Sudamérica, 1946); Víctor W. Von Hagen, *La Amante Inmortal* (Barcelona: Editorial AHR, 1958); Mercedes Ballesteros, *Manuela Sáenz, el último amor de Bolívar* (Madrid: Fundación Universitaria Española, 1976); Blanca Gaitán de París, *La mujer en la vida del Libertador* (Bogotá: Cooperativa Nacional de Artes Gráficas, 1980); Arturo Valero Martínez, ed., *En defensa de Manuela Sáenz, la Libertadora del Libertador* (Guayaquil: Editorial del Pacífico, 1988); José Rivas Rivas, *Carta de Manuela Sáenz a su PornoDetractor* (Caracas: Universidad Central de Venezuela, 1990); Martha Gil-Montero, "Manuela and Simón," *Américas* 42, no. 2 (1990): 6–15; and Ligia Elena Rojas, *Manuela Mujer Republicana* (Caracas: Ediciones Los Heraldos Negros, 1994).

30. Prieto de Zegarra, *Mujer, Poder y Desarrollo,* 203–207.

Spanish American unity, defending herself from the label of foreigner in Bogotá by declaring "my country is the whole of the American continent."[31] It was, however, a short-lived unity. By 1830, as Bolívar lay on his deathbed, first Venezuela and then Ecuador declared independence from Colombia. Sáenz, who had publicly ridiculed Bolívar's rivals, found herself out of political favor. Three years later, President Francisco de Paula Santander accused Sáenz of participation in a plot to overthrow his administration (charges she denied) and forced her to leave Colombia. From a temporary refuge in Jamaica, she wrote to Juan José Flores, a former friend of Bolívar and then president of Ecuador, who granted her safe conduct to enter the country. When Sáenz arrived in 1835, however, Flores was no longer president, and his successor Vicente Rocafuerte, comparing her to Madame de Staël, cancelled her passport and ordered her to leave the country.[32]

Crossing just over the border into Peru, Sáenz took refuge in Paita. This small town in the desert posed a stark contrast to the capitals of Quito, Lima, and Bogotá where Sáenz had been at the center of social and political events for the previous sixteen years. She would later write that "eight years in Paita dull, debase, and impoverish one."[33] Nevertheless, the port was not as isolated as it might seem. In the wake of independence, the border between Ecuador and Peru was hotly contested. Paita was central not only to such international politics, but its large exile community also played a role in the internal politics of Ecuador. Early republican Ecuador was not as unstable as neighboring countries, but still experienced its share of rebellions and civil wars. Between 1830 and 1843 power alternated, mostly peacefully, between the military leader Flores and civilian Rocafuerte. But when Flores attempted to extend his rule by rewriting the constitution in 1843, Rocafuerte joined an insurrection, which included plotters in Paita. Determined to remain politically active, Sáenz first tried to provide Flores with information on Peruvian troop movements along the border, but soon realized she could be of more use to him as a spy among the exile community.[34]

31. Letter of 1830, reprinted in Eduardo Posada, "La Libertadora," *Boletín de Historia y Antigüedades* [Bogota] 15 (August 1925): 32.

32. October 14, 1835, in Sáenz, *Epistolario*, 100.

33. June 12, 1843, in Sáenz, *Epistolario*, 140.

34. For a more thorough analysis of Sáenz's activities and political philosophy in exile, see Sarah C. Chambers, "Republican Friendship: Manuela Sáenz Writes Women into the Nation,1835–1856," *Hispanic American Historical Review* 81, no. 2 (May 2001): 225–257.

very much unelite [handwritten annotation]

Born and raised in Quito, Sáenz spent almost her entire adult life in Colombia and Peru. When Sáenz was born, then, there was no such country as Ecuador, and she never lived there when it was a nation. It was primarily during her years in Paita that national borders were increasingly defined, and it was this experience of exile that forged her own national identity. Sáenz identified herself first as a Quiteña rather than an Ecuadorian. In 1841, when she was still trying to find a way to be politically useful, she wrote to Flores, "Please pardon any foolishness I may propose to you as I have no interest in it except as a Quiteña, your friend and your faithful servant."[35] It was a personal identity closely tied to a direct experience of homeland and an affective relationship to friends and family. Indeed it was common in this period for men as well as women to identify as strongly if not more so with their home region, where local economic circuits and administrative units had deep roots in the colonial period, rather than with the new nations.[36] Flores's base of power was in Quito, for example, while Rocafuerte represented the interests of the Guayaquil elite. Because Sáenz's identification with Quito was based more on ties to people than to place, her feelings of nationalism fluctuated to some degree with the status of those relationships. She felt discouraged, for example, when she could find no one there who could effectively look after her financial affairs. "I am from Quito and I have relatives there; I had friends," she lamented, "and it is as if I never had them; I believe that even for a foreigner there would be someone to handle her matters and collect her rents."[37]

Furthermore, despite repeated expressions of love for her homeland, Sáenz never returned to Ecuador even when her exile was lifted after two years. She initially explained to Flores that she feared to return as long as Rocafuerte remained president.[38] But even when Flores returned to power, Sáenz remained in Paita. By 1842, she told Flores she never intended to return as the climate was bad for her health, and revealed that she had not intended to stay permanently in Ecuador even in 1835, but simply hoped to recover her property and leave again.[39] Nevertheless, a year and a half later, she conveyed anger and regret at her exile:

35. December 12, 1841, in Sáenz, *Epistolario,* 114.
36. Anderson, *Imagined Communities,* 54–59.
37. August 10, 1844, in Sáenz, *Epistolario,* 164.
38. May 18, 1837, and October 20, 1837, in Sáenz, *Epistolario,* 107–108.
39. January 20, 1842, in Sáenz, *Epistolario,* 115.

A terrible anathema from hell delivered by Rocafuerte has me far from my fatherland and from my friends like you, and the worst is that I have been sentenced to never return to my homeland; since as you know, my friend, it is easier to destroy something than to make it anew. An order exiled me; but the safe conduct has not been able to reunite me with my dearest affections: my fatherland and my friends.[40]

Apparently she had never intended to make Quito her permanent home, yet to have that option denied to her deepened rather than weakened her feelings of patriotism. It also strengthened her resolve to bridge distances through her correspondence. With a touch of humor, she warned Flores that he would never be free of her letters, whether she moved to Lima or even China.[41]

Politics also shaped Sáenz's sense of nationalism. Her enmity toward Rocafuerte fueled her political activism on behalf of Flores, whom she subsequently identified with the fate of the nation. Yet her alliance with Flores was based on their friendship and her confidence in his ability to maintain order, not on a territorial understanding of nationality, because Flores like Bolívar was a native of Venezuela. Exile further influenced her patriotism as she developed a sense of national identity in opposition to her experiences in and her image of Peru. Her arrival coincided with a period of border conflict between the two countries, and she took personally insults to Ecuador. In 1842, she sent a copy of a satirical poem, which depicted Ecuador and Bolivia as poor, envious neighbors, to Flores, urging him to find "a Quiteño to respond in kind in order to defend the national honor." She criticized republican leaders in Peru, moreover, for what she regarded as their ungrateful rejection of Bolívar's continuing intervention in national affairs after his troops had helped defeat the royalist army. Finally, she was disdainful of Peru's ongoing instability and civil wars, a fate she hoped Ecuador could avoid under the strong leadership of Flores. "I am a patriot," she declared, "and I do not wish my country to imitate Peru."[42]

By the end of Sáenz's life, her circle of friends—maintained either through personal contact or correspondence—came to overlap significantly with the citizenry of Ecuador. Thus her imagining of the nation had its roots

40. Sept. 7, 1843, in Sáenz, *Epistolario,* 144. Although "la patria" has a feminine article in Spanish, I have translated it as "fatherland" because of its Latin origins in "pater," the father.

41. Ibid.; June 12, 1843 in Sáenz, *Epistolario,* 140.

42. January 23, 1844 in Sáenz, *Epistolario,* 152.

in real acquaintances even if it extended to compatriots whom she had never met. In 1853 she wrote to Roberto Ascásubi, who had been in exile in Paita but had subsequently returned to Ecuador, to thank him for helping her to finally recover her maternal inheritance. She asked him to use some of the money to buy some local handicrafts, including nativity scenes, so that she could spend that Christmas Eve with friends "remembering the fatherland." She signed herself "your *llacta huasi* [countrywoman in Quichua], friend, and faithful servant, Manuela Sáenz of Quito."[43]

In contrast to Sáenz's gradual development of an identity tied to the nation of Ecuador, Mariquita Sánchez identified strongly with Argentina throughout her life, despite the young nation's changing borders and her own lengthy periods of exile in Montevideo (and a briefer stay in Rio de Janeiro) during the rule of Juan Manuel Rosas. But, Sánchez did share with Sáenz a strong character. Born in 1786, she was the daughter of a Spanish merchant and a member of the Creole oligarchy of Buenos Aires.[44] Despite her traditional upbringing, she sought legal dispensation in 1804 to marry her second cousin, Martín Thompson, over the objections of her parents. In 1819, widowed only a few months, she wed Jean-Baptiste de Mendeville, the French consul and several years her junior. Ultimately she lived independently of Mendeville, who was transferred to Ecuador and later retired to France. Sánchez also played an influential role in politics throughout her life. She supported independence from Spain in 1810, was a member and later president of the charitable Society of Beneficence, hosted for decades one of the most renowned political and cultural salons in Buenos Aires (where she patronized the young intellectuals who would later rise to national influence), and supported the Rosas opposition movements within the exile community in Montevideo from 1839 to 1852.

In her correspondence, Sánchez repeatedly and explicitly affirmed her patriotism. During ceremonies to mark the anniversary of Argentine independence from Spain in 1839, she reflected upon the excitement and optimism of those early days, and upon the fall of Rosas she wrote to her son of her strong emotions, exclaiming "So patriotic am I!"[45] Various factors may account for Sánchez's generally stronger nationalism; both her own personal history and that of Argentina were less complicated than that of

43. October 29, 1853, in Sáenz, *Epistolario,* 179.
44. For biographies of Sánchez, see Jorge A. Zavalía Lagos, *Mariquita Sánchez y su tiempo* (Buenos Aires: Plus Ultra, 1986), and María Sáenz Quesada, *Mariquita Sánchez: Vida política y sentimental* (Buenos Aires: Editorial Sudamericana, 1995).
45. Vilaseca, *Cartas de Mariquita Sánchez,* 387 and 349.

Sáenz and Gran Colombia. As a native of the capital of Buenos Aires, she had no competing provincial loyalties, and yet was supportive of meeting some provincial demands in the interests of preserving national unity.[46] Her experience of exile, while trying, was different from that of Sáenz. Whereas Sáenz found herself primarily among the political opponents of Flores, for whom she acted as a spy, Sánchez was at the heart of a large and supportive community that shared a fervent opposition to Rosas despite their political differences on other matters. She identified with them explicitly as fellow Argentines and was careful to distinguish the government of Rosas from the nation of Argentina. She frequently wrote to her daughter back in Buenos Aires of her active social life in Montevideo, once counting forty-one households that she visited regularly.[47] She took particular pride in her attendance at political gatherings along with the most prominent Argentines; of one *tertulia* in 1839, she wrote that "my friend Marín . . . came to take me by the hand and took me to the room of Miguel Irigoyen, where there was a gathering of Argentines. What a carefree time of jokes and patriotism!"[48]

Only in periods of greatest disillusionment with the state of politics in Argentina, did Sánchez waver somewhat from her firm commitment to her *patria*. In 1861, she wrote from Buenos Aires to her husband in Paris: "Sometimes I think that I have been shipwrecked and even that I am in a strange land, because not single friend from our days exists anymore, and we are always in this disagreeable politics that ruins us fruitlessly."[49] For Sánchez, as for Sáenz, a sense of national identity was intertwined with personal relationships and politics. When the high cost of living and unstable local politics spurred Sánchez to visit Rio de Janeiro for a change in 1846, she felt lonely, with fewer friends and less frequent correspondence with Buenos Aires: "I sigh for my homeland and my friends," she lamented.[50] In Rio, she had boasted, people thought she was European due to her manners, and at various times she expressed a strong desire to live in Europe (where several of her children had settled).[51] "Ah, my friend, how cruel destiny has been to me!" she exclaimed in a letter to Juan Bautista Alberdi, "so Euro-

---

46. Sáenz Quesada, *Mariquita Sánchez,* 265.
47. Vilaseca, *Cartas de Mariquita Sánchez,* 121.
48. Ibid., 378.
49. Ibid., 319.
50. Ibid., 130 and 141.
51. Ibid., 136 and 353.

What does "hostly salons" mean?

pean and not to be able to see that Europe."[52] Consistently, then, Sánchez's sense of national identity was rooted in her relationships with other Argentines, whether at home or in exile.

Interestingly, Chilean Carmen Arriagada, who never experienced exile from her homeland, displayed the most ambivalence about nationalism; perhaps exile allowed more idealized imaginings than witnessing everyday politics. Born in 1808 on the eve of independence, Arriagada was the youngest and least politically active of the three women. At age seventeen, she married, against her parents' wishes, a Prussian military officer turned landowner, but grew bored with the life of a provincial housewife. She is remembered primarily for a love affair with Austrian painter Juan Mauricio Rugendas, vividly evoked in her numerous letters.[53] Arriagada, however, was also active in the cultural life of her country: reading voraciously, hosting salons, and, although she did not publish her own writing, helping to establish a newspaper in Talca to which she contributed translations of European works. Nevertheless, her identification with the nation was relatively weak compared to Sánchez and even Sáenz, owing in part to her strong disaffection from the authoritarian form of government established in 1830 by Diego Portales. She simultaneously mocked the extravagant homages paid to slain national hero Portales—"And why don't they save as relics the bullets that pierced his benevolent heart?"[54]—and decried the political chaos that ensued after his death in 1837 with "the sentiment and mourning in which the heart of a Chilean woman should find itself upon seeing the disgraces and losses of her country. . . ."[55] Her opposition to Chile's invasion of Peru in 1837 led her to disavow at least official definitions of nationalism: "I now know that I have ceased to be a patriot; I have no interest in the blessed expedition. One tires of loving an ungrateful fatherland, and the laurels which adorn the forehead of an enemy weigh heavily . . . on the most generous heart."[56]

Arriagada identified more with the culture than politics of Chile, noting, for example, that the exile of a Chilean poet was a worse loss to the coun-

52. Ibid., 356.
53. Also like biographies of Sáenz, her life after this affair is depicted as a tragic epilogue: a slow degeneration into mental illness; Oscar Pinochet de la Barra, *El Gran Amor de Rugendas* (Santiago: Editorial Universitaria, 1984).
54. Pinochet de la Barra, ed., *Carmen Arriagada: cartas de una mujer apasionada,* 94.
55. Ibid., 90.
56. Ibid., 115; see also 118 and 160.

try than the death of Portales.[57] Nonetheless, the only national author she mentioned with any frequency was a fellow woman, Mercedes Marín, whose poetry (except for a homage to Portales) she admired, and she repeatedly voiced a desire to meet her and be welcomed into her circle.[58] Arriagada complained frequently in her letters to Rugendas about the lack of culture in the southern town of Talca, expressing her desire to visit Santiago more often and asking him to give her greetings to their common acquaintances in the capital.[59] Ultimately it was European literature that she devoured, from Shakespeare and Byron to Dumas and Hugo, which inflamed her imagination. Although she desired with all her heart that Rugendas remain in Chile, she nonetheless pointed out that "Chile is not the place for talents like yours; Italy, beautiful Italy is the fatherland of talents and the Arts."[60] By contrast, she denigrated Chileans as neither generous nor grateful. There was in fact no national character at all, she wrote: "[T]hey are imitators and by no means original."[61] As with Sáenz and Sánchez, her identity as a Chilean was rooted in social relations, but her circle of intellectual friends was small and even her closest female friend read only Spanish and so was unable to share Arriagada's interest in European literature.[62]

It is tempting to speculate on the relationship of their respective reading tastes to the relative feelings of nationalism articulated by these three women. According to Peruvian writer Ricardo Palma, Sáenz studied the classics (such as Plutarch and Tacitus), historians (including Garcilaso), and Cervantes.[63] Presumably, she also shared with Bolívar his passion for the texts of the European Enlightenment. One hopes she read the immensely popular epistolary novel of Rousseau, *La Nouvelle Héloïse.* Undoubtedly she would have identified with its protagonist, who sacrificed her virtue for the love of her tutor. Indeed Bolívar suggestively refers to Eloisa as her role model in one of his letters.[64] All these works would have bolstered Sáenz's

57. Ibid., 102.
58. Ibid., 96, 144, 150, 166, and 172.
59. Ibid., 40.
60. Ibid., 46.
61. Ibid., 41.
62. Ibid., 44, 99, and 177.
63. Ricardo Palma, *Bolívar en las tradiciones peruanas* (Madrid: Compañía Ibero-Americana de Publicaciones, 1930), 119.
64. Simón Bolívar, *Cartas del Libertador,* 2nd ed., vol. 4 (Caracas: Banco de Venezuela y Fundación Lecuna, 1964), 234.

commitment to the universal ideals of republicanism rather than to a specific patriotism. Sánchez would have enjoyed the greatest access to a wide variety of books. Buenos Aires was a central Atlantic port and even European travelers, generally so difficult to impress, remarked favorably upon its library established in 1810.[65] She refers in her letters to European literature, including George Sand, but reserves her highest praise for the early essay writers of Argentina such as Sarmiento and Alberdi. In her case, cosmopolitan tastes would not have interfered with a devotion to early nationalist works. But for Arriagada, whose passion ran to novels, there were no American romances in her youth that could compete with the European bestsellers provided to her by Rugendas. She fulfilled the fears of early national moralists on the dangers to women of novel reading: not only was she tempted into an affair, but she also transferred her sentimental attachment from her homeland to the Europe of her imagination.[66]

All three of these women were also avid readers of newspapers, the forum identified as critical to the formation of national identity by Benedict Anderson. The press allowed Arriagada, in the provinces, and Sáenz and Sánchez, in exile, to remained informed about key national events. Yet there is little evidence that such media fueled in them a deeper, more spiritual, sense of national identity; indeed these women criticized the divisive partisanship of the press. Rather it was their social relationships with fellow countrymen and women, forged by preference through face-to-face conversation but maintained through correspondence, that led to their varying degrees of identification with a more abstract imagined community of nation. For Sáenz that circle of friends stretched initially across the entire Andean region from Venezuela to Chile and supported the vision that she shared with Bolívar of pan-Americanism. It was only her confinement to a small town on the disputed border in northern Peru that gradually focused first her political aspirations and then her affective identity on Ecuador. Although Sánchez had many foreign acquaintances, the majority of her social,

---

65. Rafael Alberto Arrieta, *Centuria Porteña: Buenos Aires según los viajeros extranjeros del siglo XIX* (Buenos Aires: Espasa, 1944), 83–87; and Alexander Caldcleugh, *Travels in South America during the Years 1819–20–21; Containing an Account of the Present State of Brazil, Buenos Ayres, and Chile,* vol. 1 (London: John Murray, 1825), 174–177. One traveler commented that ladies in Buenos Aires enjoyed translations of Samuel Richardson's novels, such as *Pamela.* H. M. Brackenridge, *Voyage to Buenos Ayres, Performed in the Years 1817 and 1818, by Order of the American Government* (London: Sir R. Phillips and Co., 1820), 84–85.

66. On the alleged dangers of novels, see Unzueta's contribution to this volume.

intellectual, and political relationships were with other Argentines, even during her long periods of exile. Moreover, these relationships were continually reaffirmed by prominent national leaders, and her central role in the artistic life of the country was widely recognized within her own lifetime. Her social relations, therefore, reinforced her national identity. Arriagada, by contrast, was both more isolated from the center of Chilean cultural and political life and had a relatively small circle of compatriots in the provincial town of Talca. Although she followed politics, she did not participate, and her love of European literature even led to her disillusionment with the potential for Chilean national letters. She sought refuge, therefore, in a lengthy correspondence with a visiting Austrian artist.

Writing Women into the Republic

The distinct influences of the press and correspondence on feminine senses of national identity also shaped their efforts to find a place for women in post-colonial politics. Despite their varying degrees of identification with a nation as territorially defined, Sáenz, Sánchez, and Arriagada shared a broad commitment to the construction of stable, independent republics. They bitterly denounced civil strife and partisanship as obstacles to that goal, identifying newspapers as the partisan tools of male politicians that threatened to divide rather than unite the nations.[67] By contrast, they believed that the broader and more tolerant social relationships nurtured by women in salons and through correspondence held out the promise of national reconciliation.

Sáenz attributed partisanship and shifting loyalties to the pursuit of self-interest by male political figures. The concept of self-interest had an ambivalent place in republican ideology: if it spurred men on to glorious deeds, honor was compatible with the pursuit of the public good, but too much personal ambition could threaten the republic.[68] Bolívar attempted to lessen this contradiction by praising the pursuit of glory and public acclaim as masculine virtues, but denouncing "vulgar ambition" as rooted in the "feminine passions" of jealously and revenge. Unchecked, such "feminine pas-

    67. On the partisanship of the press in Argentina, see the essay by Tulio Halperín-Donghi in this collection.
    68. Jean Jacques Rousseau, "A Dissertation on the Origin and Foundation of the Inequality of Mankind," in *The Social Contract and Discourses,* trans. G.D.H. Cole (London: J. M. Dent and Sons, 1973), 101; and Baron de Montesquieu, *The Spirit of the Laws,* trans. Thomas Nugent (New York: Hafner Publishing Company, 1949), 25.

sions," whether expressed by women or men, led to civil discord and bloodshed.[69] Like Bolívar and other political leaders, Sáenz recognized civil war as the greatest threat to the stability of the early republican states in Latin America, but reversed its gendered connotations. From her perspective, the masculine pursuit of politics based upon interest and ambition led to disorder, as she witnessed in Peru where there was a new president "every six months," as she observed only half in jest:[70]

It is amusing to live here, since today it is one thing and tomorrow another, the variety of opinions in the same person swing back and forth according to the circumstances. Poor Country! Here there is no political faith that inspires the heart with purity, everything is done out of fear or interest.[71]

She made a similar critique of Ecuadorians Rocafuerte and Pedro Moncayo, once mutual enemies but by 1845 united in opposition to Flores.

A lack of interest could work against women's participation in politics, as Linda Kerber points out, "[b]ecause women were excluded from honors and offices, the usual methods of attaching subjects' self-interest to the outcome of national policy, women's relationship to their nation seemed to be vicarious."[72] But Sáenz turned women's exclusion from political positions into an affirmation of their greater loyalty and constancy:

[I]f I am interested in the politics of a foreign country it is only for the relation it has with the politics of my own and for my friends; the rest has little or no importance for me. When I say I take an interest, you should understand that this interest does not go beyond good wishes and intentions; since you must already know that a poor woman can neither take up arms, nor buy them, much less influence anything; but it is better to have friends, whether they be male or female.[73]

69. Bolívar, *Cartas del Libertador,* 1:168 (February 9, 1815), and 4:263 (February 23, 1825).

70. March 22, 1843 in Sáenz, *Epistolario,* 128.

71. September 22, 1842 in Sáenz, *Epistolario,* 125.

72. Kerber, "May All Our Citizens be Soldiers and all Our Soldiers Citizens: The Ambiguity of Female Citizenship in the New Nation," in *Women, Militarism, and War,* ed. Jean Bethke Elshtain and Sheila Tobias (Savage, MD: Rowman and Littlefield, 1990), 93.

73. September 7, 1843 in Sáenz, *Epistolario,* 145.

Clearly, Sáenz would not have written these letters if she literally thought that women had no political influence. She implied, however, that they could not take action in the hope of concrete rewards such as appointments and, therefore, could not easily be swayed to switch sides. By associating political loyalty with female sociability, in contrast to the betrayals caused by masculine ambition and partisanship, Sáenz asserted a central role for women in building stable nations.

Sáenz feared that divisive partisanship was inflamed by the press. Although she was an avid reader of newspapers, frequently requesting that Flores send her copies from Ecuador and reciprocating by supplying him with the publications of his opposition in the exile community, she denounced the negative power of the press to slander. Complaining of the opposition press, Sáenz reported that she had tried to convince other Ecuadorians in exile that the newspaper "was not just against General Flores but against all of Ecuador."[74] Despite her prolific correspondence, Sáenz urged Flores to find writers to refute the "libels" that she forwarded to him rather than penning the responses herself: "I regret infinitely, señor, that I cannot write. . . . [I]f I had money, I would buy [the press] to take away the source of diversion of that sarcastic man from Cauca. He has made me very, very indignant; I would like to be a man this once and never more."[75] In another letter, cited above, Sáenz acknowledged women's exclusion from military action, but it must have been especially painful to her that she could write but not be published in the press. On the other hand, her exclusion from that sphere of writing, like her inability to hold office, allowed her to continue to claim a nonpartisan position.

Sánchez similarly followed the press, but preferred to get her news directly through letters from friends, ceasing to read the papers during her periods of greatest disillusionment with politics.[76] "It has been so long that I know nothing of you," she protested to Alberdi in 1861, "except for the newspapers!"[77] Like Sáenz, she complained of the libels printed in the pro-Rosas press, including in one case a satirical barb aimed at her, and the interception and publishing of conspiratorial letters written by the opposition.[78] She denounced the aggressive tone of papers that added fuel to

74. September 11, 1843, in Sáenz, *Epistolario,* 146.
75. Ibid.
76. Vilaseca, *Cartas de Mariquita Sánchez,* 100.
77. Ibid., 355.
78. Ibid., 380 and 382.

partisan divisions: "If you had the patience to read our newspapers," she wrote to Alberdi, "you would blush to read the language in which they insult their adversaries."[79] By contrast, she praised Alberdi among all the young intellectuals and politicians of his generation: "In those ill-fated times, you were the only political man who formed opinions to my taste: with nobility, with reason, with justice. . . . You had the prudence of old age and the fire of youth."[80] She then immediately linked these ideas to the recurring problem of partisan divisions in Argentina: "They call progress the disuniting of spirits and peoples. They stir up party hatreds and close the door to all conciliation."[81]

Indeed the theme of the lack of unity is a recurring lament in Sánchez's correspondence. She praised men like Alberdi and Bartolomé Mitre, who "surprised his own party" by negotiating a peace accord in 1860.[82] But, like Sáenz, she implied that women, as friends of men in power, could serve a useful role as mediators among political factions. Although she did not explicitly attach self-interest only to men, as did Sáenz, she did complain of the power of financial interest and even bribes (which would not have been made to women) to sway political opinions.[83] By contrast, she identified herself as "very tolerant in politics as in religion."[84] Saddened by the war in 1839, she wrote, "I see in all men one family, the dead are equally mourned whichever side they were on. These unfortunates, sacrificed for ignorance, ambitions, miserable intrigues, are, for me, an object of compassion."[85] From exile in 1840, she was discouraged that no one in Buenos Aires had the conviction and bravery to advocate on behalf of the imprisoned intellectual José María Gutiérrez, whereas "[h]ow many, in the course of the Revolution, have I seen abandoned by all, and I, a poor woman, was not afraid to compromise myself to come to their aid."[86] Finally, she explicitly linked friendship with political reconciliation. When Alberdi planned a trip to Madrid in 1859, Sánchez declared her hope that he could renew his friendship with her son Juan Thompson who resided there, and

79. Ibid., 349.
80. Ibid.
81. Ibid., 349–350.
82. Ibid., 354.
83. Ibid., 40–41, 376, and 419.
84. Ibid., 349.
85. Ibid., 374.
86. Ibid., 43. Her slogan, she said in another letter, was "a tu prójimo como a ti mismo" (45).

who, she admitted, had been especially blinded by partisanship, "since each can follow his own path and still conserve friendship."[87] A year later, in the wake of a settlement among the parties in Argentina, she renewed her plea, pointing out that more than ever, "[n]ow I believe the two of you will be able to talk and renew your friendship."[88]

As the least politically active and socially connected of the three women, Arriagada voiced some of the same frustrations with political partisanship and corruption but less of the optimism that women could play a positive role through their influence upon male friends: "Do we not extol today the same figure we are ready to humiliate tomorrow?" she lamented to Rugendas, "do we not moan under the iron fist . . . and do we not conform ourselves vilely to it all rather than expose some lives or some properties that will be almost useless anyway if the slavery continues?"[89] And perhaps her sense of disconnection from the nation led her to denounce, more than Sáenz or Sánchez, foreign wars, specifically the Chilean expeditions against the Peru—Bolivia Confederation from 1836 to 1839. She observed, for example, how Portales and President Joaquín Prieto could use the call for unity in the name of a foreign enemy to quiet internal dissent with authoritarian rule.[90] And in one of her few criticisms of the female poet Mercedes Marín, Arriagada expressed her distaste for her paean to the fallen Portales, identifying in particular the poem's wish that those fugitives who escaped the troops should die of remorse as sentiments unseemly in a woman.[91]

The gendered position staked out by these literate women put them in a paradoxical position similar to that identified by Joan Scott for French feminists of the eighteenth and nineteenth centuries: how could they simultaneously highlight gender difference and yet call for equality?[92] On the one hand, they did invert some of the sex stereotypes of their own times. It is striking that all three ironically highlight how political ambitions led men to abandon principles and change their political opinions and positions, in contrast to the common image of women as fickle. "How Protean revolu-

---

87. Ibid., 352.

88. Ibid., 355.

89. Pinochet de la Barra, *Cartas de una mujer apasionada,* 150. It is possible, of course, that she tried to exert more of a positive political influence in letters to her Chilean friends, as opposed to her Austrian lover.

90. Ibid., 118 and 125.

91. Ibid., 96.

92. Joan Wallach Scott, *Only Paradoxes to Offer: French Feminists and the Rights of Man* (Cambridge, MA: Harvard University Press, 1996).

tion makes men," Sáenz exclaimed in a letter to Flores.[93] Sánchez similarly conveyed her exasperation with the mercurial opinions of men: "there are men who are worse than women, and then they ridicule us and call us charlatans."[94] And the less political Arriagada surprisingly put it most bluntly:

> I only observe that there is as much prostitution among men as there might be among women. The men say that there is no virtue strong enough in a woman to resist temptation and gold, and now, *Señores hombres,* now that a post or a somewhat higher salary has made you forget your duties, betray your oaths to one of your own principal leaders, what will you say? Will you still say that only the weak sex is weak?[95]

On the other hand, despite such forceful condemnations of the opposite sex, their claims that female sociability placed them above the corrupting power of politics closed off the option of advocating direct political rights for women in the new nations.

Nonetheless, if we consider that, unlike France, there was no potential in post-independence Spanish America to grant women the full rights of citizenship, simply the nonconformance of these women with the increasingly strict ideology of domesticity stands out as a forceful position, one that actually became less common when women began to publish their writing in the second half of the nineteenth century. Sáenz not only departed from the dominant female norms in her writing, but openly lived as a nonconformist. She refused all attempts of her English husband at marital reconciliation and never gave any indication that she shared Bolívar's own concerns "that nothing in the world can unite us under the auspices of innocence and honor."[96] Moreover, she did not limit her political influence to the salon or letter, but especially in her youth, sallied forth in uniform to do battle with Bolívar's enemies.[97] Sánchez and Arriagada were both more circumspect in maintaining proper appearances, yet deviated from domestic ideals in their private lives and semi-private writings. Both opposed their parents in making marriage choices, and then later sought various forms of escape from the

93. January 1, 1845, in Sáenz, *Epistolario,* 173.

94. Vilaseca, *Cartas de Mariquita Sánchez,* 36.

95. Pinochet de la Barra, *Cartas de una mujer apasionada,* 175.

96. April 20, 1825, *Cartas del Libertador,* 4:309; see also November 26, 1825, 4:529.

97. For the transcripts of her trial, see "Documentos inéditos," *Boletín de Historia y Antiguedades* [Bogotá] 47 (May–June, 1960): 373–402.

resulting unhappy relationships. Sánchez, who complained bitterly about her second husband, even in a letter to Alberdi, achieved a de facto independence from him when he was transferred as a French diplomat from Argentina to Ecuador. She valued that independence highly, advising her own daughter to think carefully before entering a second marriage even with a gentleman of whom she approved: "believe me, the independence of us widows has its advantages."[98] In fact, Sánchez was not technically a widow at that time, and there are indications that she had at least one affair. Finally, it is precisely because of her love affair that we have so many letters written by Arriagada. Although she initially consoled herself with the romantic notion that her relationship to Rugendas was a pure union of souls, her later letters reveal that their love was physically consummated, and that at least Arriagada's husband and most likely other acquaintances were aware of the infidelity.[99] These women may not have been representative of their class, but neither were they unique; the colonial society into which they had been born allowed for a degree of latitude between private behavior and public appearances.[100]

Not only did Sánchez and Arriagada deviate from strict norms of morality in their private lives, they also aired opinions that departed from the rising idealization of women as mothers above all else. Arriagada voraciously read all the books Rugendas lent her, but was not afraid to differ with the authors' opinions of women. She indicated that she was learning much from "Keratri," for example, but objected to "that line which he fixes for us [women] and prohibits us to pass, under the pain of becoming shocking or ridiculous should we separate ourselves from that object for which nature formed us."[101] Similarly, despite her enthusiasm for the novels of Dumas, she objected to his portrayals of women:

> Men are privileged by this famous author. If there are among his male characters criminals, there are others that are most beautiful. But among

98. Vilaseca, *Cartas de Mariquita Sánchez,* 140; see also 78, 127, and 134.

99. For the transition from a spiritual to physical relationship, see letter of August 16, 1838, and for her husband's suspicions, the earlier letter of February 18, 1837; Pinochet de la Barra, *Cartas de una mujer apasionada,* 145–147 and 65–67.

100. Ann Twinam, *Public Lives, Private Secrets: Gender, Honor, Sexuality, and Illegitimacy in Colonial Spanish America* (Stanford, CA: Stanford University Press, 1999).

101. Pinochet de la Barra, *Cartas de una mujer apasionada,* 50. Arriagada is most likely referring to French writer Auguste Hilarion de Kératry (1769–1859), who published books on art and philosophy as well as works of fiction.

the women, not one, all criminal or weak, or of an insignificant character only to decorate the picture . . . weak in moral aspects, weak in physical aspects. Poor, poor women![102]

Certainly Arriagada resented the limitations placed upon her as a woman, particularly the inability to travel freely much less set her own destiny.[103]

Sánchez, who was more politically active than Arriagada, fit better the classic image of the republican mother, yet she exercised that role in an assertive rather than passive manner, and in some cases even went beyond that model. From the inception of the Argentine nation, its male leaders recognized the potential of harnessing women's efforts in the sphere of charity and education to the service of the state. The Beneficencia, established soon after independence, sanctioned an extension of mothering by the society ladies of Buenos Aires into the management of orphanages, girls' schools, and hospitals for women. Sánchez was a prominent leader in this organization before and after her exile under Rosas, and took great pride in her role: "I have just come from a function of the Beneficencia," she wrote to her husband in 1861, "where I am the only founding member who still attends; I am always showered with attention by the highest authorities. That is my only wealth."[104] In a letter to her son Juan Thompson in 1840, Sánchez clearly articulated the dominant notion of republican motherhood:

> I cannot be of service except to girls' schools. When the war is over, we will talk about this and I will have the greatest pleasure in helping to advance, under your auspices, such an essential thing; because it is necessary to begin with the women if one wants to civilize a country, and especially among us, since the men are not enough and are always armed to destroy themselves.[105]

Similarly, she recorded the various services performed by the Argentine women in exile to the movement against Rosas, from sewing flags to organizing fundraisers.[106]

For all Sánchez's pride in playing the official role of mother to the Argentine nation, as well as being matriarch to her own extended family, there

---

102. Ibid., 165.
103. Ibid., 99–100 and 123.
104. Vilaseca, *Cartas de Mariquita Sánchez,* 319; see also 100, 310, 321, 357, and 388.
105. Ibid., 38.
106. Ibid., 388, 408, 411–412.

are indications that at times she chafed under its attendant restrictions. Her descriptions of women's support activities in Montevideo, for example, take on a somewhat distant tone as opposed to the recounting of her close personal ties to powerful leaders and central role in political salons. She also approved of the more open and active participation of even respectable ladies in business ventures that she observed in Rio de Janeiro.[107] She certainly saw herself as distinct from other women, going so far as to assert to Alberdi that they lived a similar life: "My life is necessarily more that of a male philosopher than that of a woman, with the misfortune of having the heart of a woman, a volcano for a head, and none of that frivolity of my sex to distract me."[108] Most significantly, she resented the limits placed upon women's education and the secondary role they were expected to play in carrying out, but not setting, national policy. She noted that women who wished to surpass a basic education to pursue letters at a higher level were satirically labeled as "pedantic."[109] In 1859 her resentments exploded in a relatively open conflict with Sarmiento when he published a report critical of the Beneficencia's management of the school for orphaned girls. He wished to divert funds from French and music classes, which he saw as unnecessary given the girls' station in life, to establish a normal school for teachers.[110] In letters to a newspaper (anonymously) as well as to the minister of public instruction and Sarmiento himself (in her own name), Sánchez protested that premise. Even if destined to marry artisans, she argued, only with a complete education would these women be respected by their sons and able to gently correct any cultural deficiencies of their husbands as their true companions. "You are unjust," she fulminated against Sarmiento, "you are not content with politics and boys and you want to fight with the women. Do you not know how bad it is to have them as enemies!"[111]

Conclusions

In early national Spanish America, when women were officially excluded from the public sphere of politics, not all retreated into a purely domestic arena. They continued to participate in salons, which had been important

107. Ibid., 129.
108. Ibid., 348.
109. Ibid., 40 and 338.
110. Sáenz Quesada, *Mariquita Sánchez*, 293–295.
111. Vilaseca, *Cartas de Mariquita Sánchez*, 365.

centers of conspiracy during the movements for independence, as well as maintaining broader social circles through prolific correspondence. In the cases of Manuela Sáenz, Mariquita Sánchez, and Carmen Arriagada, the intensity of their identification with a particular nation as an imagined community depended on the breadth and composition of these very real networks. Sáenz initially interacted with prominent figures from across the Andes and shared Bolívar's vision of pan-Americanism; as exile to northern Peru limited her effective sphere of influence, however, she increasingly focused upon politics in her birthplace, the new nation of Ecuador. Sánchez too spent many years in exile, but wherever she went was surrounded and respected by numerous compatriots; only in her moments of greatest disillusionment with partisan politics, therefore, did she waver from her firm identification with the Argentine nation. Finally, Arriagada, far from the cultural and political center of Santiago and with only a small group of likeminded friends, translated her frustration with politics into disaffection from the Chilean nation as a whole and sought refuge instead in the literature of Europe.

Just as social networks helped determine the degree of their nationalism, Sáenz and Sánchez held up women's role in nurturing friendships that transcended partisan factions as a justification for their ongoing influence, as mediators, in republican politics.[112] Barred from political office and therefore unable to pursue self-interested ambitions, they suggested, women were more principled in their opinions and alliances. Although Arriagada herself was less politically active, a suggestive passage from the journal of Maria Graham in Chile highlights the role of female sociability in political mediation. In early republican Chile, one of the fiercest political rivalries was between the Carreras brothers and Bernardo O'Higgins. When Graham arrived in 1822, the last of the Carreras had recently been executed. She was hosted in Santiago by the Cotapos family, political supporters of the former Carreras as well as related to them by marriage. Their daughter, Ana María Cotapos, had been married to Juan José Carrera, and she was even prosecuted for corresponding with her brother-in-law after her husband's death. Graham was surprised, therefore, when the mother and sister of O'Higgins,

112. For other analyses of the role of women writers as mediators, see Silvia Delfino, "Conversar, escribir: Dos tramas de un secreto," in *Escribir en los bordes: Congreso Internacional de literatura femenina latinoamericana, 1987* (Santiago: Editorial Cuarto Propio, 1990), 73–78, and Adriana Méndez Rodenas, *Gender and Nationalism in Colonial Cuba: The Travels of Santa Cruz y Montalvo, Condesa de Merlin* (Nashville, TN: Vanderbilt University Press, 1998), 10 and 15.

Evidence of women as "mediators"?

Doña Isabella and Doña Rosa, came to visit at the Cotapos residence. "But now that there is not one of the Carreras left, and that faction is believed to be at an end," she reflected, "it is surely the business of those at the head of the affairs of Chile to buy golden opinions of all sorts of men; and I have no doubt but they are glad I am here as an excuse to call without the formalities of reconciliation."[113] It must have been customary, therefore, for prominent ladies to take the first steps toward bringing together rival factions.

Although an argument based upon disinterest would have made it impossible for women to claim full rights of citizenship, all three of these literate women proposed and to some degree acted upon a female role that was less restrictive than that of the selfless wife and mother which was increasingly becoming the official ideal. The similarities in their lives and attitudes suggest that the domestic stereotype did not adequately represent the experiences of middle and upper-class women in early nineteenth-century South America. Their independent thinking may have derived in part from their self-education in the late colonial period, before the establishment of schools for girls where the curriculum came to emphasize domestic skills and morals, and from living through an era in which national boundaries and political institutions were in the process of formation. The intermediate nature of conversation and correspondence between the public and private spheres allowed women a space to express their desires to transcend, at least to some degree, the limitations of republican motherhood. Sáenz defended her right to advise, as well as support, prominent men in power. Arriagada, childless, refused to be defined by her biological role. And even Sánchez, who took full advantage of the limited spaces provided for women to extend their mothering efforts into charity and education, was determined to help set as well as carry out national policies in those areas.

After the middle of the nineteenth century, the expansion of education and literacy, combined with the rise of the Romantic movement in literature, provided the next generation of Spanish American women the important new opportunity of claiming a public voice. Feminine periodicals began to proliferate across the continent, and by the end of the century several female authors had gained acclaim as poets and novelists. But this achievement, as significant as it was, came with a price. In order to get their writing published, women were under ever greater pressure to uphold strict no-

---

113. Maria Graham, *Journal of a Residence in Chile, During the Year 1822 and a Voyage from Chile to Brazil in 1823* (New York and London: Praeger Publishers, 1969), 223.

tions of female domesticity. Male politicians and intellectuals considered it acceptable for ladies to write about "women's issues" for a female audience, but fewer were willing to welcome these authors as full participants in the formation of a national literature. Indeed the philosophy of Romanticism, with the value it placed on sentiment and interiority, acknowledged women's voices but circumscribed them to that terrain. Women who wrote about politics violated the apolitical space that their male counterparts were attempting to create with literature.[114] Female authors of the late nineteenth century, therefore, to a greater degree than the correspondents of an earlier generation, had to conform to the dominant ideology if they wanted official acceptance and hence potential influence. Those few who did not faced ostracism; it was no coincidence, perhaps, that their work also often conveyed a lack of connection between women and the nation, identifying more often with other marginalized groups such as African or indigenous peoples.[115] This dichotomy lasted at least into the early twentieth century as the first feminists carefully articulated their demands for civil and political rights within a discourse of domesticity and motherhood, while the art and literature of avant-garde women like Frida Kahlo or Rosario Castellanos reflected an ambivalence toward the nation.[116]

114. On the role of women in the Romantic movement, see Kirkpatrick, *Las Románticas;* Denegri, *El Abanico y la cigarrera;* and Méndez Rodenas, *Gender and Nationalism.*

115. Such as Juana Manuela Gorriti and Clorinda Matto de Turner; Denegri, *El Abanico y la cigarrera,* 85–99 and 161–192. Such authors might also idealize motherhood for women; Schlau, *Spanish American Women's Use of the Word,* 55–80.

116. For a few examples, see Jean Franco, *Plotting Women,* 102–187, Joanna O'Connell, *Prospero's Daughter: The Prose of Rosario Castellanos* (Austin: University of Texas Press, 1995); and Ileana Rodríguez, *House/Garden/Nation: Space, Gender, and Ethnicity in Postcolonial Latin American Literatures by Women* (Durham: Duke University Press, 1994).

4

Student Culture
and Nation-State Formation

Andrew J. Kirkendall

An important, if neglected, part of the story of the transition from colony to nation in South America is the history of educational institutions and their relation to nation-state and political class formation. This chapter, focusing on the experience largely of Argentina, Brazil, and Chile, explores the relationship between educational institutions and state building, the establishment of elite recruitment systems, the formation of student identities, and the search for cultural authority. I draw on primary research in Brazil, as well as on secondary research on Argentina and Chile. The coming of political independence created opportunities for the enhancement of the hegemony of the *letrados,* particularly in a country like Brazil, which saw a greater degree of continuity and political stability than other South American nations. The letrados represented the first national class, conscious of

I am grateful to the University of Nebraska Press for permission to use material from my book *Class Mates: Male Student Culture and the Making of a Political Class in Nine-teenth-Century Brazil* (2002).

its own rights and privileges and determined to improve its position at the expense of other social groups lacking the opportunities to define their own identities as they did. The nations they imagined were as limited as the oligarchical political systems they designed; they themselves constituted to a large extent what Roderick Barman has called the "official nation."[1]

Benedict Anderson pointed to the importance of elite definitions of self by speculating on the career patterns of late colonial Latin American letrados and suggesting that their spatial limits more or less defined the territorial extent of post-colonial nations. This chapter goes beyond those speculations by investigating the creation of lettered elites after independence. In doing so, it builds on the ideas of Angel Rama, who argued that the power structure he called "the lettered city" survived independence quite successfully. Rather than just colonial bureaucrats, as they had been before, early national letrados also became politicians and journalists, retaining privileged social influence through their command of lettered culture, while exercising that influence in new ways. Thus, however questionable Anderson's assertion that late-colonial bureaucratic career patterns mapped new national territories, state formation in nineteenth-century Latin America did turn, in part, on the esprít de corps of lettered elites, an esprít de corps created particularly in their experience as classmates (in more than one sense) and, eventually, "old boys."[2]

European Antecedents, Colonial Legacies

European traditions of higher education had emphasized the training of clergy and state officials. While clergy under the *patronato real* in the colonial era were beholden to the Crown for appointments and salary, the linkage between state and letrado was far more direct. As the Spanish and Portuguese Crowns enhanced their authority in the eighteenth century, they sought to limit the degree of autonomy enjoyed by the Church, particularly of the religious orders. With the coming of independence, however, the relationship between church and state became more contentious. As new na-

---

1. See Benedict Anderson, *Imagined Communities: Reflections on the Origin and Spread of Nationalism,* rev. ed. (London: Verso, 1998); and Roderick Barman, *Brazil: The Forging of a Nation, 1798–1852* (Stanford, CA: Stanford University Press, 1988), 235–240.

2. Angel Rama, *The Lettered City,* trans. and ed. John Charles Chasteen (Durham, NC: Duke University Press, 1996), 13–28, 45–47.

tions were formed, the letrados sought to ensure their own cultural authority, often at the expense of men of the cloth.

To understand the evolution of the letrado, we must look at Iberian antecedents and colonial legacies. Spanish and Portuguese policy in the Americas differed in what was, for my purposes, one crucial respect. While Spain established the first universities in the Western Hemisphere, Portugal expected its subjects to return to the mother country in pursuit of higher education. Primary and secondary education were also relatively neglected. In Portuguese America, the only significant educational institutions that were allowed to develop were those related to the Roman Catholic Church and particularly to its most important representatives in Brazil, the members of the Society of Jesus.[3] But when the Jesuits were expelled from Brazil in 1759, as a result of pressures from colonists who resented their role as protector of the indigenous population of Brazil, as well as a drive for greater centralized control of the colony by the "enlightened despot," the Marquis of Pombal, Brazil's educational system, such as it was, virtually collapsed.[4]

To understand the model Brazilian legislators had in mind in forming national institutions after independence, one must therefore look at the University of Coimbra in Portugal. Established in the 1300s it grew significantly while an overseas trading empire developed in the 1400s and 1500s. Coimbra provided the training ground in canon and civil law for bureaucrats who served the Crown in Asia, Africa, and the New World. Brazilians ambitious to rise in the royal service were drawn to Coimbra and served the Crown not only in Portuguese America but also in other parts of the empire. A Coimbra education had primarily been, as Stuart Schwartz has argued, a socializing experience that "readied a man for the robe of office." Extracurricular activities, most particularly, according to Schwartz, "drinking and brawling," created a certain esprít de corps and long-lasting personal ties among the young men, amounting to a virtual "class consciousness" that mitigated against blind loyalty to the king.[5] The role of law school experi-

---

3. For a discussion of the Jesuits' contribution to Brazilian culture, see Fernando de Azevedo, *Brazilian Culture: An Introduction to the Study of Culture in Brazil,* trans. William Rex Crawford. (New York: Macmillan, 1950), particularly 145–146, 155, 327.

4. Azevedo, *Brazilian Culture,* 170, 355; John Hemming, *Red Gold: The Conquest of the Brazilian Indians* (London: Macmillan, 1978), 451–482; Kenneth Maxwell, *Pombal: Paradox of the Enlightenment* (Cambridge and New York: Cambridge University Press, 1995), 57–59, 84–86.

5. Stuart Schwartz, *Sovereignty and Society in Colonial Brazil: The High Court of Bahia and Its Judges, 1609–1751* (Berkeley: University of California Press, 1973), xii–xiv, xx, 14, 15, 72–77, 361–362.

ence in defining identities would be just as strong in the schools established in the new nation of Brazil after political independence in 1822.

Coimbra students were a privileged lot, enjoying special exemptions from civil jurisdiction until 1834. Visually, students were distinguished from the townsmen of Coimbra by the cap and gown that from 1718 to 1834 they were required to wear both in and out of class. School uniforms were intended to enhance the feeling of corporate solidarity as it lessened distinctions between rich and poor students. Given their protected legal status, the uniform may also have served as an additional shield from punishment for their actions, although it also must have made them the target of occasional acts of violence by those who resented their privileges.[6]

The Spanish equivalent of Coimbra was the University of Salamanca, also a product of the Middle Ages that similarly thrived as the Spanish empire was constructed. The Spanish Crown also wanted state agents, not independent professionals. The Crown served as the ultimate magistrate and mediator of social conflict in Spain and its American colonies. Salamanca, like Coimbra, was a product of the medieval scholastic mindset. Although a royal university, here as elsewhere during the colonial period, the influence of the Church and clergy was strong. As the Spanish empire was established, Salamanca became the premier university in Europe.[7] As at Coimbra, Salamanca students also had special privileges, including the "right . . . to obtain absolution for assaults on" professors and clerks. In general, students were immune from prosecution.[8] The privileged status of Salamanca students continued after graduation for they, like the nobility, were not subject to direct taxation.[9]

Salamanca students favored studying law over the burgeoning humanities. As in Coimbra, the university created a kind of "administrative nobility." Those interested in serving the Crown increasingly had to get an education. "It appears that the principal aims of the colleges is more political

6. Alberto Sousa Lamy, *A Academia de Coimbra, 1537–1990* (Lisbon: Rei dos Livros, 1990), 22, 27, 651, 689.

7. For a discussion of the rise of Salamanca, see Richard L. Kagan, *Students and Society in Early Modern Spain* (Baltimore: Johns Hopkins University Press, 1974).

8. John Tate Lanning, *Academic Culture in the Spanish Colonies* ([1940] Port Washington, NY: Kennikat Press, 1971), 5–8. See also George M. Addy's discussion of these issues in *The Enlightenment in the University of Salamanca* (Durham, NC: Duke University Press, 1966), 48–52.

9. Mark A. Burkholder, "Honor and Honors in Colonial Spanish America," in Lyman L. Johnson and Sonya Lipsett-Rivera, *The Faces of Honor: Sex, Shame, and Violence in Colonial Latin America* (Albuquerque: University of New Mexico Press, 1998), 37.

than spiritual," it was said in 1636, "because most of the" students "are train-ing for Your Royal Service in secular posts."[10] As the absolutist monarchy's demand for their services expanded, those who received advanced training in the law enhanced their special status and prestige. "[T]he doctors of law were accorded the privilege of constant access to the person of the king."[11]

Twenty-five universities were established in Spanish America during the colonial period; most had strong ties to the religious orders. Perhaps as many as 150,000 men received degrees from colonial universities during the period of Spanish rule.[12] Universities were founded even in such relatively marginal parts of the Spanish American empire as Argentina and Chile. The University of Santo Tomás provided theological education in Chile from the early seventeenth to the mid-eighteenth centuries.[13] The Royal University of San Felipe opened its doors in 1758 in Chile. After its founding, the re-ligious schools declined in popularity and importance because San Felipe offered new and eagerly awaited opportunities for young men from Chile and surrounding regions (including Paraguay and Argentina) to study law. While 128 men during the period received doctorates in law from San Fe-lipe, an additional 106 received doctorates in theology, and only a handful in medicine. Attempts to foster technical education were, by and large, not successful.[14] In Argentina, the primary institution during the colonial period was the Jesuit school in Córdoba, founded in 1617, which mainly of-fered theological education. Following the expulsion of the Jesuits in 1769, the Franciscans operated the university until it was transformed into a royal institution in 1800. Legal studies were first offered there in 1791, and by and large, Argentines interested in serving the empire looked to the University of Chuquisaca (present-day Sucre), perhaps the most eminent institution on the South American continent after the University of San Marcos in Lima. Graduates of the University of Chuquisaca prominent during the transition

10. Quoted in Kagan, *Students and Society,* 78. Regarding the preference for law, see pp. xix, 214–219.

11. Lanning, *Academic Culture in the Spanish Colonies,* 9.

12. The best book available in English on Latin American education during the colo-nial period is still Lanning, *Academic Culture in the Spanish Colonies.* See especially p. 53.

13. See Bernardino Bravo Lira, *La Universidad en la Historia de Chile, 1622–1992* (Santiago: Pehuén Editores, 1992), 17.

14. Simon Collier and William F. Sater, *A History of Chile, 1808–1994* (Cambridge: Cambridge University Press, 1997), 21. See also Amanda Labarca H., *Historia de la En-señanza en Chile* (Santiago: Imprenta Universitaria, 1939), 43–44.

to independence included Mariano Moreno and Juan José Castellí, among others.[15] Both men were loyal to the port city of Buenos Aires and its interests. While they clearly would have preferred to incorporate Upper Peru into a larger national confederation, neither would have been influenced primarily by a trajectory defined by their educational experience, as the Anderson model would suggest.[16] The silver of Bolivia mattered more than the intellectual riches of Chuquisaca, and the limits of their imagined community were not to be defined by the larger administrative divisions of the Spanish empire as much as by diverging regional economic interests, political factionalism, and armed conflict.

Although Spanish American students maintained many of the same privileges of their Spanish counterparts, the university rector had a certain measure of authority over where students lived and how they dressed. Students were forbidden to wear ostentatious clothing and required to wear the cap and gown "upon pain of suspension and loss of credit for courses." Prohibitions against bringing weapons to classes suggest continuing discipline problems among the students. Universities even maintained their own jails.[17]

Throughout the colonial period, in both Portuguese and Spanish America, the relatively small group of university-educated men retained their privileged position. As Angel Rama argued, "writing consolidated the political order by giving it rigorously elaborated cultural expression." Men of the city, agents of empire, they controlled the paper flow that helped legitimate Spanish and Portuguese authority in the New World. "Their services in the manipulation of symbolic languages were indispensable."[18] Although Brazilians generally suffered more from Portuguese education policies than Creoles in Spanish America did, Portuguese Americans able to afford to go to study in Coimbra confronted fewer barriers to advancement in the colonial bureaucracy than did their Creole counterparts in Spanish America during the period of the Bourbon reforms in the eighteenth century.[19] Influenced by Enlightenment ideals, but tied to their sometimes unreliable protector, the Crown, the letrados after independence would seek a way to guarantee their continued social prominence while increasing their politi-

15. Ricardo Levene, *A History of Argentina,* trans. and ed. William Spence Robertson (Chapel Hill: University of North Carolina Press, 1937), 94–95, 160–161.

16. Anderson, *Imagined Communities,* 52–58.

17. Lanning, *Academic Culture,* 44–46.

18. Rama, *The Lettered City,* 7, 16–22, 29–30.

19. See Mark A. Burkholder, *Politics of a Colonial Career: José Baquíjano and the Audiencia of Lima,* 2d ed. (Wilmington, DE: Scholarly Resources, 1990).

cal power.[20] The coming of independence created the need not only for an independent bureaucracy but also for a political class. If anything, the importance of access to higher education was enhanced by the creation of new nation-states. A crucial component in the dynamic of nineteenth-century life was the attempt by the letrados to ensure that their cultural authority against the Church and their political authority against the caudillos, the men on horseback.

Change and Continuity in the New Nation-States

The newly independent nations of South America inherited inadequate educational infrastructures, which had been further damaged late in the late colonial period with the expulsion of the Jesuits. With the coming of independence, political leaders had to decide how education would serve the nation. What kind of education would be offered and for whom would it be intended? Educational policy and the formation of nation-states were directly linked. Political leaders had to decide whether the primary goal of an educational system was to fashion a political class or an active citizenry. Although they could hardly neglect the latter entirely, national resources tended to be disproportionately focused on the former. Continuities between the colonial and post-independence period, in this regard, were particularly strong. If anything, the new states tended to reinforce and exaggerate the colonial emphasis on legal education and on the production of state agents. Perhaps nowhere were pre-existing Iberian models linking education to the creation of state agents adopted more faithfully than in Brazil, which in so many ways was the nation least transformed by the transition to independence. The accelerating secularization of education marked the most distinct departure from tradition in most South American countries, and the clergy lost much of its cultural authority and economic power throughout the course of the nineteenth century. Secularizing reforms helped undermine the Church while promoting the hegemony of the (frequently anti-clerical) liberals and those trained in law.

20. This discussion is influenced by Tulio Halperín-Donghi, "The Colonial Letrado as a Revolutionary Intellectual: Dean Funes as Seen through His Apuntamientos para una Biografía," in Mark D. Szuchmann and Jonathan C. Brown, eds., *Revolution and Restoration: The Rearrangement of Power in Argentina, 1776–1860* (Lincoln: University of Nebraska Press, 1994), 54–73.

Brazil

By adopting a constitutional monarchy with the son of the Portuguese king as Brazil's first emperor, Brazil avoided many of the political problems associated with the coming of independence in Spanish America. Coimbra graduates educated in civil law, with experience as magistrates, were central to the consolidation of the Brazilian state as they transferred their loyalty to a new empire. Brazil's ruling class was united by a commitment to the maintenance of an export economy made possible by the labor of imported African slaves. Like the powers-that-be in slave societies throughout the hemisphere, Brazilian elites had a special fear of disorder that caused them to embrace a more centralized political system that enhanced political stability even if it did not always serve diverging regional economic interests. The power of the large landowner in Brazil was strong, but limited in its reach. The monarchical system maintained the social dominance of the patriarch on the plantation, while inhibiting his political aspirations.[21]

In Brazil, the founding of the law schools in the decade following independence was a highly self-conscious exercise in state building. Brazilian legislators, the majority of whom were educated at the University of Coimbra, saw that Brazil needed a magistracy trained in Brazilian law, not Portuguese law. Early debates revolved around whether to have a law curriculum within a larger university or a law school independent of a larger university. Although critics later lamented the failure to establish a more broadly based system of education, the Brazilian legislators were probably correct when they argued that Brazil lacked the resources to support a university.[22] The primary concern of the legislators, in any case, was more political than educational, per se. The new state required men to fill its positions, and the number of Brazilians educated at Coimbra was insufficient. The law school would train "able men" who would one day be "wise magistrates." The need for legally trained men to staff the bureaucracy of the Brazilian Empire was clear, while the central government would leave the provinces to fund primary education or not as they saw fit. The men trained in the law schools would be not only judges but also professional politi-

21. See José Murilo de Carvalho, "Political Elites and State Building: The Case of Nineteenth-Century Brazil," *Comparative Studies in Society and History* 24 (July 1982): 383, 386–389.

22. See the discussion in "Criação do Curso Jurídico no Brasil" (circa 1825), particularly the comments of Estevão Ribeiro de Rezende. In Arquivo Nacional, Rio de Janeiro, Brazil, microfilm 006.0-076.

cians, serving as provincial presidents and eventually in the Chamber of Deputies, the Senate, and the cabinet. Independence had created a need for a larger supply of letrados, while enhancing their importance and broadening the scope of their ambitions.[23] Throughout the imperial period, the law schools in Olinda (Recife after 1854) in the northeastern province of Pernambuco and in São Paulo in the south remained the only significant institutions of higher education in the empire, other than the medical schools in Salvador and Rio de Janeiro. (Medical doctors also became government officials and politicians, although to a much more limited degree.) Northerners tended to go to the Pernambuco school, while southerners went to São Paulo, but a significant minority (an estimated 10 percent) transferred from one to the other at some point in their law school career.[24] These young men would have greater opportunities to establish truly national ties and a more national orientation. As it had under Portuguese rule, the monarchy enhanced the power of the letrados (called *bacharéis* in Brazil). By the 1850s and 1860s, 74 percent of cabinet ministers were graduates of the two Brazilian law schools.[25] Brazil's system of elite recruitment became the most highly developed in the Western Hemisphere. Large landowners found their interest in order facilitated by the centrally controlled imperial political system and sent their sons to the law schools to establish their credentials to serve the state and to further family interests in the patronage networks that informally undergirded the formal power of the state. Although most recent graduates would serve the monarchy in a position in the centrally appointed magistracy somewhere in their home province, building on family ties, the most successful among them would later serve as

23. See the comments of the Viscount of Cachoeira, Luiz José de Carvalho e Mello, in his "Projeto de Regulamento ou Estatutos para o Curso Jurídico Mandado Crear n'esta Corte pelo Conselheiro D'Estado Visconde de Cachoeira e Apresentado em Março de 1825" (Rio de Janeiro: Typographia Imperial e Nacional, 1826), 3. In Arquivo Nacional, Rio de Janeiro, IE354, Ministério do Império, Curso Jurídico de São Paulo, Relatórios e Ofícios do Diretor. Two key works on the imperial law school graduates are Eul-Soo Pang and Ron Seckinger, "The Mandarins of Imperial Brazil," *Comparative Studies in Society and History* 14, no. 2 (March 1972): 215–244, and Roderick Barman and Jean Barman, "The Role of the Law Graduate in the Political Elite of Imperial Brazil," *Journal of Inter-American Studies and World Affairs* 18, no. 4 (November 1976): 423–450.

24. Barman and Barman, "The Role of the Law Graduate," 439.

25. José Murilo de Carvalho, "Elite and State-Building in Imperial Brazil" (Ph.D. diss., Stanford University, 1975), 90.

provincial presidents far from their homes and eventually at the heart of imperial life in Rio de Janeiro itself.[26]

On the secondary level, Colégio Dom Pedro II also served to further the empire's centralization. Founded in 1837 and named in honor of the young boy emperor, the school's location in Rio de Janeiro made it a favorite place for national politicians living in the capital to send their sons. Graduates of the school were automatically admitted into either the law schools or medical schools without having to take entrance examinations.[27] (Other secondary schools thrived insofar as they prepared students to take these exams.)[28]

Despite the centralized nature of the Brazilian political system, the provinces were left to their own devices in funding public education. The frequent rotation of provincial presidents made it difficult to create sustained education policies. Obligatory education was seen as being linked to "communist and socialist movements," as one fairly progressive politician of the late nineteenth century noted. Even as late as the 1870s, only 14 percent of the population was literate.[29] In a society defined by ties of patronage and clientele, illiterate clients, even when they voted, remained something less than active citizens.

Chile

By the 1830s, Chile had achieved political stability to a degree exceeded in South America only by Brazil and which it maintained throughout much of the nineteenth century. Chile's relatively smooth path to independence had been aided by a colonial bureaucracy that had continued to function during the transition to independence.[30] Although internal struggles over the loca-

---

26. See Richard Graham, *Patronage and Politics in Nineteenth-Century Brazil* (Stanford: Stanford University Press, 1990). For a discussion of career patterns, see Pang and Seckinger, "Mandarins of Imperial Brazil," 223–226.

27. Barman, *Forging a Nation,* 194; Needell, *Tropical Belle Epoque,* 54–58.

28. Maria de Lourdes Mariotto Haidar, *O Ensino Secundário no Império Brasileiro* (São Paulo: Editora Grijalba Ltda., 1972), 22, 53, 62, 92, 262.

29. Mariotto Haidar, *O Ensino Secundário,* 30; Afonso Arinos de Melo Franco, *Rodrigues Alves: Apogeu e Declínio do Presidencialismo,* vol. 1 (São Paulo: Editora da Universidade de São Paulo, 1973), 41; Robert Conrad, *The Destruction of Brazilian Slavery, 1850–1888* (Malabar, FL: Krieger Publishing Company, 1993), xiv.

30. See Jay Kinsbruner, *Chile: A Historical Interpretation* (New York: Harper and Row, 1973), 21.

tion of power continued in the 1820s, centralizing forces triumphed under Diego Portales. Portalian Chile had a strong executive and a weak legislature. A fairly homogenous and geographically concentrated political class developed, whose economic interests were largely consonant and who were able to agree on fundamentals of social and political organization. In Chile a fairly small number of interrelated family groups dominated politics. Of 599 members of the nineteenth-century Chilean parliament, there were, at least, 98 sets of brothers, 61 fathers and sons, 20 cousins, 12 fathers and sons-in-law, and 32 brothers-in-law.[31] Between 1830 and 1930, there were three presidents and at least fifty congressmen from the Errázuraz family alone.[32] As a group, Chilean politicians of the period were described by contemporary observers as "austere, taciturn, and reserved," coming "to politics from the classroom, from the office, and the courtroom."[33]

As early as 1811, Juan Egaña proposed at the meeting of the first national congress that a secondary institution be created for sons of the Chilean elite to train to become future governors of the independent nation.[34] The Instituto Nacional, originally founded in 1813, although closed following the reestablishment of Spanish control and not reopened again until 1819, became a "national preparatory school," somewhat in the manner of Brazil's Colégio Dom Pedro II, and for similar reasons, not least of all its location in the capital city. Largely a secondary institution providing instruction in the humanities, including Latin, mathematics, rhetoric, and an introduction to legal studies on the secondary level, it was "popularly believed to have educated three-quarters of all Chile's leaders between 1830 and 1891." The Instituto Nacional also offered professional degrees in law, theology, medicine, and mathematics. As with the Brazilian law schools, the Instituto Nacional was expected to train "men to build the state," according to Egaña, one of its primary shapers. The Instituto Nacional sought to "instill an overriding responsibility to the nation" and is said to have shaped Chilean po-

31. See Gabriela Marcella, "The Structure of Politics in Nineteenth-Century Spanish America: The Chilean Oligarchy, 1833–1891" (Ph.D. diss., University of Notre Dame, 1973), 33–34, 106, 110, 112. Like the Hapsburgs, Marcella notes that Chile's ruling class "accomplished more through marriages than through warfare."

32. Simon Collier, "From Independence to the War of the Pacific," in *Chile since Independence,* ed. Leslie Bethell (Cambridge: Cambridge University Press, 1993), 21–22.

33. Justo Arteaga Alemparte, quoted in Marcella, "Structure of Politics," 73.

34. Julia Heise Gonzalez, *Años de Formacion y Aprendizaje Politicos, 1810–1833* (Santiago: Editorial Universitaria, 1978), 225.

litical style.[35] Meanwhile, Chile's university from the colonial period, the formerly Royal University of San Felipe, which had educated many of the most important Chilean magistrates and politicians in the early post-independence period, including Diego Portales, was abolished in 1839 after decades in decline.[36]

Unlike Brazil and Argentina under the caudillo Juan Manuel de Rosas, Chile even in the era of oligarchical politics was a center of educational reform, due in part to the infusion of talent from outside the country, some of whom, but not all, were political exiles. These included luminaries such as the Venezuelan Andrés Bello, the first rector of the University of Chile, and Argentine Domingo Sarmiento, who established a normal school in Santiago in the 1850s and who laid the groundwork for innovations that would bear greater fruit in his native land.[37]

The University of Chile, established by the Chilean government in 1843, looked to the Institut de France of the Napoleonic era as a model. In his inaugural address, Bello spoke of "purging" the university of the "stains acquired under the malevolent influence of despotism" in order to "accommodate" it to "republican institutions."[38] During the early decades the university was devoted to administration rather than to teaching. It oversaw the operations of the nation's network of provincial *liceos* and primary schools, designing the curriculum and choosing, writing, and, when necessary, translating the textbooks.[39]

35. Collier and Sater, *History of Chile,* 101. See also Bravo Lira, *Universidad en la Historia,* 79, and Marcella, "Structure of Politics," 85. "Guillermo Feliú Cruz went so far as to attribute the 'style' of Chilean national and intellectual life to the ability of the Instituto Nacional to mold young men into open-minded adults regardless of personal and family background," according to Gertrude Yeager, in "Elite Education in Nineteenth-Century Chile," *Hispanic American Historical Review* 71:1 (February 1991): 104. See also 74–75, 78–79, 95.

36. Collier and Sater, *History of Chile,* 63; Bravo Lira, *Universidad en la Historia,* 75.

37. See the intellectual biography by Iván Jaksić, *Andrés Bello: Scholarship and Nation-Building in Nineteenth-Century Latin America* (Cambridge: Cambridge University Press, 2001).

38. Quoted in Bravo Lira, *Universidad en la Historia de Chile,* 407. See also Jaksić's discussion of the "problem of training the new generation of public officials that republican Chile required," in *Andrés Bello,* 111.

39. Bravo Lira, *Universidad en la Historia,* 115; Labarca, *Historia de la Enseñanza,* 109; Jaksić, *Andrés Bello,* 124.

Argentina

Early Argentine legislators also felt the need to establish new institutions of higher education after independence was achieved. The University of Buenos Aires, a state institution, was founded in 1821 to offer a more diverse and modern curriculum than the formerly Jesuit institution in the interior, as well as to establish the cultural supremacy of the port city.[40] Secularizing liberals argued that the University of Córdoba with its "monastic" and "scholastic . . . spirit" was inadequate for the new nation. There the "intellect" was "welled up" within a "mental cloister," its critics charged.[41] In comparison to its colonial antecedents, the University of Buenos Aires would provide a wider variety of courses, including those in the hard sciences.

In the short term, however, Argentine progress in education was hampered not only by scholastic colonial legacies but also more fundamentally by post-independence regional fragmentation and caudillo rule.[42] Diverging economic interests between Buenos Aires and the interior kept nation and state fragmented. The University of Buenos Aires played "an unrivaled role in the intellectual reproduction, propagation, and refinement of liberalism," but it could not thrive when a constitutional framework had not been solidified in which the letrados' own authority would be assured.[43] Financial problems hindered the development of the *porteño* university in the early decades. Under Juan Manual de Rosas, governor of Buenos Aires province, the university suffered further. Professors lost their positions for political reasons, and the quality of teaching clearly declined as political allies of Rosas prospered. Students receiving degrees had to declare their loyalty to the caudillo. All university employees were required to provide evidence of their dedication to the cause of Rosismo. In order to limit the number of students, as much as to address concerns about finances, tuition

40. The major study of the university is Tulio Halperín-Donghi, *Historia de la Universidad de Buenos Aires* (Buenos Aires: Editorial Universitaria de Buenos Aires, 1962).

41. Domingo Sarmiento, *Life in the Argentine Republic in the Days of the Tyrants: or Civilization and Barbarism*, trans. Mrs. Horace Mann (New York: Hafner Press, 1868), 116.

42. A book that provides a fundamental and nuanced understanding of the difficulties of the transition to independence is Tulio Halperín-Donghi, *Politics, Economics, and Society in Argentina in the Revolutionary Period* (Cambridge and New York: Cambridge University Press, 1975).

43. Jeremy Adelman, *Buenos Aires and the Legal Transformation of the Atlantic World* (Stanford, CA: Stanford University Press, 1999), 167.

was now charged, and the university received infrequent and inadequate financial support from the state.[44] In 1846, Rosas tightened his grip on the school by appointing a commission to examine curricular matters. The university only began to revive after his fall in 1852 and the subsequent return of Argentina's leading intellectuals from exile.[45] Vicente Fidel López, who studied law at the university during the Rosas years, bitterly recalled classes devoted to plodding explications of outdated texts in which the larger social and global context of the historical development of law was absent.[46]

In a purely negative way Rosas inspired Argentina's "education president," Domingo Sarmiento, to promote free public education, arguing that "an ignorant people will always elect a Rosas."[47] More committed to public education than any other leading intellectual on the continent, Sarmiento was strongly influenced by educational reformers in Western Europe and the United States such as Horace Mann. He brought female normal school teachers from the United States to teach in Argentina in the 1860s and 1870s. He helped lay the groundwork for Argentina's remarkable social and cultural development by the end of the nineteenth century.[48]

In both Chile and (after the fall of Rosas) in Argentina, there was a greater understanding of the role that education could play in preparing those who had been subjects of a distant Crown to become citizens than there was in Brazil, but even reformist Chile was, to some degree, suspicious of disseminating education too broadly. In an address marking the opening of the University of Chile's faculty of philosophy, Enrique Good Ross warned that

permitting education to be disseminated indiscriminately and with excessive liberality to the inferior classes will inspire them to despise their

44. Halperín-Donghi, *Historia de la Universidad de Buenos Aires,* 51–53.

45. Levene, *History of Argentina,* 411. See Vicente G. Quesada's description of student life under Rosas in *Memorias de un Viejo* (Buenos Aires: Ediciones Ciudad Argentina, 1998), 145–160.

46. See Vicente Fidel López, *Evocaciones Históricos* (London: W.M. Jackson, Inc., 1945), 45–46.

47. Quoted in David Bushnell and Neill Macaulay, *The Emergence of Latin America in the Nineteenth Century* (New York: Oxford University Press, 1988), 229.

48. Mark D. Szuchman tends to focus on education as a form of social control, but a comparison with other South American countries during this period leads one to highlight the positive aspects of Argentina's approach. See his *Order, Family, and Community in Buenos Aires, 1810–1860* (Stanford, CA: Stanford University Press, 1988), 151–163.

status and their peers, and they will develop haughtiness out of a false sense of superiority. They will regard manual labor, domestic service, and even the exercises of those honorable but humble arts—those activities which permit us to enjoy the prime necessities of life—as tedious.[49]

Despite calls for the expansion of technical education in Chile and elsewhere throughout the nineteenth century (inspired in part by the need for engineers to build railroads) and the partial advance of the sciences, educational reformers in both Argentina and Chile found that the new subjects failed to attract students. Law continued to be the preferred subject for ambitious youth (65 percent of all degrees from the University of Chile, for example, were in that subject).[50] "All the 'fathers of families,'" one Chilean wrote in 1833, "yearn for their sons to become lawyers, as they should."[51] Even in countries without explicit systems of elite recruitment comparable to those that Brazil developed, law remained the preferred field of study for those who were to follow careers in politics. Law only increased in popularity in Chile, for example, as the century progressed.[52] In Buenos Aires, as well, it had been the favorite subject of the sons of the commercial bourgeoisie since the late colonial period, and the need for men with legal training accelerated thereafter.[53] In that sense, Brazilian leaders were not unreasonable to have focused on legal training for their political class, since cultural predispositions led South Americans in the nineteenth century to continue to regard education primarily as an avenue for social and political advancement, or as an instrument for confirming the already existing social status of a fairly small number of families. (University administrators and teachers, nevertheless, almost universally bemoaned the student's focus on acquiring a title.[54]) By linking access to education so closely to access to political life, South American society in the nineteenth century further enhanced the legitimacy of existing authority by giving an oligarchy the added appearance of seeming to be a meritocracy. As a Chilean student wrote in

49. Quoted in Marcella, "Structure of Politics," 18.
50. Collier and Sater, *History of Chile,* 101–102. See also Serrano, *Universidad y Nación,* 176.
51. Quoted in Labarca, *Historia de la Enseñanza,* 97.
52. Of the nineteenth-century members of Chile's parliament studied by Marcella, 66 senators and 160 deputies had law degrees; and 26 members of parliament had engineering degrees, and 14 had medical degrees. See Marcella, "Structure of Politics," 87.
53. Halperín-Donghi, *Historia de la Universidad de Buenos Aires,* 21.
54. Yeager, "Elite Education," 103.

1842, the colonial aristocracy had been replaced by "a new class based on the virtues of knowledge and talent."[55]

Clearly, there was a large degree of continuity between the colonial and post-independence periods in this regard. Society remained divided into the *gente decente* and the popular classes. Education served the interests of oligarchical political systems. Although education could provide an avenue to political power, access to education was fairly limited. Unless a young man from the popular classes acquired a patron from the upper echelons of society, his options would be limited indeed.[56]

Student Culture and Identity in Oligarchical Societies

Education existed primarily to serve the interests of oligarchical political systems and patriarchal societies. To some degree, the schools sought to impose certain models of personality and behavior, as well as common values. According to historian Gertrude Yeager, Bello in Chile sought to encourage the development of traits such as "diligence, precision, concentration, self-discipline, perseverance, [and] attention to detail." He thought that the study of grammar and Latin would produce "cautious administrators and legislators."[57] Professors were to act as "agents of socialization" by inviting students to weekly *tertulias* in their homes.[58] (Faculty-directed tertulias seems to have been more central to Chilean student life than to Brazilian student life, where the students focused their energies on their own student organizations and their own autonomous group living arrangements known as "republics.") Although women were admitted to many of these universities as early as the 1870s (1871 in Chile and 1879 in Brazil), they did not arrive in large numbers until well into the twentieth century.[59] University education remained a prerogative predominantly of the upper-class male and the university provided a setting in which elite male identities were formed.

55. Quoted in Allen Woll, *A Functional Past: The Uses of History in Nineteenth-Century Chile* (Baton Rouge: Louisiana State University Press, 1982), 12.

56. See, for example, Serrano, *Universidad y Nación,* 164 and 165; Richard Graham, *Patronage and Politics in Nineteenth-Century Brazil* (Stanford, CA: Stanford University Press, 1990).

57. Yeager, "Elite Education," 93–94.

58. Ibid., 91.

59. Collier and Sater, *History of Chile,* 101–102.

In Argentina in the wake of independence, concerns about the breakdown of social order led to tighter controls over student behavior than in Brazil. Administrators and faculty could request help from police in apprehending students absent from class. Authorities, furthermore, tried to restrict student access to public space to a much greater degree than they did in Brazil, in both liberal eras and the more repressive Rosas period.[60] Students were, to a certain degree, public figures; the results of their performance on examinations, even the numbers of times they missed class, were published in local newspapers in all three countries.[61] Authorities tried to shame these students into appropriate behavior (but, in the Brazilian case, at least, they were not altogether successful in this regard).

If we really want to understand the role of the schools in forging a political class, we have to look at the worlds the students themselves made and the identities formed during their years of higher education. Even during the repressive period under Rosas, students in Buenos Aires fought against the intellectual and political restrictions imposed in the classroom and maintained their own active extracurriculum in the city's "salons and bookstores." In their life outside of the classroom, they forged an identity as a political class. According to Argentine Vicente Fidel López, his personality was formed in the company of friends who entered university when he did and within the larger context of his university environment.[62] To understand these young men's process of identity formation, one has to look at the meanings they attached to their actions and to their persons.[63]

One of the central institutions of Brazilian law student culture, and a key component in the formation of their identities, was the *república,* a private space in which they practiced being public men. The república is an example of a *panelinha,* which anthropologist Anthony Leeds has described as "a relatively closed, completely informal primary group, held together by ties of friendship or other personal contacts acting for common ends."[64] The república marked a social space in which the student, distant from the pa-

---

60. See Mark D. Szuchman, *Order, Family, and Community in Buenos Aires, 1810–1860* (Stanford: Stanford University Press, 1988), 103–104.

61. Bernardo Subercaseaux, *Cultura y Sociedad Liberal en el Siglo XIX: Lastarría, Ideologia y Literatura* (Santiago: Editorial Aconagua, 1981), 37–38. See also Szuchman, *Order, Family, and Community,* 145–146.

62. See López, *Evocaciones Históricos,* 31–32.

63. Adelman, *Republic of Capital,* 168.

64. Anthony Leeds, "Brazilian Careers and Social Structure: An Evolutionary Model and Case History," *American Anthropologist* 66, no. 6 (December 1964): 1330.

triarchal big house of the large landowners, experienced a measure of independence absent in a world defined by bonds of patronage. Within this space, students developed a strong sense of common identity, creating a family of brothers, as the students frequently called each other, in a community without chiefs. Within these repúblicas, and the student literary and political associations that grew out of them, young elite men in Brazil developed the affective ties that helped create a cohesive national political class.[65]

An important aspect of the law school experience was to differentiate the students from the rest of society.[66] In this sense, the five years spent in Pernambuco or São Paulo or Santiago or Buenos Aires were as much a "rite of institution" as a rite of passage, in Pierre Bourdieu's useful distinction. Their time as students separated them from those who would never experience higher education.[67] As one Brazilian student poet wrote in the 1860s, "Perhaps he never wrote a book / and didn't devote himself to knowledge / But his name on this list of São Paulo law students / was all that really mattered."[68] To be on that list was to mark a young man as an agent of the state in the short term and a representative of the nation as a deputy, senator, or cabinet minister in the long term.

Central, as well, to creating a sense of identity was a recognition of "others" in relation to themselves.[69] Brazilian law students, for example, made a clear distinction between themselves and the rest of the community. "Futrica," an "ordinary, egotistical man of low sentiments," continued for most of the nineteenth century to be the dismissive designation for those outside of the community.[70] For their part, elite women's contrasting condition and lack of access to public space helped define the students' identity as young men. Until late in the nineteenth century in São Paulo and well

65. See, for example, J. V. Couto de Magalhães, *Revista de Academia* (April 1859): 40–41; *O Constitucional,* August 11, 1882; José Manuel Cardoso de Oliveira, *Dois Metros e Cinco* (Rio de Janeiro: H. Garnier, 1905), 2, 24–25.

66. According to Yeager, this was true for Chilean education as well. See her "Elite Education," 98.

67. Pierre Bourdieu, "Rites of Institution," in *Language and Symbolic Power* (Cambridge, MA: Harvard University Press, 1991), 117–126.

68. L. N. Fagundes Varella's poem is cited in Celio Debes, *Na Propaganda,* vol. 1 of *Campos Salles: Perfil de um Estadista* (Rio de Janeiro: Livraria Francisco Alves, 1978), 30.

69. See Gertrude Yeager's brief discussion of this issue in "Elite Education," 98.

70. Aurelio Buarque de Hollanda Ferreira, *Pequeno Dicionário Brasileiro da Lingua Portuguesa,* 11th ed. (Rio de Janeiro: Editora Civilização Brasileira, 1983), 581.

into the twentieth century elsewhere, women of the upper classes were expected not to leave the house unless accompanied by the male head of household. They were frequently transported in enclosed sedan chairs carried by slaves, while the law students occupied the streets of São Paulo and Recife at all times of the day and night.[71]

Although Brazilian students did not maintain the Portuguese tradition of wearing a cap and gown as had their forefathers in Coimbra, they did adopt a semi-official uniform that was centuries removed from the medieval traditions of Coimbra, but just as clearly an emblem of their status and identity. Instead of wearing academic robes, they chose the wool suits favored by the business classes of France and Great Britain, outfits ill-designed for the Brazilian climate, but which symbolized their membership in the "official" Europeanized "nation" they sought to create. The student type, par excellence, was a bit of a dandy; to appear more serious, law students chose to wear glasses even when they did not need them. When other young males, such as clerks, chose to dress the same way, the law students resented it, and conflict could result. The right to wear a frock coat was one of the prerogatives that accompanied their status.[72] Students began to "play the gentleman" in their dress, deportment, and leisure activities.[73] In Chile, as well, clothes made the gentleman; an Instituto Nacional student from the provinces like the fictional Martín Rivas had to learn to dress like someone from Santiago as part of the often painful process of identity formation and socialization into the dominant group.[74] The political dominance of the capital city over provincial Chile was reflected in styles of clothing and the tendency of people from the countryside to refer to the city as "Chile."[75] In

71. See, for example, Affonso A. DeFreitas, *Tradições e Reminiscências Paulistanas* (São Paulo: Livraria Martins Editora, 1955), 51; Gilberto Freyre, *The Mansion and the Shanties,* trans. and ed. Harriet de Onis (New York: Alfred A. Knopf, 1963), 36; Mario Sette, *Arruar, História Pitoresca do Recife Antigo* (Rio de Janeiro: Livraria Editora da Casa do Estudante do Brasil, 1952), 7–8.

72. See, for example, José Luis de Almeida Nogueira, *Academia de São Paulo: Tradições e Reminiscências: Estudantes, Estudantões, Estudantadas* (São Paulo: Vanorden and A Editora, 1907–1912), 1:125; 2:48, 244, and 3:244. See also Graham, *Patronage and Politics,* 68, 69; Needell, *Tropical Belle Epoque,* 166–168; and Yeager, "Elite Education," 101–102.

73. On "playing the gentleman," see Henry Abelove, *The Evangelist of Desire: John Wesley and the Methodists* (Stanford: Stanford University Press, 1990), 7–9.

74. Alberto Blest Gana, *Martín Rivas* (Madrid: Ediciones Cátedra, 1983), 60–61, 101–104.

75. Collier and Sater, *History of Chile,* 103.

Brazil, the law schools were not located in the capital, but students who had grown up in Rio de Janeiro, particularly those who were sons of national politicians, tended to set the tone for personal style in both São Paulo and Pernambuco. Rio de Janeiro, city and province, the capital of a highly centralized empire and for decades the empire's economic motor, was the site of these young men's ultimate aspirations. As students, they tried to shed their provincial accents and adopt a more national style of speech.

Even as they developed their own more European and national identities, Brazilian students took other social groups' sense of identity cavalierly, parodying publicly the practices of military men, for example. In 1854, this led to a near state of war between members of a local military battalion and the students of São Paulo. What became known as the "incident of the cadets" started when a young soldier stood in line for a theatrical performance with his soldier's hat on his head. (Theaters were places that students felt they owned, as sometime actors and playwrights and inveterate patrons.) A fifth-year student began making loud noises in order to draw attention to the cadet and to what he considered his inappropriate attire and location. Other students joined in by yelling and shouting, as well as beating their walking sticks and stamping their feet on the ground. Francisco Gonçalves Meirelles, the law student, then stood on a bench and started giving orders as if he were an officer himself. "Turn to the right! Present arms! Aim! Fire!" The sound of whistles and canes built to a deafening roar. Finally, the young soldier could no longer bear it and ran away, much to the students' delight; they continued hooting at the fleeing man mercilessly. Other soldiers, who happened to be nearby, and who did not appreciate Meirelles's attempts to impersonate an officer, tried to seize him, but his fellow students prevented them. In the following days and nights, there were recurring conflicts between law students and military men around the city. As a result of one incident, a young cadet who had been thrown into a ravine by some students was gravely, perhaps even fatally, injured. His fellow soldiers responded by threatening that if he should die, they would take their revenge on the students, not leaving one alive. The students, in response, marched two by two to the provincial president's palace, demanding to know "if the government could and wanted to guarantee their safety." "If not," they declared, "the students would be ready to defend themselves." The president cautioned the students to take no untoward steps and sent the whole battalion to the port city of Santos to cool off. Of the fate of the injured cadet, history remains silent. The incident confirms the students' privileged, protected status within imperial society; the military had suffered reduced prestige and status since the creation of the National Guard in the early 1830s. (Civilian politicians had been concerned by the participation of military men in popular riots and rebellions.) Unlike in much of South America, the Brazilian military clearly was subordinate to civilian authority in all ways until the fall of the empire in 1889, and the letrados' cultural authority was unchallenged until the waning years of the empire.

Students saw themselves as being uniquely the representatives of youth and, in turn, of the legitimate aspirations of the nation. Autonomy and legitimacy were theirs alone. The students embraced youth in the way that was typical of the Romantic period. "My heart is elevated like a mountain top," one Brazilian student wrote in 1860, "and when I feel great and noble passions, I feel immense pleasure in comparing my heart to that of the paltry souls I see around me."[76] Politically, idealistic youth was marked by the "noble spirit of independence and liberty."[77] Only the uncorrupted young could save Brazilian society. "It is to youth that the Empire should appeal in the hopes that it will be more zealous in promoting the happiness and glory of the fatherland and moral principles, thereby civilizing the great Brazilian family."[78]

For the generation of the mid-1840s, the influence of French Romanticism was paramount in Brazil. Students looked to figures like Lord Byron for examples of appropriate personal behavior as well as literary production.[79] Student newspapers and associations, both largely devoted to literature during this period, proliferated. As many as thirteen student newspapers were being published in 1860 in São Paulo alone.[80] Although the "grand mission" of founding a newspaper was "a difficult and burdensome business," as one student editor proclaimed in 1856, it was also an "eminently patriotic task, a glorious sacrifice that those who aspire to work for the aggrandizement of their country cannot refuse."[81] The newspapers were frequently tied to student associations, which were often launched in cele-

76. Antônio Simplício de Salles, "Physiognomias Acadêmicas," *A Legenda* (21 October 1860): 92.

77. "Indifferentismo Político: Continuado do n. antecedente," *O Argos Olindense* (11 August 1838): 4.

78. "A Civilisação no Brasil," *O Album dos Acadêmicos Olindenses* (30 June 1850): 118–120.

79. See my discussion in "Orators and Poets: Language and Elite Male Identity at the São Paulo Law School, 1850–1889," *South Eastern Latin Americanist* 38, no. 4 (spring 1995): 43–48.

80. Augusto Emílio Zaluar, *Peregrinação pela Província de São Paulo (1860–1861)* (São Paulo: Universidade de São Paulo, 1975), 127–128.

81. J. Campos, "Introducção," *O Clarim Litterário* (May 1856): 1.

brations on Independence Day, September 7. One law school professor lamented in 1858 that the "most talented and most admired students are those who most take advantage of these associations and least apply themselves to the law."[82]

The young men at the law schools in Pernambuco and São Paulo dedicated themselves to the cause of literary nation building. They discussed critically the efforts of Brazilian authors to establish a national literature and considered themselves to be making contributions, as well.[83] Such activity was in the "service of the holy cause of our country," to which they offered "great sacrifices."[84] For the students, the "cause" of letters was "sacred." The "written word," one student wrote in 1859, "is the most powerful element of social progress."[85] Students at both schools shared the products of their literary efforts with each other, distributing their newspapers through the mails and reinforcing their strong ties and sense of common identity and destiny.

The young men fully embraced the Romantic notion of the artist as a superior man with a mission to redeem society.[86] Although Romanticism had become the predominant literary style in Brazil with the publication of Gonçalves de Magalhães's *Suspíros Poéticos e Saudades* (Poetic Sighs and Longings) in 1836, Romanticism took hold at the law schools only in the mid-1840s. From then on the law schools were the "great focus of the Romantic infection," as one critic of the Brazilian letrado has written, which "dominated the national spirit until the end of the 1870s."[87]

Born after Brazil had achieved independence, the generation that arrived in law school after 1845 knew no other reality than Brazil as an independent nation. What Brazil lacked to become recognized as a full-fledged member of the civilized world, according to the students, was the cultural autonomy that a national literature would symbolize. Many students, along with their elders, looked to indigenous themes for inspiration in the creation

82. Francisco de Paula Baptista, "Memória Histórica dos Acontecimentos Mais Notáveis do Anno Findo" (Recife, Pernambuco: N.p., 1858), 6–7.

83. See, for example, "Chrônica Litterária," *Ensaios Litterários* (August 1859): 17–18; *O Clarim Litterário* (May 1856): 3–4; M.S. de Bueno, *Memórias da Associação Culto à Sciência,* May 10, 1859, p. 7.

84. "Chrônica Litterária," *Ensaios Litterários* (May 1849): 18.

85. "Introdução," *Ensaios da Sociedade Brazília* (October 15, 1859): 1.

86. On the mission of the Romantic poet, see Roque Spencer Maciel de Barros, *Significação Educativa do Romantismo Brasileiro: Gonçalves de Magalhães* (São Paulo: Editora da Universidade de São Paulo, 1973), 84–87.

87. Paulo Prado, *Retrato do Brasil: Ensaio Sôbre a Tristeza Brasileira* (Rio de Janeiro: Livraria José Olympio Editora, 1962), 145.

of a Brazilian literature. A poem printed in an 1850 Pernambuco student newspaper *O Album dos Acadêmicos Olindenses* was a good example of this brand of literary nationalism; the poem made extensive use of Tupí words, all of which were helpfully defined by the author.[88] Another poem from this time employed the language of the Brazilian backlander, the *sertanejo*.[89] The need to explain the vocabulary of the indigenous population or that of the sertanejo demonstrated the social gap between the literati and their ostensible inspirations. Literary nationalism inevitably had its artificial tendencies. Although it had its own culturally democratizing tendencies, bridging the gap between an oral cultural and a hyperliterate one, it was also an example of cultural appropriation of the popular classes' language. Moreover, the elite's real interest in the "people" was limited. The Indianist movement in Brazil was a diversion from Brazil's all-too-obvious African heritage and a sentimental celebration of a people who were safely dead or at least largely out of sight in the Brazilian context.

In any case, an interest in the African component of Brazilian national culture developed more slowly. Indeed, in one of those rare moments in the 1840s and 1850s when the careful control of language exhibited in the student newspapers slipped, one can glimpse some of the hidden prejudices of the student body. Students used the phrase "the language used by Africans in our kitchens" to attack writing in a student newspaper that was published solely to deflate the literary pretensions of their colleagues.[90]

There were other inherent contradictions in the students' literary nationalism, as well. Their models for creating a national literature and the proper roles and sensibilities for poets were drawn from Europe, most particularly from England and France. As one graduate recalled of his classmates in the São Paulo in the 1840s, "Every student with some imagination wanted to be Byron, and had as his inexorable destiny to copy or translate the English bard."[91] Favorite authors of the students besides Byron included Hugo, Chateaubriand, Scott, and Balzac. National independence, one student wrote, brought with it expanded possibilities for relations with "civilized" Europe,

88. M. A. Machado, "O Canto do Índio," *O Album dos Acadêmicos Olindenses* (June 1850): 157–158.

89. José M. deFreitas, "O Sertanejo," *Atheneu Pernambucano* (May 1857): 30.

90. The "kitchen" language contained in the newspaper *Zoilo* (named for a critic of the poet Homer) is criticized in *O Brado da Indignação* (September 1850): 3. See also "Sandices em Guisa de Crítica, pelo Senhor Figueira," *O Brado da Indignação* (October 1850): 21.

91. Quoted in Heitor Martins, "Byron e *O Guarani*," *Luso-Brazilian Review* 2 (December 1965): 69–74.

the "sphere of knowledge being broadened after Portugal ceased to be the exclusive spring from which we could drink." Literary inspiration from other countries created the possibility for a new literature that they hoped would surpass Portuguese antecedents.[92]

Of all the forms of literary production, none was as important as poetry for these young men. The Romantic exaltation of the artist, and particularly the poet, helped provide these young men with an especially strong sense of themselves as people above and beyond the ordinary. "The poets are the true apostles of God," one student wrote in 1856.[93] The sense of the poet as someone with a "mission" was the "typical contribution of Romanticism" to world literature and art. As a literary style, moreover, Romanticism was particularly tied to a stage in personal development, indeed to adolescence itself. In the context of the Brazilian law schools, Romanticism helped solidify the identity of a national political class.[94]

In Argentina, as well, the brief moment of respite during which Rosas retreated from power in 1832 created an opportunity in which the flux of French ideas transformed the mentality of young Argentines like Vicente Fidel López. Elsewhere in South America, as well, the influence of Romanticism was particularly strong among adolescents.[95]

As they defined themselves, these young Brazilians also defined the nation. In more explicitly political terms, the law schools were seen as the "two forces that maintain us [i.e., the Brazilian empire] in equilibrium."[96] The young men embraced the centralized nation-state that prevented Brazil from being fragmented into tiny republics like many of their Spanish American neighbors, destined, as they saw them, for no importance in world affairs. A decentralized state would break up in "incoherence, rivalries, and an internal antagonism that would destroy the sentiment of nationality which consists in the perfect fusion and brotherhood of the same people," one student warned. Nationality was "above provincialisms."[97] For decades after his premature accession to power in 1840, the young Emperor Dom

92. "Esboços Crítico-Litterários," *O Clarim Litterário* (May 1865): 4.
93. Pedro de Calasans, "A Gonçalves Dias," *O Clarim Litterário* (May 1856): 4.
94. See Antônio Cândido, *Formação da Literatura Brasileira (Momentos Decisivos), 1836–1880,* vol. 2 (São Paulo: Livraria Martins Editora, 1971), 26, 28, 178, 184, 284. See also Rama, *The Lettered City,* 36–37, 43.
95. López, *Evocaciones Históricas,* 39–40; Labarca, *Historia de la Enseñanza,* 108–109; Adelman, *Republic of Capital,* 168.
96. Coelho Duarte, *Ensaios Litterários* (August 1849): 28.
97. Manoel Pereira de Sousa Arouca, "Melhor Forma de Governo," *Memórias da ssociação Culto à Sciencia* (10 November 1859): 76–79. See also A. A. de Souza Carvalho, "A Centralisação no Brasil," *Aurora* (May 1849): 45–49.

Pedro II, the letrados' patron and himself a letrado in spirit as well as the Empire's supreme magistrate, served as the reflection of how these young men saw themselves, as well as the ultimate national symbol. In a revealing way, students spoke of the empire itself as being "still adolescent."[98] The students must "make the state the image of man; like him, the state should be free, and like him, the state should be intelligent."[99] These young men looked at the nation and the state and saw themselves.

While the Brazilian law students were largely left alone to define their own identities and political understandings, in Chile, the limits of appropriate behavior for even elite male students were clearly defined. Consider the example of Francisco Bilbao, the son of a congressman who had lived in exile in Peru when Bilbao was growing up in the 1830s. A student at the Instituto Nacional in the 1840s, he was, like so many of his South American contemporaries, infused with the spirit of Romanticism that was gradually displacing colonial scholasticism. Bilbao criticized Chilean society and the Catholic Church in *El Crepúsculo,* a monthly periodical published by La Sociedad Literaria. After copies of the publication were burned, Bilbao was put on trial on charges of immorality, blasphemy, and sedition. Bilbao directly challenged the authority of the judge and prosecutor in court. Fined and expelled from school, he left for exile in France. On his return in 1848 he joined with some of the more progressive student members of the Club de la Reforma to form the Sociedad de la Igualdad, an organization that tried to incorporate artisans in a broader project of opposition to Chilean oligarchical politics. When the Sociedad was suppressed in 1850, Bilbao went into exile again, as did many student members of the Sociedad de la Igualdad such as Benjamin Vicuña Mackenna.[100]

A safer extracurricular activity for Chilean students to define their identity was through literary production, which helped define them as gentlemen, and provided the key to entrance into the club of letrados. La Sociedad

98. See, for example, Rangel Pestana, "As Lettras, Sciencias e Artes no Brasil," *Memórias da Associação Culto à Sciencia* (April 1860): 43; A. F. Vianna, "Discurso," *Ensaios Litterários do Atheneu Pernambucano* (September 1852): 27.

99. Francisco Gomes dos Santos Lopes, "Discurso," *Ensaios Litterários do Atheneu Pernambucano* (September 1852): 27.

100. Collier and Sater, *History of Chile,* 104; Solomon Lipp, *Three Chilean Thinkers* (Waterloo, Ontario: Wilfrid Laurier University Press, 1975), 12–20; Alberto J. Varona, *Francisco Bilbao, Revolucionario de América: Vida y Pensamiento: Estudio de sus Ensayos y Trabajos Periodísticos* (Panama City: Ediciones Excelsior, 1973), 75–91, 109–119, 136–138.

Literaria, for whom Bilbao had written his controversial polemic, was perhaps the most important of the literary organizations with which students were associated. Chilean student publications included plays, novels, and short stories, although they do not seem to have developed the autonomous life that Brazilian student newspapers did.[101] While the earliest intellectuals operating in Chile, like the Venezuelan exile Bello, wrote neoclassical prose, members of younger generations like Alberto Blest Gana were admirers of Balzac and Stendahl.[102] National history developed a particular following among Chilean students, as it did among nineteenth-century Chilean elites generally. (Witness, for example, the 1839 Instituto Nacional student group, the Society of Chilean History.[103]) As in Brazil, Chilean students "in their writings . . . often found their own political education to be the cornerstone of national stability."[104]

Within oligarchical and patriarchal societies, mechanisms had to be created to guarantee stability and continuity. Students expected and (by and large) received deference from their social inferiors. In Brazil, students in the first year of law school expected to be referred to as "doctor" by those they met on the street, even during their first year of study. Yet the new state of political independence could not guarantee that traditional patterns of deference could be maintained in countries like Argentina. As Domingo Sarmiento complained about conditions under Rosas, "Implacable is the hatred which these people [from the popular classes] feel for men of refinement, whose garments, manners, and customs, they regard with invincible repugnance."[105] The caudillist state had eliminated much that Sarmiento admired about the colonial world. Prior to independence, Sarmiento lamented, "The judicial chairs and the administrative offices were then occupied by educated men." He lamented the loss of "the elegance of manners, the refinement of customs, the cultivation of literature, . . . the public spirit which animated the people."[106] As Tulio Halperín-Donghi has argued, Sarmiento's "gospel of renewal by means of education is tied . . . to the desire to restore—in the context created by the revolutions of the nineteenth century—the sovereignty of intelligence in which Sarmiento recognized an

101. Yeager, "Elite Education," 91; Varona, *Francisco Bilbao,* 64–73.
102. Collier and Sater, *History of Chile,* 102.
103. Woll, *A Functional Past,* 30.
104. Yeager, "Elite Education," 100–101.
105. Sarmiento, *Life in the Argentine Republic,* 22.
106. Ibid., 70.

enduring legacy of the colonial order."[107] Caudillos and military men, however, continued to challenge letrados for cultural and political authority in
Argentina for the rest of the nineteenth century.

The roles these young men adopted and the identities they embraced,
helped define aspects of South American political culture for more than a
century. In Chile and Brazil, in particular, oligarchical systems restricted
political participation and access to political power. The letrado provided
the model for appropriate political behavior. This in turn became a further
impediment to a more active role by citizens from the popular classes, and
it restricted access to membership in the official nation.

Higher Education and Mass Society

In the late nineteenth century, educational reforms accelerated in all three
countries, although once again, with Brazil trailing the others in the breadth
and significance of its initiatives. After the fall of the Brazilian empire in
1889, new schools were established. Most of these new institutions were
law schools, founded to serve the interests of Brazil's newly sovereign states
in the highly decentralized republic, as the law schools in Pernambuco and
São Paulo had served the centralized empire. In Argentina and Chile, as
well, new educational institutions were created. Law continued to dominate,
although informally and intellectually, social science began to have a measure of cultural authority, and technical education began to gain more prominence, as well. Both were partly consequences of the influence of positivism
on South American thinkers in the late 1800s and early 1900s.[108] In Brazil,
the military's overthrow of the empire in 1889 had been inspired, in part, by
a desire to challenge the authority of the "*casacas*" or suits. By the mid-
1890s, however, the military had retreated to the barracks in an attempt to
protect its own professional identity, leaving the political arena once again
largely to the letrados.[109]

In Chile and Argentina, more than in Brazil prior to the 1930s, social
change accompanied a greater integration into the North Atlantic econ-

107. Tulio Halperín-Donghi, "Sarmiento's Place in Post-Revolutionary Argentina,"
27–28.
108. See my "From 'Liberty and Order' to 'Order and Progress': Republican Discourse
among São Paulo Law Students, 1878–1889," *SECOLAS Annals* (March 1996): 91–96.
109. See June Hahner, *Civilian-Military Relations in Brazil, 1889–1898* (Columbia:
University of South Carolina Press, 1969).

omy.[110] An increasing percentage of the Chilean population had access to at least some level of education by the late 1800s. By 1920, Chile had achieved fifty percent literacy.[111] Certainly no country in South America experienced the economic boom that Argentina did in this time period. Long-term investment in education at lower levels began to pay off. Male literacy rates made even more impressive gains in Argentina than in Chile; the literacy rate increased from 19 percent in 1869 to 62 percent in 1914.[112] This led to a dramatic increase in university attendance in a short period of time, beginning in the 1880s but accelerating after the turn of the twentieth century, from 3,000 in 1900 to 14,000 in 1918.[113]

In the later years, reforms at the University of Córdoba, although largely limited to relatively parochial issues of university governance, pointed the way for a different relationship between university and society. A new, although still relatively small and inchoate, middle class found its way into the ranks of the letrados. Their educational backgrounds would be more diverse, with the expansion of offerings in the social sciences in particular, but their social function would remain much the same.[114] The twentieth-century state agents would look to incorporate, rather than merely expect deference from, the popular classes. Students involved in the university reform movement in Argentina in 1918 called for the offering of more educational opportunities for the working classes and established direct linkages with working class organizations, following the example, to some degree, of Francisco Bilbao.[115] In other South American countries, figures inspired by the Argentine movement, such as Peru's Victor Raúl Haya de la Torre, would open "popular universities" in which university students would themselves serve as instructors of manual laborers. Over the course of the next few decades, as a tutelary state was created, populist leaders would devise a more expansive definition of the nation, as well.

110. See Bushnell and Macaulay, *The Emergence of Latin America in the Nineteenth Century,* 228–234; William Glade, "Economy, 1870–1914," in *Latin America: Economy and Society, 1870–1930,* ed. Leslie Bethell (Cambridge and New York: Cambridge University Press, 1989), 9–15.

111. Yeager, "Elite Education," 92–93; Collier and Sater, *History of Chile,* 179–180.

112. Levene, *History of Argentina,* 522.

113. David Rock, *Argentina, 1516–1982: From Spanish Colonization to the Falklands War* (Berkeley: University of California Press, 1985), 200.

114. Rama, *The Lettered City,* 57–58.

115. See Richard J. Walter, *Student Politics in Argentina: The University Reform and its Effects, 1918–1964* (New York: Basic Books, 1968), 50, 56–57. See also Varona, *Francisco Bilbao,* 117–120.

The Critics

5

Scenes of Reading:
Imagining Nations/Romancing History
in Spanish America

Fernando Unzueta

If the "crux of the modern nation" is, according to E. J. Hobsbawm, the "formation of a nation-state,"[1] in the Americas, the territorial dissolution of most of the Spanish monarchy and its recomposition into independent republics took place during the first half of the nineteenth century. During this period, the American kingdoms fought for and gained independence and began to produce the lettered configuration of their nations. Nevertheless, most studies of Latin American nations measure them against social and material indicators associated with contemporary nationalisms, such as the struggle for social justice, full territorial articulation, national popular movements in an era of increasing social mobilization, and the overall

A shorter version of this essay appeared as "Novel Subjects: On Reading and National (Subject) Formation," *Chasqui* 31, no. 2 (2002): 75–94. I am grateful to Cheryl S. Unzueta for her editorial suggestions.

1. E. J. Hobsbawm, *Nations and Nationalism since 1780: Programme, Myth, Reality* (Cambridge and New York: Cambridge University Press, 1990), 64.

"modernization" process. From these traditional sociological and political perspectives, Latin American history has been interpreted as the oligarchic manipulation of nationalisms against the people in nation-less republics.[2] In a different vein, much has been written on the conceptual oxymoron of a "continental nationalism," usually to condemn shortsighted localized nationalism in favor of an ideal pan-Americanism.[3] Just as frequently, many essays defined the nation in essentialist terms related to its racially mixed composition, using concepts related to expressions such as *raza cósmica, continente mestizo,* or *pueblo enfermo.* Independently of the merits of many of these studies and their more contemporary versions, they say little about how the nation came into being and the shapes it took in the nineteenth century. Additionally, by imposing modern criteria to its early forms, they are destined to portray the nation as an incomplete or failed project.

   In a gradual change, some recent interpretations of the nation center on the formation of national cultures through writing and other cultural manifestations and trace the roots of twentieth-century popular nationalism to nineteenth-century liberalism.[4] While the objective elements that constitute Spanish American nationalities were forged later on, the imagery of national identity (the symbols and the language of nationalism) is contemporaneous to the first discourses and political institutions that proclaimed independence from the Spanish Crown and were well in place by the 1860s.[5] Furthermore, however popular or well integrated a modern nation is, the associations

---

   2. See Víctor Alba, *Nationalists without Nations: The Oligarchy versus the People in Latin America* (New York: Praeger, 1968); and the more recent book by Danièle Demelas, *Nationalisme sans nation? La Bolivie aux XIXe–XXe siècles* (Paris: Editions du CNRS, 1980).

   3. See Arthur Whitaker, *Nationalism in Latin America* (Gainesville: University of Florida Press, 1962).

   4. Angel Rama describes the first three decades of the twentieth century as the "nationalist" period when, for the first time, the old liberal formula of "popular education + nationalism" translated into "true community participation," in *La ciudad letrada* (Hanover: Ediciones del Norte, 1984), 106, 142. Mabel Moraña, as well, writes that "national-popular movements" around 1910 to 1940 redefined many "topics" (populism, nationalism, Americanism) of nineteenth-century liberalism. See her *Literatura y cultura nacional en hispanoamérica (1910–1940)* (Minneapolis, MN: Institute for the Study of Ideologies and Literatures, 1984), 355.

   5. See Germán Colmenares, *Las convenciones contra la cultura. Ensayos sobre la historiografía hispanoamericana del siglo XIX* (Bogotá: Tercer Mundo, 1987), 200. Likewise, Nicolas Shumway shows that Argentina's "guiding fictions and rhetorical paradigms were founded well before 1880," in *The Invention of Argentina* (Berkeley: University of California Press, 1991), xii.

among the individuals who belong to it are always, as it was early pointed out by Ernest Renan, more cultural than material.[6] In the last analysis, rather than simply searching for the roots of the nation in an earlier period, a conceptual shift is in order, a change that provides a new interpretive model to study national formation, namely, a new way of reading the nation.

Reading and Writing the Nation

Benedict Anderson's *Imagined Communities* (1983/1991) has almost single-handedly provided the basis for this new approach to the problem of nationalism. While modern political doctrines and practices are still central to his approach to the rise of nations, his major insight consists of seeing nationalism as a cultural system (instead of a political ideology) that comes into being against centralizing religious communities and dynastic realms, and thanks to the technical advances of print culture.[7] From this constructivist perspective, as opposed to strictly material or essentialist orientations, the nation can be seen as an artifact (Anderson) produced through a wide range of symbols, narratives, and discursive formations, including newspaper writing, history, and literature.

Such a redefinition of the nation's "conceptual object"[8] began to have a considerable impact on discussions of Spanish American nationalities in the 1980s, thanks to the reception of Anderson's work and, probably more significantly, of Angel Rama's *La ciudad letrada* (1984). While I do not want to conflate the approaches of these two important books, some parallels seem obvious, most notably, with regard to the roles they attribute to intellectuals and bureaucrats and, more generally, to print media and cultures

6. "A nation is a spiritual principle, the outcome of the profound complications of history; it is a spiritual family not a group determined by the shape of the earth." This "spiritual principle," according to Ernest Renan, implies the possession of common memories and customs, contemporary consent, and a program for the future. See Renan, "What Is a Nation?" (1882), in *Nation and Narration,* ed. Homi Bhabha (London: Routledge, 1990), 18–19.

7. Benedict Anderson, *Imagined Communities: Reflections on the Origin and Spread of Nationalism,* rev. ed. ([1983] London: Verso, 1991). I also find it relevant that Anderson has stressed the "New World origins of Nationalism," and condemned the "Eurocentric provincialism" of many scholars who have largely ignored the "crucial chapter" of his book, retitled "Creole Pioneers" in its second edition. See *Imagined,* xiii.

8. Homi K. Bhabha, "Introduction: Narrating the Nation," in *Nation and Narration,* ed. Bhabha (London: Routledge, 1990), 3.

vis-à-vis national and state formation. In the field of literary and cultural studies, Homi Bhabha's collection of essays entitled *Nation and Narration* (1990) brought Anderson's paradigm to the forefront, and focused the study of the nation in its "narrative address," that is, "as it is written," particularly through novels.[9] Accordingly, Doris Sommer's *Foundational Fictions: The National Romances of Latin America* (1991) showed the "inextricability of politics from fiction in the history of nation building," and more specifically of romantic novels and patriotic history.[10]

The impact of Sommer's book probably prompted my invitation to address the role of the *romance nacional* at the interdisciplinary conference that motivated this essay.[11] One of the conference's goals was to produce historicized explorations of how the nation was written and read in nineteenth-century Latin America. While there is considerable work on how the nation was written, unfortunately, the bibliography of that period's ways of reading literature (or those of the present, for that matter) is extremely limited and basically nonexistent when dealing with reading the nation in romances. Thus, new and sometimes oblique approaches to this topic are needed. One such possibility is considering national romances as a historical genre. Sommer, for instance, rightly observes a "generic coherence" that would be missed in individual readings of the historical romances she studies. She further argues that they "became national novels . . . not so much [due] to their market popularity, although to be sure many of these novels were immediately popular, but to the fact that they became required reading by the first decades of the twentieth century."[12] The popularity of romances is worth noting but by itself gives little indication as to how their national dimension was read. And whereas the institutionalization of the *ro-*

9. Bhabha, "Introduction: Narrating the Nation." Such a culturalist, even "textualist" approximation to the study of the nation, would also seem to be supported by prominent historians, such as E. J. Hobsbawm. As he argues, quoting himself, "in approaching the 'national question,' 'it is more profitable to begin with the concept of 'the nation' (i.e. with 'nationalism') that with the reality it represents.'" See Hobsbawm, *Nations and Nationalism since 1780*, 9.

10. Doris Sommer, *Foundational Fictions. The National Romances of Latin America* (Los Angeles: University of California Press, 1991), 5–7. Even though Shumway follows a different approach, in his *The Invention of Argentina* (also 1991), he comes to a similar conceptual shift.

11. Reading and Writing the Nation in Nineteenth-Century Latin America conference, Woodrow Wilson International Center for Scholars, Washington, DC, April 28, 2000.

12. Sommer, *Foundational Fictions,* 31, 51.

mance nacional as required reading in the school system may be a later phenomenon, the fact that it can be considered a (historical) genre implies the
existence of a range of literary conventions that informed the reading and
writing of these works at the time they were published. Thus, I argue that
the nation was an integral part of the ideas and practices involved in the production and reception of Latin America's sentimental novels.

I appeal to the notion of a "horizon of expectations," or "the literary experience of contemporary and later readers, critics and authors," to talk
about some of the conventions that inform the ways of writing or reading
literature, and writing or reading the world. According to Hans Robert
Jauss, this concept includes factors such as the "familiar norms or imma-
nent poetics of the genre," the literary historical tradition, and the readers'
possibilities to establish comparisons between a "narrower horizon of literary expectations" and the "wider horizon of experience of life."[13] While the
first two elements are habitually taken up by the study of historical genres,
the third one rarely is, in spite of its significance. A contextualized and historicized analysis of reading practices illuminates the socially formative
function of literature,[14] and therefore seems highly relevant to any discussion of subject and national formation through narrative that wants to move
beyond the text. Accordingly, one of the ways in which I historicize my
comments on national romances will be by insisting that the constructivist
approach to the nation and the romance genre itself, besides being a part of
contemporary conceptual paradigms, was a key preoccupation of many
nineteenth-century texts and most often their working assumption. Intellectuals of the period had enormous faith in the power of the written word,
both formative and corruptive. Like Jauss, they believed that literature in
fact influences the way readers behave and see themselves and their worlds.
Most importantly, they trusted (and sometimes feared) that romances
helped define personal character and national identities.

In an article entitled "La educación," published in 1857 in a short-lived
Bolivian newspaper, the anonymous columnist starts by describing the suicide of a 20-year-old man in front of a school and moves on to comment on
the lax education of the youth of the day, and the effect reading has on them:

13. Hans Robert Jauss, *Toward an Aesthetic of Reception* (Minneapolis: University
of Minnesota Press, 1982), 22, 24.
14. "The social function of literature manifests itself in its genuine possibility only
where the literary experience of the reader enters into the horizon of expectations of his
lived praxis, preforms his understanding of the world, and thereby also has an effect on
his social behavior." Jauss, *Toward an Aesthetic of Reception,* 39.

Los resortes de familia se hallan completamente relajados. La niñez está abandonada a sí misma: su carácter distintivo, la obediencia, desaparece. . . . Y la juventud ¿cómo podrá educarse de su propio esfuerzo? . . . No hai un principio superior que regle sus movimientos. Desapareciendo las verdades relijiosas ni aun le quedan las mácsimas de la honradez exterior y decencia social. *La fuente de su filosofía, de su literatura, de su relijion, de su historia, de su política, la de todas sus ideas y sentimientos, son las novelas* [my emphasis].[15]

Given a modern sense of the diminishing hold of traditional or transcendental values, novels, much like television in today's society, are perceived as the most important influence on the readers' thoughts, feelings, and even their actions—that is, on every aspect of their lives. Furthermore, the influence of novels on the readers' subjectivities and behavior is not just a private concern but also a public issue, a matter of state, as family and the nation are conceived as parallel social organizations:

La situacion doméstica ha sido, es y será siempre la palabra que esplica las revoluciones, los triunfos y las derrotas nacionales. El despotismo privado engendra el despotismo político: el desorden de la familia es la anarquía del estado.[16]

Latin American romances consistently entangle both of these themes. As Sommer suggests, they often set European sentimental texts right by patching up the cracks in "the ideal of the bourgeois family" and turning love and marriage into foundational projects.[17] Family works as the natural model of the nation. More significantly, the public's affective involvement with family romance provides the cornerstone of novels' contribution to nation-build-

---

15. "Family ties have been completely loosened. Childhood has been abandoned to its own devices, and obedience, the distinctive characteristic of children, is disappearing. . . . How can youth educate itself with no principle to govern it? . . . When religious truths vanish, young people are left even with out the principles of honorable behavior and social decency. *Novels become the source of everything for them: philosophy, literature, religion, history, and politics—the source of all their ideas and all their sentiments*" [my emphasis]. "La educación," *La Lira* 2 (March 3, 1857): 1–2.

16. "The state of family life has always been, is now, and will always be the factor that explains both revolutions and national defeats and triumphs. Despotism in private life engenders despotism in public life. The disorder of the family produces anarchy in the state." Ibid., 2.

17. Sommer, *Foundational Fictions,* 17–18.

ing efforts. In other words, fictional representations of family and romance mediate relations and establish bonds between readers and the nation.

Critical essays and other programmatic pieces of the period clearly develop the connection between literature and the process of national formation in the young republics. Around mid-century, the novel, in particular, participated in this process by rewarding instances of exemplary behavior (and thus avoiding the bad influences of European literature that may lead to the suicide of stray youths or other types of immoral acts) by merging personal and family destinies to those of patriotic history and by representing, or hinting at, the symbolic unification of the nation. Interpretations relating romances to nation building correspond both to present-day critical readings of nineteenth-century novels and to the general tenor of the "horizon of expectations" surrounding the writing and reading of these novels when they were originally published.

Reading is a creative and thus variable activity, centrally involved in the complex process of the production of meaning, including the meaning of nationness. I do not accept a passive notion of reading, where meaning is forever fixed by the author or the text (as written) and univocally available to readers. Having said that, in the other half of the "hermeneutic circle," the texts themselves provide directions for their own interpretation, a road map for reading and making sense of them.[18] Thus, I do not advocate total free play by the reader, nor an absolute textualist position of free-floating signifiers.[19] Instead, I consider that a text's structure and contents provide a limited range of "subject positions" for their readers, and while not all readers comply with those "guidelines" or circumscribe themselves to those positions, certain dominant readings remain. Additionally, besides textual relationships, contextual, and institutional grounding, the ways in which contemporaries actually read the nation were also determined by reading practices and conventions. Consequently, outside evidence about how people read would greatly enrich this type of analysis.[20] Building on avail-

18. Tzventan Todorov develops this argument in "Reading as Construction," in *The Reader in the Text: Essays on Audience and Interpretation,* ed. Susan R. Suleiman and Inge Crosman (Princeton, NJ: Princeton University Press, 1980), 67–82. On the "hermeneutic circle," see Wilheim Dilthey, "The Rise of Hermeneutics," *New Literary History* 3, no. 2 (1972): 229–244.

19. Either of these positions would undermine the notion that nations were in fact written and read in the nineteenth century, that some of these constructions were more effective than others, and that they were "embedded" in unwritten and historical contexts.

20. Further research is needed to get a range of readings. There is ample "evidence"

able readings and genre conventions, I explore the models that national romances provide for how to read themselves, literature, and the world, and
keep in mind that, to the extent that they are "dialogical," they incorporate
and anticipate readers' responses.[21]

Rather than reiterating the associations among romance, family, and nation, something Sommer does rather well, I will concentrate on additional
but related points about how the nation was written and read in Latin America's novels and sentimental romances. First, I will provide interpretations
(readings) of two different ways of figuring (writing) the nation in order to
suggest that historical romances provide a narrative means ideally suited to
represent the dominant national imagination in the mid-nineteenth century.
I will assert that a new historical consciousness enters literature as a key in-
gredient of the national imagination and that the romance nacional ably in-
corporates this novel way of seeing history and society. As a genre, the
broad outlines of national romances were defined around 1850, and these
conventions inform my own readings. Second, I will argue that nineteenth-
century novels introduce a radical shift and an opening of the "scenes of
reading" in Latin America. This shift is related to changes in the cultural,
publishing, reading, and writing practices of that era, and provides for a
closer identification between readers and characters, and the public and the
nation. My inquiry into the scenes of reading of the novel provides important contextual background for the interpretations presented and new insights into the horizon of expectations involved in reading and writing the
nation. Finally, I will explore some of the actual mechanisms by which romances seduce readers into national belonging, and suggest that similar
ways of reading are at work in oral situations and in autobiographical writings, bridging the oral/written and the fiction/nonfiction divides.

Imagining Nations

In the first decades of the nineteenth century, Creole identity formation, either as a way to legitimize rebellion against the Spanish crown or as an ar-

---

of actual readings by contemporaries in the form of letters, prologues, reviews, and essays. These, however, make up the historical genre and do not necessarily open alternative readings. Thus, I am aware of the skewed nature of the actual readings I will consider, marked in some cases by their closeness to state power, and most often to the
institutionalization of literature and its self-perceived role in nation-building projects.

21. For a discussion of the novel as a "dialogical" genre, see Mikhail M. Bakhtin,
The Dialogical Imagination (Austin: University of Texas Press, 1991).

ticulation of an "incipient nationalism . . . almost entirely devoid of social content,"[22] benefited from the crux of Anderson's conceptualizing of the nation, a new sense of time and space articulated through the diffusion of print capitalism. Anderson argues that national communities arise from the spread of novels and newspapers: new "modes of apprehending the world" that make it possible "to 'think' the nation."[23] In Spanish America, this "spread" occurred later and had a more limited readership than its North American counterpart. Nevertheless, several newspapers and periodicals were established towards the end of the eighteenth century and they mushroomed in the first decades of the next.[24] They were instrumental in the struggle for political independence from Spain, as many of the ideas producing *patriotismo criollo,* if not directly published in the periodicals of the era, were argued, attacked, debated, and re-printed in them. With some hindsight (in 1846), the Venezuelan writer, Juan Vicente González, cryptically summarized the political and ideological impact of independence-era newspapers as follows: "[T]he press has been the itinerary of the revolution."[25]

Even before emancipation was an imminent issue, or when government or Inquisitorial censorship muted direct political calls for independence, Creole periodicals played a crucial role in forging a sense of identity among the colonial communities. Most of these newspapers were edited by enlightened economic or patriotic societies of "friends of the country." Through them, the notion of the *patria* acquired a more precise meaning as its members began to have a clear conscience of their common territory, past and

22. John Lynch, *The Spanish-American Revolutions, 1808–1826* (London: Weidenfeld and Nicolson, 1973), 340.

23. Anderson, *Imagined Communities,* 22. I will not dwell on Anderson's scant use of Latin American historiography, particularly because I am more interested in his general model rather than in the facts that he presents (or not). That is, I take his insights into the narrative construction of the nation as an imagined community more as a heuristic tool than as a historically accurate representation of how Latin American nations came into being.

24. See Mariano Picón-Salas, *De la conquista a la independencia: Tres siglos de historia cultural hispanoamericana* ([1944] Mexico City: Fondo de Cultura Económica, 1985), 212; and Jean-Pierre Clement, "El resurgimiento de la prensa periódica en la América española: el caso del *Mercurio Peruano,*" in *La América española en la época de las luces,* Proceedings of Coloquio Franco-Español, Instituto de Cooperación Iberoamericana, Burdeos, France, September 18–20, 1986 (Madrid: Cultura Hispánica, 1988), 311–325.

25. Juan Vicente González, "La reforma de la ley de imprenta," in *Libertad de imprenta: Selección (1820–1864)* (Caracas: Presidencia de la República, n.d.), 123. All translations from the Spanish originals are mine.

present, through the writings on the country's geography, history, and politics.[26] A few years later, on the eve of Mexican independence, periodicals were part of a "civilizing effort" related to the formation of national communities, a "sense of a wider culture in the making," and the need for "concerned citizens to benefit a developing society as a whole."[27] Colonial newspapers, therefore, began to articulate land, culture, and community into more coherent units, lending some weight to Anderson's claim that print capitalism (largely newspapers and novels) allows territorial stretches to be "imagined as nations."[28]

The novel, like the newspaper, also provides a means for imagining nations. At least since Ian Watt's study of the "rise" of this form in the eighteenth century, the "bourgeois novel" has been associated with the forging of the nation through the self-awareness of the middle class, particularly in England.[29] The mimetic representation of a rather ample social community living in the broad geographical space of country, town, and city was instrumental in developing the sense of nationality. Indeed, it has been argued that the spaces and times of modern nations are "embodied in the narrative culture of the realist novel."[30]

This experience, however, should not automatically be applied to Spanish America, where long narrative fiction was not a widespread phenomenon until the second half of the nineteenth century. During the first quarter of the century, neoclassicism was still the dominant literary aesthetic. Accordingly, patriotic poetry, odes, hymns, and other verse forms were the preferred genres; neoclassical tragedies, comedies, and dramatized discourses were popular as well; prose works consisted mostly of political essays, manifestos, and speeches dealing with the reality and ideals of the independence

26. Clement, "El resurgimiento," 320.

27. Nancy Vogeley, "Mexican Newspaper Culture on the Eve of Mexican Independence," *Ideologies and Literature* 4, no. 17 (1983): 358–359, 373.

28. Anderson, *Imagined Communities,* 61. For additional studies on the role of the press in the formation of national consciousness in Colombia, Perú, and Bolivia, respectively, see Renan Silva, *Prensa y revolución a finales del siglo XVIII: Contribución a un análisis de la formación de la ideología de la independencia nacional* (Bogotá: Banco de la República, 1988); Ascensión Martínez Riaza, *La prensa doctrinal en la independencia del Perú, 1811–1824* (Madrid: Cultura Hispánica/ICI, 1985); and Fernando Unzueta, "Periódicos y formación nacional: Bolivia en sus primeros años," *Latin American Research Review* 35, no. 2 (2000): 35–72.

29. Ian Watt, *The Rise of the Novel: Studies in Defoe, Richardson, and Fielding* (Berkeley: University of California Press, 1957).

30. Bhabha, "Introduction," 2.

movements.[31] As very few novels were written, narrative poetry was the main literary vehicle for the national imagination in this period. Furthermore, the foundational *parnasos* or literary anthologies published throughout the century contained poetry almost exclusively, and not the more popular narrative forms like the novel or *cuadros de costumbres*.[32]

The ideas forging a Creole national identity provided the major themes for emancipation verses. The riches of the American soil were sang as a way to show nature's (God's) favoring of the economic prosperity and independence of these lands. According to Andrés Bello's classic "La agricultura de la zona tórrida" (1826), the soldiers who defeated the "Lion of Spain" should now become hardworking "citizens" of peaceful and glorious "young Nations." Another canonical work of neoclassical poetry of the period, José Joaquín de Olmedo's "La victoria de Junín: Canto a Bolívar" (1825), also touches on key points of early nationalist discourses. In this poem, the modern hero Bolívar, under the "benign" shadow of the Inca, is celebrated as he "restitutes" the nations' freedom and lands after three centuries of "servitude" under the Spanish "oppressors" and "usurpers." Similarly, most national songs written at this time (whether or not they would become official national anthems), repeated the same topics of hero worship and myth making, the formation of good citizens, and patriotic celebrations of freedom and (an abstract) American nature.[33]

In contrast to patriotic poetry and newspaper writing, novelistic discourse had a less prominent role in the national imagination of the independence period, perhaps due to the fact that the narrative process of this genre was quite discontinuous and had significant lapses before the 1840s.[34] Nevertheless, given its considerable importance and ambiguities, *El Periquillo Sarniento* (1816) merits consideration in relation to literary representations of the nation during the emancipation era. The relevance of this novel was reaffirmed by Anderson's comments on José Joaquín Fernández

---

31. See Emilio Carilla, *La literatura de la independencia hispanoamericana (Neoclasicismo y prerromanticismo)* (Buenos Aires: EUDEBA, 1964), 39–43.

32. For an insightful analysis of these anthologies, see Hugo Achugar, "Parnasos fundacionales, letra, nación y estado en el siglo XIX," *Revista Iberoamericana* 63, nos. 178–179 (1997): 13–31.

33. For a good collection of these poems, see Emilio Carilla, comp., *Poesía de la independencia* (Caracas: Biblioteca Ayacucho, 1979).

34. Benito Varela Jácome, "Evolución de la novela hispanoamericana en el XIX," in *Historia de la literatura hispanoamericana: Del neoclasicismo al modernismo,* coord. Luis Iñigo Madrigal (Madrid: Cátedra, 1987), 91.

de Lizardi's work as an exemplary text of the "national imagination," and by the fact that in its interpretive history in Mexico, it was read as the first and quintessential national novel throughout the nineteenth century.[35]

In Lizardi's work, the old and reformed protagonist, Pedro Sarmiento, writes his life story as the *pícaro* Periquillo Sarniento, a lazy youth who does almost everything in order to avoid manual labor, something he considers unfitting to his "noble" birth, even though he has no money to keep a lifestyle in accordance with his aspirations. Although he meets virtuous men along his travels, he seems inevitably attracted to imitate and outdo the most corrupt.[36] For years he errs through the ample social landscape of late colonial Mexico, allowing us to witness the "national imagination" at work.[37] The novel portrays a vivid and complex image of the viceroyalty of New Spain, one closely related to the emergent newspaper culture of the time. The dramatized editor and eventual publisher of Periquillo's life is none other than Fernández de Lizardi himself, under his pen name *El Pensador Mexicano* (The Mexican Thinker), also the title of a periodical he published in 1812–1814.[38] A lively journalistic style and the work's innovative use of the picaresque form facilitated the representation of the "totality of colonial society"[39] in the best tradition of realist novels.

Lizardi's work deploys two ideological lines, one dealing with the critique of the viceroyal order, the other with enlightened, reform-oriented thought. In a widely supported interpretation, Mabel Moraña notes that the reformist program pushes the "formation of the idea of 'nation' as a stable and productive totality" and promotes a populist, socially "integrative na-

35. Anderson, *Imagined Communities,* 29–32. Altamirano states unequivocally that *El Periquillo* "fue la primera novela nacional," in his *Revistas literarias de México* (Mexico City: SEP, 1988), 59. For an overview of the novel's interpretive history a century after its publication, see Alfonso Reyes, "*El Periquillo Sarniento* y la crítica mexicana," in *Obras completas* (Mexico City: FCE, 1956), 169–178.

36. José Joaquín Fernández de Lizardi, *El Periquillo Sarniento* ([1816] Mexico City: Porrúa, 1967). "Periquillo Sarniento" has been loosely translated as "Itching Parrot." The discursive and behavioral "mimicking" of the character is central to the book.

37. Anderson, *Imagined Communities,* 30.

38. He was imprisoned for attacking the viceroy in this paper, one of the many he published or to which he contributed articles. See Jean Franco, "La heterogeneidad peligrosa: Escritura y control social en vísperas de la independencia mexicana," *Hispamérica* 12, no. 34–35 (1983): 12. Nancy Vogeley argues that Lizardi turned to fiction writing "as a strategy to outwit the censor," in "The Concept of 'the People' in *El Periquillo Sarniento,*" *Hispania* 70, no. 3 (1987): 458. Significantly, he returned to journalism after 1820, abandoning the novel, once censorship was lifted.

39. Franco, "La heterogeneidad," 18.

tionalism."[40] Or, as Antonio Benítez-Rojo puts it, the protagonist's displacement through diverse settings "helped awaken in the novel's readers the desire for nationness."[41] A closer reading, however, shows the ambiguities and elitism of *Periquillo*'s concept of "the People," and even questions whether Lizardi favored independence from Spain when he published the novel. In fact, the novel portrays the "kingdom" of New Spain as an integral part of the Spanish nation and under the supreme authority of the king. Thus, the representation of Lizardi's novel as Mexico's first national and populist work of fiction has more to do with its nationalist interpretive readings than with the novel itself.[42]

Nonetheless, the work produces an "incipient bourgeois consciousness," an "awareness and understanding of colonial identity" and, perhaps to that extent, it helps in the construction of a "a new sense of nationhood."[43] Likewise, it portrays the commercial class and the bureaucracy as the emergent social groups, and promotes a whole set of bourgeois liberal values: a work ethic, a new type of family (still paternalistic), and individualism, all of them associated with national formation.[44] After repenting, Periquillo ends up as a successful business and family man and a most pious person. According to Benítez-Rojo, the fact that he inherits "his master's tavern and store, symbols of a commercial activity carried out almost exclusively by the Spanish group," shows Lizardi's support for the rise of Creoles to power in Mexico.[45]

In the final analysis, however, *El Periquillo Sarniento*'s imagining of the nation is problematic, particularly because it fails to launch its community

40. Mabel Moraña, *"El Periquillo Sarniento* y la ciudad letrada," *Revista de Estudios Hispánicos* 23, no. 3 (1989): 115, 120. Additionally, for the colonial critique, see Nöel Salomon, "La crítica del sistema colonial de la Nueva España en *El Periquillo Sarniento,"* *Cuadernos Americanos* 138, no. 1 (1965): 167–179. For Lizardi's reform efforts, see Antonio Benítez-Rojo, "José Joaquín Fernández de Lizardi and the Emergence of the Spanish American Novel as National Project," *Modern Language Quarterly* 57, no. 2 (1996): 325–339.

41. Benítez-Rojo, commenting on Anderson's interpretation, in "José Joaquín Fernández de Lizardi and the Emergence," 335. Although I do not question Benítez-Rojo's statement, I will use the notion of "desiring the nation" mostly in the context of the seductions of romantic novels.

42. For futher development of this line of questioning, see Fernando Unzueta and Cristina Bruch, *"El Periquillo Sarniento* as (and) Mexico's Populist Fiction(s)," *Papers in Comparative Studies* 8 (1993–94): 221–229.

43. Vogeley, "Concept," 461–463.

44. See Franco, "La heterogeneidad," 20–24; and especially Edmond Cros, "The Values of Liberalism in *El Periquillo Sarniento,"* *Sociocriticism* 2 (1985): 85–109.

45. Benítez-Rojo, "Fernández de Lizardi and the Emergence," 333.

toward the future. The popular insurgency of 1810 that eventually led to Mexican independence, for instance, is described as a "popular mutiny" whose results produced a "truly fatal and disastrous era for New Spain."[46] More importantly, the causes of this significant historical event (the only major one alluded to in the novel) are not explained or given a narrative context. Events and actions in this novel have personal consequences but are not influenced by, or have an impact on, society as a whole. A life's adventures, and not the protagonist's organic relation to history or society at large, are the organizing principle of this novel.

Similarly, Periquillo's life path of repentance and finding of bourgeois and Christian values is paralleled and reinforced by the individual destinies of the other "good" characters. Whereas his friends of "low" origin and lifestyles die or disappear thanks to a series of twists in the plot, all the originally "noble" men (in both senses of the term) who had helped or favorably impressed the protagonist along his way but had come to suffer from poverty and ridicule due to social injustice, find their way back (with the intervention of the reformed hero in some instances) to riches, nobility, and a virtuous life of high social standing. In spite of its strong criticism of contemporary colonial society, the moral high ground of this novel posits the *restoration* of an ideal social order, one that could be projected toward the future, but only in terms of *recovered* universal virtues (the many wise lessons Periquillo heard and ignored) and not in terms of the clear historical ascendancy of a new national class.

The Creoles' rise to economic (but not political) power, like the desired liberal reforms, figures as a call for local autonomy and not necessarily for independence. Additionally, considering the shifting connotations of concepts such as patria and nation in this work, it is safe to note that the novel represents both the political ambiguities of the times (c. 1816), and the fact that the concept of a (modern) nation, besides being a matter of dispute, was just in the process of being formed in Latin America.

Romancing History

In the second edition of *Imagined Communities,* there seems to be an awareness of the early (late eighteenth-century) nationalism's lack of historical

46. Lizardi, *El Periquillo,* 412, 414. In all fairness, alluding to censorship, Lizardi points to the dangers of writing about these issues in Mexico in 1813; he also notes that a "summary" of American history (one he does not provide) would allow the readers to decide whether the Spanish government or the Americans wanting independence were right. See Lizardi, *El Periquillo,* 415.

concern. Although not clearly articulated, at issue is the discontinuity of "national" consciousness: the shift from an enlightened and universalistic way of imagining the nation to the romantic and historicist one that became dominant a few decades later.[47] The nation is constantly being redefined under changing social, political, and cultural circumstances. Anderson appears to grasp the importance of history for "second-generation" nationalist movements, not only in Europe but also in the Americas: "the two groups thus began the process of reading nationalism *genealogically*—as the expression of an historical tradition of serial continuity."[48] Unlike their European counterparts that gave "depth to nationality" via ethnic and linguistic means, for Spanish American nationalists who after 1830 had "inherited" independent national states, "The solution, eventually applicable in both New and Old Worlds, was found in History, or rather, History *emplotted* in particular ways" [emphasis added].[49] As I will argue, around 1850, history was given narrative coherence by means of the plot of romance as a way to forge national unity textually.

In the nineteenth century, nation-building movements were vehicles for "national" unification and nations were seen as the proper phase in "human evolution or progress."[50] In Spanish America, "progress" was measured by comparisons with the powerful North Atlantic economies: England, France and, increasingly, the United States. The Eurocentric and teleological vision of history was hardly questioned. The few voices who questioned that vision and called for an alternative cultural model of development (à la German philosopher Johann Gottfried Herder) were largely ignored, negating to a large extent the continent's "difference." This meant that Spanish America's own "other"—its indigenous or black populations, and the "noncivilized" hinterlands—were mostly excluded from the models of the nation that were produced through the writings of the intellectual elite. One of the ways in which the other was marginalized from these models of the nation

47. With regard to this "shift," Anderson acknowledges that "nationalism in the age of Michelet and Renan represented a new form of consciousness—a consciousness that arouse when it was no longer possible to experience the nation as new." In *Imagined,* 203. The absence of the concepts of "history" and "nation" in an important "nationalist" text of the previous century, like the U.S. Declaration of Independence, highlights the significance of an ingrained historical consciousness to the nineteenth-century idea of the nation.

48. Anderson, *Imagined Communities,* 195.

49. Ibid., 197. Hayden White, in *Metahistory: The Historical Imagination in Nineteenth-Century Europe* (Baltimore: Johns Hopkins University Press, 1973), has studied the ways in which history is emplotted, that is, given meaning, through the use of different plot structures, romance among them.

50. Hobsbawm, *Nations and Nationalism,* 33, 38.

was by displacing it/them beyond their borders. In some cases, but not necessarily, this had spatial connotations. In Domingo F. Sarmiento's paradigmatic *Civilización y barbarie* (1845), for instance, the first term of the title's duality was located in the capital city (the Buenos Aires that modeled itself after Europe) and was supposed to "spread" from there to the provinces. "Barbarism," however, was not only what lay beyond the frontier but also the Spanish colonial past that had survived and lived in the republics (and perhaps at their centers). Thus, nationalist liberals developed other exclusionary strategies for modeling the nation, including the one I choose to call "romancing" history and the nation.

At the same time that novel writing and literature in general were being institutionalized (around 1840 to 1850), a new historical sense was introduced in all narratives. History became the hegemonic discourse as all other disciplines appealed to it to explain their subject matter and acquire legitimacy.[51] Just as national consciousness shifted under different historical and discursive conditions, there was a corresponding change in the literary means of imagining the nation. By the mid-nineteenth century, in Spanish America, historical romances, much more than a realist/satirical novel such as *El Periquillo Sarniento,* are the "foundational fictions" (Sommer) engaged in the symbolic production of the region's nationalities. To be more precise, and using Raymond Williams's terminology, I consider the romance nacional an emergent narrative form in the 1840s, dominant in the 1850s and 1860s, and residual, to different degrees, ever since.[52]

51. Michel Foucault has noted that history is the defining element of the modern *episteme:* "the human being has become historical through and through, none of the contents analysed by the human sciences can remain stable in itself or escape the movement of History," in *The Order of Things: An Archaeology of the Human Sciences* (New York: Vintage Books, 1973), 370. Likewise, Peter Brooks insists on the generalization of explanation by means of "historical" or genetic narratives and the role of history as "the key discourse and central imagination," in *Reading for the Plot: Design and Intention in Narrative* (New York: Vintage Books, 1985), 5–6. The new historical sense was widely accepted in Spanish America, as Sarmiento's article "Los estudios históricos en Francia" (1848) shows; in the article, he points out that "everything related to social institutions, customs and beliefs has become history, because history has been asked to explain [give reason for] the development of the human spirit." In *Obras de D. F. Sarmiento,* vol. 2 (Buenos Aires: Gobierno Argentino, 1883–1900), 199.

52. See Raymond Williams, "Dominant, Residual and Emergent," *Marxism and Literature* (Oxford: Oxford University Press), 121–127. In a few decades, say by the 1880s, with an increased awareness of the importance of and differences among regions, cultures, and populations, the idealizing characteristics of romances would no longer allow them to be the "dominant" form to represent the nation.

The historical "shallowness" of the early nationalisms, including that of Spanish American independence and Lizardi's work in particular, was partially overcome thanks to the temporal depth that became an integral part of narrative. In novelistic discourse, as Erich Auerbach has convincingly shown, "romantic historism" distinguishes the modern realist novel from eighteenth-century or earlier versions and allows an organic connection of humanity, environment, and history: "[R]ealism of modern times cannot represent man otherwise than as embedded in a total reality, political, social, and economic, which is concrete and constantly evolving." I will take Auerbach's arguments further and suggest that the literary representation of "the present as history" made possible by this new historical consciousness provided a more appropriate means for imagining the nation.[53]

The incorporation of historical discourse and historicism in Spanish American narrative can be readily appreciated in many historical, socio-political, *costumbrista* or "realist" novels, works explicitly representing the "national imagination." But it is more productive to explore an extreme case: the relation between "romance" and history. I will show how this genre, apparently far removed from its social context, given its idealized and conventional representation of history and social reality, is tightly related with historical reality and, particularly, with the formation of nationalities in the new republics.

The romance was the dominant novelistic genre in Latin America around 1850. I define Spanish American national romances by establishing a dialogue between a historicized critical tradition, meta-textual discourses of the period, and the romances themselves.[54] In the broadest of terms, the ro-

53. Erich Auerbach, *Mimesis* (Princeton, NJ: Princeton University Press, 1974), 463, 480. Anderson, in *Imagined Communities* (p. 28), notes the radical change in the "handling of time" of two Phillipino novels he comments on, written in 1838 and 1864, respectively, but fails to make the distinction, made by Auerbach and Bakhtin, among others, in terms of the nineteenth-century "historicist" novel and earlier versions. This is possibly due to the significant tradition of eighteenth-century English novels ("realist" but not in Auerbach's sense, that is, "historicist") that he seems to have in mind. Even in this "national" context, however, Raymond Williams writes that while "perhaps" this form was dominant between 1730 and 1750, the "emergence of the novel as the major literary form" started in the 1830s, as "new kinds of experience, in an essentially different civilization flowed into the novel." Williams, *Writing in Society* (London: Verso, 1983), 72–73. Eighteenth-century novels (and *El Periquillo* falls under that model) begin to explore "socioscapes" in "calendrical" time, as Anderson suggests, but the full development of these possibilities only begins to take place a few decades later, when the new historical consciousness makes it possible.

54. My use of the concept of *romance nacional* is more circumscribed (temporally

mance is a love story full of idealized literary conventions such as the polarized characterization of its protagonists. It contains a teleological vision of history associated with "liberalism," the ideology of the ascendant class, and it actively participates in the cultural configuration of Spanish American nations. In all these aspects, Bartolomé Mitre's *Soledad* (1847) is a paradigmatic national romance.[55] I will also note that several of the literary characteristics of this and other national romances, like their use of stock characters, ideal and exceptional protagonists, stylized settings, and their overall abstractness, (re-)produce the values of other contemporary nonfictional constructions of the nation, such as those provided by constitutions. They work as a rhetorical strategy of inclusion and exclusion that resembles the hierarchical social practices and realities of the period, and they also signal the desire for (and not the reality of) national unity and a homogeneous citizenry.

Soledad is a sentimental work that tells the story of a young and beautiful woman (Soledad) married to an old Spaniard, Ricardo, who represents the past and the abuse of power. She obeys him as her husband, even though she was forced to marry him, but takes pride in keeping "the freedom of [her] heart."[56] This small space of innocence, not to be overlooked in the realm of romance, is threatened by the seductive powers of Eduardo, a young Creole womanizer. Soledad's cousin, Enrique, returns victorious from the wars of independence just in time to prevent her "fall." Finally, Soledad's husband becomes ill but repents and blesses her union to Enrique before dying. They, in turn, are happily married a year later. As a typical sentimental romance, then, *Soledad* retrospectively tells a predestined love story that materializes after a series of trials; in the end, the young, valiant, and handsome hero obtains the legitimate love of the angelically romantic protagonist.

In order to see the "national imagination" at work, however, it is necessary to establish symbolic relationships between the family romance and the romance of national history. In such a reading, the hero represents the

---

and otherwise) than Sommer's (*Foundational Fictions*). Besides developing the argument for a historical genre by more fully integrating same period self-definitions, I highlight the importance of a new historical sense and the fact that the novels' love and family relations to patriotic history are mediated by historical discourse. See Fernando Unzueta, *La imaginación histórica y el romance nacional en Hispanoamérica* (Lima and Berkeley, CA: Latinoamericana Editores, 1996).

55. Bartolomé Mitre, *Soledad* ([1847] La Paz: Ediciones Abaroa, 1972).
56. Ibid., 6.

people and a new national movement (as he has just defeated the loyalist colonial Spanish troops); Soledad, the desired object, is related to the nation, land, and culture; the antagonists, intent on appropriating the nation for themselves, are forces from the past and abusive forms of power, or from a conservative and irresponsible Creolism.[57] Upon collectivizing the romance, the hero's mission consists of rescuing a usurped nationality in order to return it to its legitimate owner, that is, himself (and by integrative synecdoche, the people). The marriage can thus be interpreted as the union by which the people, land, and culture come together in the process of national formation.

Likewise, by studying the text as a "historicized romance," it can be shown how the several dichotomies of the work containing some of its organizing ideologemes are produced.[58] Mitre associates all positive values, such as youth, nature, art, honesty, and the future, with the national; on the other hand, old age, tradition, deceit, and the past are a part of negative Spanish values. This binary axiological system of characterization and description, perceived as "natural" in the romance, is actually part of a collective imaginary narrative (i.e., an ideologeme) used to explain the necessity of the historical triumph of liberal national elements over a despotic colonial past. The literary conventions of romance articulated in *Soledad* become much more meaningful in the context of a national(-ist) interpretation of the past, and the historical moment is hardly represented in this highly aestheticized work. At the same time, by romancing history, Mitre's text produces an idealized, future-looking, and exclusionary imagining of the nation.[59] What needs to be highlighted is that the representational strategies used in producing this national imaginary are subsumed under the narrative coherence provided by the romance as a literary form.

57. The historian Bradford B. Burns reads the main characters in the following terms: "Soledad encapsules the Latin American people, while Don Ricardo Pérez represents the Iberians, master of the land and people. In Enrique and Eduardo, the reader encounters the two major divisions of the creoles, the liberal and the conservative." He further notes that *Soledad* allegorizes Mitre's views of Spanish American independence as expressed in his later and well-known historical works. In "Bartolomé Mitre: The Historian as Novelist, the Novel as History," *Revista Interamericana de Bibliografía/Inter-American Review of Bibliography* 32, no. 2 (1982): 155–167.

58. See Frederic Jameson, "Magical Narratives: On the Dialectical Use of Genre Criticism,"*The Political Unconscious* (Ithaca: Cornell University Press, 1981), 115–119.

59. Shumway rightly notes that Argentine liberal intellectuals, like Mitre, contributed to create a "mythology of exclusion" as part of their national "guiding fiction,"in *The Invention of Argentina,* xi.

Soledad, as most romances, produces a symbolic transformation of its referent by which it provides imaginary solutions to real contradictions in the social context.[60] The narrator, for instance, ignoring the deep political, economic, and racial conflicts (among others) dividing the society that he was writing about, states categorically: "Then [1826] Bolivia was not what is now [1847]; a homogeneous nation, one that does not understand nor can understand a [political] system other than representative republicanism."[61] In the teleological and romantic vision of this work, social problems disappear and the historical progress of the republic is inevitable. The concept of a "homogeneous nation," however central to Mitre's work and to nineteenth-century historiography and liberal discourse in general, was at that time as distant from reality as it is now, but it flows naturally from the idealized vision of romance, a vision forging the ideals of national unity inherent in Creole configurations of the nation. Thus, even though romances often represent national unity where none exists, the desire for such unity and its related ideals, precisely because of its unfulfilled nature, remains in the political imagination of readers as a blueprint that guides projects of national formation.[62]

A strong historical consciousness is an integral part of the idea of the nation. The inextricability of these two concepts partially explains the mixed legacy of *El Periquillo Sarniento*'s imaginings of the nation. On the one hand, it promotes the ideal of the good-natured man and citizen as the basis of bourgeois individualism and the liberal nation, makes a rather thorough inventory of the territory and peoples it comprises, and begins to insert its community in calendrical time of forward-moving history. Likewise, this novel is accessible to a wider audience, appealing rationally to its readers' Christian and civic virtues as the basis of a future national community. On the other hand, it does not resolve the conflict between its inclusionary posture (with regards to Indians in particular) and Creole elitism, or provide a clear historical sense of the emergence of nations and their developmental processes. In spite of these limitations, the enlightened principles proposed in *El Periquillo Sarniento,* as well as its inscription of a country's natural and social resources, articulate the feelings of local and regional

60. Jameson makes this argument for the romance genre in general, in "Magical Narratives," 117–118.

61. Mitre, *Soledad,* 32.

62. The idealization of history in national romances like *Soledad* also provides a symbolic "solution" to two usually contradictory needs of nationalism: to ground itself in the past and to forge a modernizing project.

identity. Furthermore, it can be argued that a sense of community needs to be developed and cultivated before that community sees itself in national terms. To that extent, Lizardi's novel, much like the earlier enlightened newspapers, begins to shape the ever-changing communities called nations, and republican nationalism builds on late colonial patriotismo criollo and on *El Periquillo Sarniento*'s early national imaginings.

In a few decades, a new historical outlook permeated all discourses and, consequently, the concept of the nation. Under romantic historicism, past and present became more closely related; individual destinies (just as those of novelistic characters) were interconnected with society and their inexorably changing environment at large. Interpretations of the past articulated explanations of the present and set models for future societies; history, in most cases, provided further narrative unity and depth to national imaginings, even in the more conventional literary forms. In Mitre's idealized and socially exclusionist (and yet, acutely historicist) novel, family romance leads to the forward-looking romance of history. In order to imagine a nation with certain internal cohesiveness, this work romances the past to explain it and make it meaningful in the present, forges narrative coherence, transforms reality, and proposes more or less utopian solutions to Spanish American history and social problems. *Soledad* produces the symbolic formation and unification of nationality; it imagines the nation as it romances its history.

Scenes of Reading I: Novels and the Promise of National Communities

Whereas Lizardi's novels were practically isolated efforts in the configuration of this literary form, the situation of national print media in Spanish America would change considerably in a few decades. In addition to celebrating the exponential growth of the periodical press, several mid-century writers perceived the novel as a literary genre uniquely appropriate to expand the reading public and promote nation formation.[63] In a sense, however, *El Periquillo Sarniento* already inaugurated a new type of reading

---

63. I explore these issues in light of the role of the novel and its poetics in the formation of a public sphere in Fernando Unzueta, "The Nineteenth-Century Novel: Toward a Public Sphere or a Mass Media?" in *Beyond the Lettered City. Latin American Literature and Mass Media,* ed. Edmundo Paz-Soldán and Debra Castillo (New York: Garland/Hispanic Issues, 2001), 21–40.

scene in the continent's letters, thanks to three related phenomena. First, this novel opened itself to a much wider readership; second, its publication and dissemination were closely connected to newspapers, and (thus) third, it entered into a market of consumer goods, with increasing numbers of cultural goods among them.[64]

Lizardi's (first) prologue, echoing an old colonial grievance, points out the "material difficulties" involved in "publishing" in the Americas a work like *Vida de Periquillo;* departing from tradition, however, he also noted the novelty that it would be to see it "in print."[65] The novel was a new genre in Latin America and its circulation, as Ignacio M. Altamirano would observe later on, unlike that of other literary forms, depended on the print industry and its technological advances.[66] Instead of calling on a traditional "patron" to subsidize the publication of the book, the Mexican Thinker accepted the suggestion that the readers should pay for its printing. By doing so, this work entered a possible "mass culture," both in terms of its market orientation and with regard to the breadth of its public, acknowledged by the author to be quite heterogeneous, and possibly including some unlikely traditional readers.[67]

Latin America's novel, since its very beginnings, was much closer to a budding mass culture than to the Kantian ideal of disinterested art. While the absence of an autonomous literary field has been noted before, particularly in terms of the political orientation of many of the literary trends of the period (such as *romanticismo social*), the importance given to market issues in discussions about novels has not been properly foregrounded.[68] The commercial nature of novels, for instance, clearly pointed to their (relatively) widespread readership. In the abovementioned prologue, Lizardi invited each of his readers to buy and subscribe to several chapters.[69] While Benítez-Rojo mentioned a "probable printing" of 300 to 500 copies and suggested that *El Periquillo* "must not have had much impact on public

---

64. Even though Anderson refers to the role of both newspapers and novels in imagining the nation, he fails to mention *El Periquillo*'s obvious connections with Lizardi's journalistic writings.

65. Literally, "en letra de molde," in Lizardi, *Periquillo,* 1.

66. Ignacio M. Altamirano, *Revistas literarias de México* ([1868] Mexico City: SEP, 1988), 40–41.

67. "Sé que acaso seréis, algunos, plebeyos, indios, mulatos, negros, viciosos, tontos y majaderos." Lizardi, *Periquillo,* 4.

68. Julio Ramos acutely explores these issues in *Desencuentros de la modernidad en América Latina. Literatura y política en el siglo XIX* (Mexico City: FCE, 1989). As many others, however, he is mostly concerned with the last two decades of the century.

69. Lizardi, *Periquillo,* 4.

opinion in its day,"[70] I believe he underestimated the presence of illiterate readers and the importance of "public readings" (to both literate and illiterate audiences) that took place in reading salons, coffeehouses, and private homes. Enrique Flores has documented the existence of such public reading salons and the common practice of nonliterate "readings" in Lizardi's Mexico; he has also noted the author's involvement in some of these activities, and the novel's incorporation of these themes and strategies.[71] Additionally, since the "copies" mentioned were newspaper-like *entregas,* it is very likely each copy passed through several hands, greatly increasing the novel's "informal" but literate readership as well.[72]

Open invitations (and exhortations) to the public to buy a subscription, like Lizardi's, were a recurrent journalistic topic of the period; and the proximity between newspapers and novels is not accidental. Whereas a detailed analysis of the links between these two types of discursive formations lies beyond the scope of this article, I will mention that from *El Periquillo* to *Los de abajo* (1910), by way of *Soledad* (1847), *Guatimozín* (1846), *Martín Rivas* (1862), *Clemencia* (1869), and *Juan de la Rosa* (1885), many if not most nineteenth-century Latin American novels (and other important works, such as *Facundo*) were first published as *folletines* or in some type of newspaper format. Folletines appeared in the most important newspapers of the continent in the 1840s, at the same time that the first national romances began to be published.[73] Likewise, several newspapers around the middle of the century offered their readers copies of "original" (i.e., Latin American or "national") or European novels as a way to get them to buy subscriptions, attesting to the popularity of the genre in terms of its market value, to the close ties between novels and newspapers, and to their parallel efforts to broaden their largely shared readership. Finally, romances, like many literary sections of newspapers or the increasingly more specialized journals, catered to the growing female readership as well. Besides opening up to new publics, I will maintain, they call for new ways of reading.

70. Benítez-Rojo, "Fernández de Lizardi and the Emergence," 334.

71. Enrique Flores, "El loro de Lizardi: Lectura en voz alta del *Periquillo Sarniento," Literatura Mexicana* 3, no. 1 (1992): 7–39.

72. For a discussion of these informal distribution channels of newspapers, and the perceived obstacles they presented to their commercial success, particularly around mid-century, see Unzueta, "Periódicos y formación nacional," 57–58.

73. See Sarmiento's "Nuestro pecado de los folletines" (1845) for a description of the beginnings and popularity of *folletines* in Chile. In *Obras de D. F. Sarmiento,* vol. 2 (Buenos Aires: Gobierno Argentino, 1883–1900), 314–317.

As suggested earlier, Mitre's *Soledad* may be considered a prototypical national romance. The way it was published was also common to many other folletines. It first appeared on the bottom third of La Paz's *La Epoca,* the first Bolivian daily, from October 7 through October 25, 1847. Shortly after, it was published as a separate volume by the same press, with its "elegant edition" being duly advertised in the newspaper.[74] The same procedure was repeated in 1848, when Mitre moved to Chile. The novel appeared as a folletín in Valparaíso's *El Comercio,* and was immediately published in book form in the same city.[75] While I do not have printing figures at hand, given the fact that *La Epoca* listed about 200 subscribers in its first month of existence (April–May, 1845), it is not difficult to surmise that *Soledad* reached a much wider audience than *El Periquillo,* when comparing the first appearance of both works.[76]

In addition to an enlarged but still limited readership, the 1840s, when national romances first appeared, witnessed the increased publication of literary journalism and periodicals, the beginnings of the institutionalization of literature (with a capital "L"), and the formation of an incipient critical community.[77] Intellectuals used their meta-literary texts—newspaper and journal articles, as well as prologues to literary works—to urge their fellow

74. *La Epoca,* November 5, 1847.

75. See Paul Verdevoye, "Littérature et américanisme: auteur de *Soledad* (1847), roman de Bartolomé Mitre," in *Le roman romantique Latino-Américain et ses prolongements,* ed. Olver Gilberto de Leon et al. (Paris: L'Harmattan, 1984), 14. In a different but related publishing situation, Altamirano mentions the case of a Mexican novel of the 1860s for which the demand for subscriptions exceeded the author's expectations and required a second printing. Altamirano, *Revistas literarias de México,* 70.

76. *El Periquillo,* however, had a much more (re-)productive subsequent history. While *Soledad* was not re-edited until 1907, Lizardi's work went through nine editions by that time. See Verdevoye, "Littérature," 14, and Lizardi, *El Periquillo,* xiii. The informal circulation of *folletines* through several readers that I alluded to, and some popular reading practices, are attested in Blest Gana's description of a character: "La segunda hermana, Edelmira, es una niña suave y romántica como una heroína de algunas novelas que ha leído en folletines de periódicos que la presta un tendero aficionado a las letras." In Alberto Blest Gana, *Martín Rivas (Novela de costumbres político-sociales)* ([1862] Madrid: Cátedra, 1983), 123.

77. For the significance of literary journals and magazines, see Boyd G. Carter, "Revistas literarias hispanoamericanas del siglo XIX," in Luis Iñigo Madrigal, coord., *Historia de la literatura hispanoamericana: Del neoclasicismo al modernismo* (Madrid: Cátedra, 1987), 75–86. Beatriz González Stephan, in *La historiografía literaria del liberalismo hispanoamericano del siglo XIX* (La Habana: Casa de las Américas, 1987), has shown the importance of literary histories and historiographies, particularly after the 1840s, in the process of liberal national formation.

citizens to create an American literature, independent and different from Spain's. Under this program of *americanismo literario,* itself part of the broader romantic movement for "mental emancipation," the national or American literature to be produced would be "original" if it focused on the nature, mores (*costumbres*), and history of the new republics. These literary conventions are really ways of reading and writing the nation. Ways of writing because most of the authors had them in mind when producing their works of fiction, as witnessed by their own prologues and essays, many of which, including Mitre's own prologue to *Soledad,* can be considered among the key manifestos of americanismo literario. Ways of reading because there is ample evidence, in the same type of critical texts, that the conventions about what elements made a literary piece "original" were indeed used as evaluative and interpretive criteria when reading works of this period.[78]

In many of these programmatic texts, novels or romances are presented as the most appropriate literary forms to represent history, costumbres, and nature as national elements. Their length allowed for the dynamic incorporation of a range of elements as well as a sense of social mobility and historical change. They were popular and, perhaps more importantly, they provided a sense of totality, both social and geographic. All these aspects were related to the period's conceptions of the nation, and novels, better than other genres (but by no means exclusively), were able to represent them. Therefore, to read Latin American sentimental novels as *national* romances is far from an anachronistic move or a theoretical imposition. It is certainly a critical choice, but one that is supported by the conventions for reading and writing literature prevalent in the period.

The nineteenth-century novel's "interested" character, its intent to have an impact on the lives of its readers, permeates several of its defining features, including an openness toward the market and a broader audience, a marked didacticism, and its political, social, or "extra-literary" contents. Continuing an Enlightenment tradition, most of the novelists of this century, from Lizardi to Matto de Turner, sought to educate the people, to improve their costumbres, and to better their societies. The novelty is that they wrote for a much wider public thanks to the genre's larger circulation, and

78. For an indication of how novelists forged many of the conventions of the genre with their critical texts, in addition to the few authors I mention, see the selections included in Norma Klahn and Wilfrido H. Corral, comps., *Los novelistas como críticos,* vol. 1 (Mexico City: FCE, 1991). Also, see Unzueta, "El romance nacional en Hispanoamérica," *La imaginación histórica,* 89–124.

to the languages and styles that they used. In other words, the novel as a literary form became more popular, in both senses of the term.

In comparison to most other literary forms, and to earlier narratives, nineteenth-century novels radically democratized literature by portraying lower social classes, previously excluded from serious representation, and by broadening its reading public. Echoing Lizardi, Alberto Blest Gana also noted that the novel should "study" all the "diverse social spheres."[79] Similarly, he trusted in its growing "popularity" and effectiveness in its civilizing mission.[80] The novel not only represented the lower classes, but it did so in a language that they could understand. Its target audience, in addition to the generic and supposedly universal "hombre," had been broadened to include women and members of all social classes (including the "menos cultas"). In summary, the novel was supposed to be accessible to everyone ("está al alcance de todos"). These were, according to the Chilean author, along with a socially and historically accurate representation, the main characteristics that allowed a novel to be "national in its essence."[81]

Even though these statements with regard to the social depth and reach of the novel may seem like exaggerations, they were shared by most Latin American intellectuals and authors at the middle of the century. Ignacio M. Altamirano, for instance, considered the novel as "reading for the people," particularly because of "the influence it has had and will continue to have in the education of the masses." The "education" to which he alluded, how-

---

79. Alberto Blest Gana, "Literatura chilena: algunas consideraciones sobre ella" (1861), in Norma Klahn and Wilfrido H. Corral, comps., *Los novelistas como críticos*, vol. 1 (Mexico City: FCE, 1991), 56.

80. "La novela . . . cuenta entre la generalidad de los lectores con un número mucho mayor de aficionados que la poesía, porque la primera *está al alcance de todos.* . . . El estudioso y el que no lo es, el viejo y el joven, *la madre de familia y la niña . . . todas las clases sociales, todos los gustos,* cada uno de los peculiares estados en que las vicisitudes de la vida colocan al *hombre,* encontrarán en la novela un grato solaz. . . . [L]a novela, por el contrario, tiene un especial encanto para toda clase de inteligencias, *habla el lenguaje de todos,* pinta cuadros que cada cual puede a su manera comprender y aplicar, y *lleva la civilización hasta las clases menos cultas de la sociedad,* por el atractivo de escenas de la vida ordinaria *contadas en un lenguaje fácil y sencillo*" [emphasis added]. Blest Gana, "Literatura chilena," 52–53.

81. "Estudiando, pues, *nuestras costumbres tales como son,* comparándolas en las *diversas esferas sociales,* caracterizando los tipos creados por esas costumbres y combinándolos, a fin de ofrecer *una imagen perfecta de la época con sus peculiaridades características, la novela no puede dejar de ser esencialmente nacional,* según el mayor o menor acierto de los que a ella consagran sus esfuerzos" [emphasis added]. Blest Gana, "Literatura chilena," 56.

ever, embraced a much wider scope than the narrow Christian morality promoted by Lizardi, as it implied nothing short of the "induction of the people
into modern civilization."[82] Under the "liberal" conception of culture and
society, "civilization" was associated with European or urban and high-cul-
ture Latin American values; for the Mexican novelist and critic, the novel
was an "artifice" used by intellectuals or "thinking men" in order to make
certain ideas more palatable to the masses.[83] In spite of their elitist attitude,
for authors like Sarmiento, Blest Gana, and Altamirano, the novel had a mediating role in a modern republican society: it built bridges among different
social classes, forging national unity. Altamirano made this point eloquently
when he wrote that novels contributed to the "leveling of social classes
through education and customs," and went on to add that "novels, like folk
songs, like journalism, like oratory, *will be* a uniting link to them [the
masses], and perhaps the strongest one" [emphasis added].[84]

The optimism that lettered culture had with regard to its diffusion and effects was somewhat nuanced by Altamirano's use of the future tense ("será,"
or will be) in the previous quote. While they often used the present tense,
most of the poetics of the novel that I am discussing formulate a "project"
more than represent a reality. In a sense, they are "performatives of nationality": they enact the nation as they inscribe it.[85] Nevertheless, by comparing the novel with songs, newspapers, and political discourse, Altamirano
was basically describing, or perhaps desiring, a "popular" literary genre. He
did both (and mixed his tenses accordingly), when he observed the fact that
"there already is a thirst for reading among the people [el pueblo]," a "thirst"
("avidez de lectura") that, according to him, "will be satisfied with national
works."[86] The Mexican author expected that many more "national works,"
in addition to the several he examined, would be forthcoming. The key is-

82. Altamirano, *Revistas,* 56.
83. In Altamirano's words: "[para] hacer descender a las masas doctrinas y opiniones que de otro modo habría sido difícil que aceptasen" *Revistas,* 39.
84. Ibid., 48, 56.
85. Analyzing Latin American poetic anthologies that circulated throughout the
nineteenth century, Achugar notes that the texts are published with their "reading community," in the form of lists of subscribers. He further adds that these texts are "performatives of nationality," much like the essays on the novel or a national literature I am
discussing here. See Achugar, "Parnasos fundacionales," 20.
86. "La avidez de lectura que hay ya en el pueblo, va a ser satisfecha con obras nacionales." In Altamirano, *Revistas,* 70. The calls for the creation of "national works" are
actually one of the topics of the manifestos of *americanismo literario* and poetics of the
novel.

sue seemed to be that this literature be national. As he put it, "[W]e *desire* the creation of a literature that is absolutely ours," a literature involved in the nation-building process: "[Such] literature will now have a patriotic mission" [emphasis added].[87] Like national romances, the poetics of the novel around mid-century in Latin America were socially integrative in their rhetoric, forward looking in their historical outlook, and liberal in their politics and ideology. Most importantly, as the previous quotes make clear, they advocated themselves to projects of national formation and deploy a romantic "desire" for the nation.

Reading and Subject Identification

Reader identification with a text's protagonists, its national contents, and values is crucial to the construction of an imagined community. The novel in general and romances in particular introduced significant changes from this angle to the process or reading the nation in literature. In order to explore this phenomenon, I will build on the Bakhtinian notion that the texts themselves incorporate their audiences' responses and, at the same time, I will refer to actual readings by contemporaries in the form of letters, responses to reviews, and essays.

As I pointed out earlier, patriotic poetry was the main literary outlet for the national imagination at the beginning of the century. Olmedo's "La victoria de Junín: Canto a Bolívar" (1825) is one of the paradigmatic texts of this genre. I will not dwell on the poem itself, but rather on Simón Bolívar's reading of it, as contained in two letters he wrote to Olmedo, from Cuzco, on June 27 and July 12, 1825. The first letter begins as follows:

> Querido amigo: Hace muy pocos días que recibí en el camino dos cartas de Vd. y un poema: las cartas son de un político y un poeta, pero el poema es de un Apolo. . . . Vd. se hace dueño de todos los personajes: de mí forma un Júpiter; de Sucre un Marte; de La Mar un Agamenón y un Menelao; de Córdoba un Aquiles. . .[88]

---

87. Ibid., 37.
88. "Dear Friend: Only a few days ago on the road I got two letters and a poem from you. The letters were written by a politician and a poet, but the poem was written by an Apollo. . . . You have taken charge of all the characters, making me into Jupiter, making Sucre into Mars, making La Mar into Agamemnon, and making Córdoba into Aquilles."

Like most epic poetry, "La victoria de Junín" provides a sense of community to the extent that lofty heroes embody its ideals and (under neoclassical aesthetics) conform to classical models. Whereas the poem largely succeeds in its myth-making function, reader identification is indirect, in the best of cases. Only Bolívar, perhaps, could see himself as Jupiter and identify with that representation. In fact, in the second letter, he seems to resent the overarching role given to Huaina-Capac in the "Canto," and complains that the Inca is the poem's "hero."[89] Other mortals, including most "good citizens," read this poem and others like it as privileged instances of hero worship and as homages to national or Latin American independence. Thanks to their tone and contents, these poems and their heroes become as monuments, which are easily recognizable but not conducive to personal identification. Accordingly, readers ritually come back to poems like Olmedo's, particularly in patriotic celebrations and the appropriate anniversaries, but are not likely to keep copies by their nightstands.

El Periquillo Sarniento initiates a different type of reading scene. Beyond recognizing familiar settings, the novel asks readers to witness and learn lessons from the protagonist's life story, a story full of sins and, eventually, ethical and religious transformation. Reader identification is supposed to be both rational and moral. This fact may explain the coherence of the many long and digressive *sermones* within the novel, which the author justifies in terms of his stated goal to educate his readers. In this vein, Flores convincingly argues that Lizardi mixes writing and orality. Thanks to the sermones, the incorporation of speeches and other passages related to public readings (often targeting "lectores iletrados," those who "read" by listening to someone else reading), the novel reflects a culture where written and oral cultures are interconnected and "reading" has much broader connotations than today.[90]

Lizardi is aware of the "oral" contents of his novel and their implications. Responding to a harsh reviewer of his novel, he wrote:

Simón Bolívar, *Itinerario documental de Simón Bolívar* (Caracas: Ediciones de la Presidencia, 1970), 268.

89. This is how Bolívar critiques this "flaw" of the poem: "Vd. ha trazado un cuadro muy pequeño para colocar dentro un coloso que ocupa todo el ámbito y cubre con su sombra a los demás personajes. El Inca Huaina-Capac parece que es el asunto del poema; él es el genio, él la sabiduría, él es el héroe, en fin." In Bolívar, *Itinerario,* 275.

90. See Flores, "El loro de Lizardi."

Hablando del estilo dice "que yo soy el primero que he novelado en el estilo de la canalla." Ahora bien: en mi novela se hallan de interlocutores colegiales, monjas, frailes, clérigos, curas, licenciados, escribanos, médicos, coroneles, comerciantes, subdelegados, marqueses, etcétera; yo he hablado en el estilo de esta clase de personas. . .[91]

Two issues were at stake here: social breadth in the novel's contents and the use of appropriate language codes that were accessible to socially differentiated subjects, from "*gente soez,*" to the characters listed above. Lizardi's use of words like "interlocutores" and "hablado" (rather than "character" and "written") is, in itself, significant, and backs Flores's insight into a strong oral context for the novel. Likewise, the author defended his choice of inserting the protagonist in "filthy pictures" and "lowly scenes" in similar terms: it is only "natural" for a youth gone astray to wander around the worst dives and situations. He also noted, however, that these are not the only environments included in his novel.[92]

Realistic representation of characters from a wide social spectrum, in terms of the verisimilitude of their language, and the plurality of the settings they inhabit, allowed the audience the possibility of identifying with some of the characters and settings, and the direct or indirect recognition of others that occupied the same national space. In marked contrast with Olmedo's poem, this novel created for its readers a sense of familiarity and self-recognition that seemed to be key for the construction of the nation. In this and other aspects, *El Periquillo* and novels throughout the century shared an affinity with the idea behind collections of cuadros de costumbres, such as *Los mexicanos pintados por ellos mismos* (1854), where a wide array of social types, from different ethnic, economic, and geographical backgrounds, are placed next to each other, sharing their nationness in spite of all their differences.[93] More importantly, perhaps, these national types

91. "Speaking of style he says that 'I am the first to have written a novel in the style of the lowlife.' But in fact, my novel includes many kinds of interlocutors: students, nuns, friars, priests, lawyers, scribes, doctors, colonels, businessmen, bureaucrats, nobles, etc. I have written in the style of each of them." José Joaquín Fernández de Lizardi, "Apología de *El Periquillo Sarniento*" (1819), in Norma Klahn and Wilfrido H. Corral, comps., *Los novelistas como críticos,* vol. 1 (Mexico City: FCE, 1991), 17.

92. "Pero además de que no siempre se presenta en escenas bajas, ni siempre trata con gente soez, cuando se ve en estos casos es naturalemente, y por lo mismo éste no es defecto, sino requisito necesario según el fin que se propuso el autor." In Lizardi, "Apología," 19.

93. See *Los mexicanos pintados por ellos mismos. Tipos y costumbres* (Mexico: M.

and their stories were placed in front of the readers (and spectators, as they normally contain visual reproductions as well), so that they see themselves in their (self-) portrayals. In a direct response to the perceived distortions of foreign travelers' representations, these texts intended to be thoroughly national (in the characters represented, authors, and audience) and promote collective self-recognition. The self-reflexive instance, so crucial to (modern) personal identity, was also at work in these collections as in the novels. They displayed the diverse members of a community, their costumbres, and stories, always embedded in the places where they lived, and interacting with each other. Both novels and cuadros de costumbres fostered communal identity construction and affirmation.

Unlike *El Periquillo Sarniento,* national romances contain idealized representations of reality, but they appear in a much more open reading scene. Given both of these phenomena, and considering that romance has traditionally been related to "wish fulfillment,"[94] I would argue that reader identification in romance, in addition to direct recognition of familiar environments and human types, is mediated by a *desire* projected onto the text and characters, much as it occurs with contemporary mass media.

Around the middle of the nineteenth century, the novel's "popularity" was welcomed because of its potential to educate, and feared on account of its supposed threat to the minds and hearts of readers, particularly the "weaker" ones, women and the young. The corrupting potential of novels was often associated with its "frivolous" nature; novels, after all, were often considered mere forms of fiction and entertainment, as opposed to the gravity of "serious" writing, such as history, science, and religious or moral treatises. Juan Poblete has shown that in an increasingly bourgeois society (in Santiago, around 1860), that nevertheless retained distinctive conservative attitudes toward cultural issues, the leisurely, "easy," and feminine reading of novels was perceived negatively when contrasted with the more "difficult"—and therefore more "productive" and "masculine"—reading of traditionally sanctioned topics. He further adds that Blest Gana's *Martín*

Murguia y Comp., 1854). I write "collection" because only through them a sense of totality, similar to a novel's, is achieved. A single *cuadro de costumbres,* poem or *tradición,* no matter how representative or symbolic, provides only a limited snapshot of a larger picture, or a single tile in the larger mosaic of nations.

94. "The romance is nearest of all literary forms to the wish-fulfillment dream." In Northrop Frye, *Anatomy of Criticism* (Princeton, NJ: Princeton University Press, 1957), 186.

Rivas plays a "transactional" role between these two ways of reading, tempering some romantic excesses with an agenda of national and cultural politics.[95] This mediating role of gendered ways of reading easily can be extended to most national romances, as they combine, by definition, the sentimental with the patriotic and the historical.

Whereas "frivolity" may have been an issue, more commonly novels, and sentimental novels in particular, were simply criticized for their excessive and uncontrolled sensuality. Altamirano makes this point clearly:

> En la leyenda de amores, lo confesamos, puede haber gran peligro. . . . Los cuadros *seducen,* las reticencias malignas despiertan la curiosidad, el lenguaje de la lectura *embriaga,* y si no se encuentra en la *pasión* una fuerte dosis de moralidad, el alma se extravía [my emphases].[96]

The nonrational aspects of the novels, associated with the "feelings of the heart," much more than Lizardi's moralistic digressions, have the ambivalent capacity to modify the costumbres, behaviors, and subjectivities of the readers. In a modern gesture, national romances foreground feelings and emotions as essential to personal and collective identities. At the same time, in a decidedly "antimodern" critical consensus, novels were not only supposed to be national but also ethical. In spite of questions with the appropriateness, from a contemporary perspective, of using ethical aesthetic judgments, a novel's "morality," or lack of it, was a basic evaluative criteria in the poetics of the period, in Latin America as in the United States.[97]

There is likely a distance between "popular" and "elite" or programmatic readings, the former more concerned with pleasure and entertainment, the latter with moral nation-building projects. Earlier on, Lizardi also made a

---

95. Juan Poblete describes Blest Gana's theory (or poetics) and practice of the *novela nacional de costumbres* in terms of its "transactional" role, particularly between gendered ways of reading. See his "La construción social de la lectura y la novela nacional: el caso chileno," *Latin American Research Review* 34, no. 2 (1999): 75–108.

96. "In the legend of love, let us confess, may lie considerable danger. . . . The scenes *seduce* the reader. That which is suggestively left unsaid awakens curiosity. The language itself becomes *intoxicating.* And if a strong dose of morality does not accompany the *passion,* souls may go astray" [my emphases]. Altamirano, *Revistas,* 53–54.

97. For the critical climate in the United States, see Nina Baym, *Novels, Readers, and Reviewers: Responses to Fiction in Antebellum America* (Ithaca, NY: Cornell University Press, 1984).

similar distinction between *leer con gusto* and *leer con fruto*.[98] For him, as for the writers of romances, the key was merging both ways of reading in the same work, strengthening the novel's mediatory role. In national romances, mixing pleasure and education implied marshaling sentimental strategies that affected the readers' selves in order to pursue moral, political, and cultural goals. Sentimental novels educated, as Sarmiento noted, the readers' *"facultad de sentir,"*[99] their ideas, passions, and imagination. They changed the "interior" of persons, or, in the language of the period, their "character," "hearts," or "spirit." As another critic put it, when the young read "good novels" they were "moved to their cores" and "feel inclined" to imitate good deeds.[100]

Reader identification is eminently "personal," that is, affective and sentimental, but also rational and moral and concerned with the collective wellbeing. In the same essay in which Altamirano warned of the dangers of novels' abilities to "seduce," he also suggested that "feelings of the heart . . . can easily be directed toward individual good and toward public happiness."[101] This transition between "feelings" and the "public good," the sentimental and the political, is at the core of national romances. Indeed, these novels foster such a transition by deploying a "justified seduction" as a means to educate individuals and to promote social values, always under strict codes of morality.[102] The key was, as Altamirano would argue, "reunir el encanto a la moral,"[103] not just to bring the novel's seductive powers under control, but to use them productively in their moralizing and nation-building projects. Sentimental novels, therefore, were part the broader goal of educating good and modern citizens.[104]

98. "Leer *con gusto* y leer *con fruto* son dos modos de leer, dos descripciones de la lectura que Perico emplea en varios momentos de la novela." In Flores, "El loro de Lizardi," 28.

99. See Sarmiento, "Nuestro pecado de los folletines."

100. Pedro de Prado y Torres, "La historia y la novela," *La Ilustración Mexicana* 5 (1855): 311.

101. Altamirano, *Revistas*, 54.

102. I take the expression "seducción justificada" ("justified seduction") from Poblete, "La construcción social de la lectura," 95.

103. Altamirano, *Revistas*, 55.

104. According to Sarmiento's educational program, while "philosophical, religious, political and social" matters come later, children should be taught "aquello que eleva el corazón, contiene las pasiones y los prepara para entrar a la sociedad." In Domingo F. Sarmiento, *Recuerdos de provincia* ([1850] Málaga, Spain: Anaya, 1992),

Scenes of Reading II: Novels and Seduction

The ways in which the moral and patriotic "seductions" work in national romances can be explored by examining a few "scenes of reading," in the more narrow and literal connotation: namely, fictional reading scenes, where characters read privately and silently, or where some type of group or collective reading takes place.[105] In most reading scenes, a partly oral activity (of one person reading out loud to others) is framed within the written text of the novel. Such scenes are commonplace in novels throughout the period, from *El Periquillo Sarniento* (1816) at the beginning, *Amalia* (1851/1855) and *María* (1867) in the middle, and *Suprema ley* (1896) at the end, to name a few. They often involve young characters in the process of learning how to read and, at the same time, become part of the nation, as in *Juan de la Rosa* (1885) and *Aves sin nido* (1889).[106] Aural readings were a very common practice in the Hispanic world, well into the early twentieth century.[107] Besides connecting different publics, aural readings also provide a transition to the art of telling and listening to stories, practices often incorporated in novels.[108] It is also worth noting that while characters in the first half of the century read mostly European (French) romantic literature,

---

356. National romances, I have been arguing, include both the "high questions," appropriate for "mature reason" (Sarmiento), and the sentimental dimension (properly "contained") required to participate in modern societies.

105. Danny J. Anderson discusses this type of scenes of reading, particularly in Federico Gamboa's *Suprema ley,* as crucial to the literate imaginings of late nineteenth-century Mexico, in "Reading and Modernity: Literate Imaginings during the Porfiriato, 1876–1991" (paper presented at Symposium on National Subjects and Discourses in Latin America's Nineteenth Century, Ohio State University, Columbus, OH, April 20, 1996). See also Richard H. Brodhead, *Cultures of Letters: Scenes of Reading and Writing in Nineteenth-Century America* (Chicago: University of Chicago Press, 1993). Both D. Anderson and Brodhead highlight the socially and culturally mediating role of reading (as a cultural practice) in specific contexts.

106. Antonio Cornejo Polar makes a similar argument for *Aves sin nido* in "El aprendizaje de la lectura: novela y formación nacional en Hispanoamérica," *Osamayor* 2, no. 4 (1991): 3–6.

107. For the phenomenon in Spain, see Jean-Françoise Botrel, "Teoría y práctica del la lectura en el siglo XIX: el arte de leer," *Bulletin Hispanique* 100, no. 2 (1998): 577–590. Botrel cites many examples from the Cuban experience.

108. Given these continuities, but without ignoring the differences, I will also refer to the oral practice of listening to nonwritten stories as "reading." Decoding and reacting to narratives is the key, and not whether these narratives are oral in nature or in print.

increasingly they read Latin American poetry and, by the end of the century, national romances.[109]

Novels also describe discussion groups commenting on the newspapers, or literary or political pieces just read, and to that extent they represent an incipient public sphere being formed on the continent, both in the public forums of cafés, academies, and associations, as in the salons of private homes.[110] In this context, it is also worth remembering that the novel's mediating role between different social classes is due, in part, to its closeness with more popular and/or oral genres (Altamirano mentioned folk songs, journalism, and oratory). Lettered culture and novels in particular are not as far removed from nonwritten cultural practices as it is commonly thought. In addition, just as the role of print media in the construction of the nation and its public spheres needed to be highlighted, so can it be argued that national romances introduced in fiction the more intimate and domestic settings as privileged spaces where public and private issues, including the always contextualized subjectivity of individuals, came together and took shape. Perhaps like no other genre, novels combine in their representations diverse social groups, orality, and literacy and, after the romantic revolution, the public and the private, actions and feelings. Their role in the constitution of subjectivities and the individual cannot be underestimated; and the individual, as François-Xavier Guerra notes, is at the core of modern nations.[111]

The "conclusion" of Gertrudis Gómez de Avellaneda's *Sab* (1841) includes a reading scene where some of these issues are developed. This long, confessional type of letter, written by the protagonist, the mulatto slave Sab, reads in part as follows:

Había nacido con un tesoro de entusiasmos. Cuando en mis primeros años de juventud Carlota leía en alta voz delante de mí los romances,

109. See Thomas Bremmer, "Historia social de la literatura e intertextualidad: Funciones de la lectura en las novelas latinoamericanas del siglo XIX (el caso del 'libro dentro del libro')," *Revista de Crítica Literaria Latinoamericana* 11, no. 24 (1986): 31–49. As Bremmer notes, characters in José Martí's *Amistad funesta* read both *Amalia* and *María*.

110. See Unzueta, "The Nineteenth-Century Novel."

111. See François-Xavier Guerra, "Una modernidad alternativa," *Modernidad e independencias. Ensayo sobre las revoluciones hispánicas* (Madrid: Mapfre, 1992), 85–113. Guerra also highlights the importance of modern forms of socializing and the configuration of a public sphere in the Hispanic revolutions and wars for independence.

novelas e historias que más le agradaban, yo la escuchaba sin respirar y una multitud de ideas se despertaban en mí, y un mundo nuevo se desenvolvía delante de mis ojos. Yo encontraba muy bello el destino de aquellos hombres que combatían y morían por su patria. Como un caballo belicoso que oye el sonido del clarín me agitaba con un ardor salvaje a los grandes nombres de patria y libertad: mi corazón se dilataba, hinchábase mi nariz, mi mano buscaba maquinal y convulsivamente una espada, y la dulce voz de Carlota apenas bastaba para arrancarme de mi enajenamiento.[112]

This particular fragment brings together, through the art of reading, a literate and educated slave, Sab, with his master, Carlota. In an intimate atmosphere, Sab reflects upon the ambiguous formative role of reading in his life, a rhetorical commonplace also customary in autobiographies and biographies. The use of the imperfect tense of the past alludes to the habitual and repeated nature of the reading scenes and their consequences. The types of literature actually read ("romances, novelas e historias") had traditionally been socially constructed as male reading, given their connection with war and patriotic sacrifice. The fact that they are liked by the young *criolla,* however, seems to indicate that historical (and national) romances appealed to both a male and female readership. Sab, the aural reader, clearly identifies with the fictional, as well as, possibly (the two meanings of "historia"), historical characters of the nonspecified works. The abstractness and nonspecificity of romances commonly allows readers to adapt them to their own circumstances. In Sab's case, his identification, the texts' seduction, not only "awakens ideas" and "opens a new world" for the reader, but also produces physical changes in him ("me agitaba . . . mi corazón se dilataba. . ."). More significantly, it moves him to act ("mi mano buscaba. . ."), even though the same novel "disciplines" Sab into forsaking his leadership potential in a

112. "I had been born with a wealth of enthusiasms. When, during my early years, Carlota read aloud for me the novels and other romantic fiction that she enjoyed, I listened with bated breath. A multitude of ideas were awakened in my breast. A new world was revealed to my eyes. The destiny of men who fought and died for their country seemed beautiful, indeed. Grand words like *liberty* and *fatherland* agitated me with savage ardor, like a warhorse at the sound of the trumpet. My heart swelled, my nostrils flared, my hand groped mechanically for a sword, and the sweet voice of Carlota could hardly bring me back to myself." Gertrudis Gómez de Avellaneda, *Sab* (Madrid: Cátedra, 1999), 266–267.

slave rebellion.[113] In this scene, fictional models, characters, histories, and/or stories, trigger the potentially nationalist feelings of the reader, just as Latin American poetics of the novel and other literary manifestos of the period argued they would.

Finally, I do not believe the "enajenamiento" mentioned at the end implies that the patriotic feelings aroused are a romantic dream per se. Rather, I would argue, it refers to Sab's inability, as a slave, to fulfill the same "destiny of those men," a destiny he wishes were also his.[114] It refers, basically, to the disconnect between Sab's actual world and the "new world" that romances entice him to imagine. A Creole reader, if only there had been one with Sab's sensibilities, would not have had the same obstacles. And indeed, in other national romances, Creole protagonists do go off to war to fulfill their destinies at the incitement of nationalist discourses and conversations with their lovers. In the world of this novel, however, the protagonist's aspirations are curtailed not because they are the result of a reader's seduction by fiction, but because Sab lives under the unjust historical and social condition of slavery. In other words, while romances provide an impetus for action, here "reality" inhibits it.

National romances inspire feelings and actions, both romantic and patriotic. Their historical and ideological contents, their constructions of gender and the contexts and resolutions of each specific work determine how these latent forces are channeled. In *Sab*, patriotic and romantic desires are elicited but frustrated by the trope of an "impossible or romantic love" and vetoed by a colonial situation. Nevertheless, the "national" dimension of these "tragic" romances is achieved both by the readers' recognition of the topoi of americanismo literario, namely, the representation of nature, costumbres, and history in national terms, and by the unfulfilled desire for a "new world" imagined or a more perfect romantic relation that could symbolize national union. While the novel seduces readers into believing in the possibility of a romantic relationship between Sab and his master Carlota, and later, between Sab and Carlota's poor cousin, Teresa, Enrique Otway (Carlota's foreign and selfish future husband) feared a socially more suit-

113. According to Sab, "[L]os esclavos arrastran pacientemente su cadena: acaso sólo necesitan para romperla oír una voz que les grite '¡Sois hombres!' pero esa voz no será la mía." In Gómez de Avellaneda, *Sab,* 206–207.

114. "Neither do I have a *patria* to defend . . . because slaves do not have a *patria.*" In Gómez de Avellaneda, *Sab,* 219.

able romance with a Creole.[115] Furthermore, unlike Enrique, the first three characters as well as the potential "passionate" Creole, in addition to being *cubanos,* can also be considered "superior souls," with a special affinity toward "feelings," "affections," and "emotions," and for whom great "passions," virtues," and "sorrows" are reserved.[116] According to the romance's own criteria, romantic unions should be sentimental and ethical in nature, and national in character. Therefore, any of the three unrealized but suggested romantic possibilities would have provided more ideal unions as the foundations of (quite different, to be sure) national projects.

Other sentimental novels combine romantic and patriotic impulses in more "productive" ways. *Soledad,* for instance, begins with the two clearly gendered ways of "reading" that tend to be present in national romances. While Soledad is seduced by the libertine Lovelace while reading Rousseau's *Julie,* the male protagonist is enticed to join the patriotic troops in the wars of independence after listening to stories about one of its "heroes."[117] These two modalities of relating to texts, namely being seduced by reading romantic texts (or by hearing a lover's words), and by "reading" (or listening to) patriotic stories, are socially constructed as female and male, respectively. Accordingly, in national romances, female agency is represented mostly in terms of feelings and words, while action defines male agency. Nevertheless, beyond uniting the protagonists in matrimony, romances mediate between female and male cultural representations and reading practices by merging them in their endorsement of national causes. Soledad's romantic inclinations, for instance, are eventually guided to sup-

---

115. "Luego (y este último cuadro le afectaba más vivamente), luego la veía consolada de su perfidia con el *amor ardiente y desinteresado de un apasionado criollo,* y le juzgaba dichoso a ella también dichosa" [emphasis added]. In Gómez de Avellaneda, *Sab,* 230. Enrique's fears and his own materialism and foreignness mark some of the key aspects that make up ideal romances: they should be ethical ("desinteresado"), romantic ("ardiente," "apasionado") and national ("criollo").

116. Gómez de Avellaneda, *Sab,* 133.

117. See chapters five ("La nueva Eloísa") and six ("Reminiscencias"), respectively. In the last one, while telling how Enrique grew up, a secondary character narrates his story as follows: "Pasado algún tiempo empezó a figurar el nombre del general Lanza como uno de los caudillos más terribles que combatían contra los españoles en el Alto Perú. La relación de sus hazañas entusiasmaba al joven Don Enrique, a lo que contribuía mucho las ideas que le había comunicado Don Pedro en su educación. Un día se presentó a la madre de Soledad, a quien él también llamaba su madre, y le dijo que estaba resuelto a irse a incorporar al general Lanza para pelear por la independencia de su patria. . . . [H]a vuelto por fin a La Paz con el grado de capitán, después de haberse hallado en las batallas de Junín y Ayacucho." Mitre, *Soledad,* 53–54.

port her lover-to-be's patriotic efforts, in a typical resolution for a national romance. What needs to be highlighted is that listening to his stories ("reading") leads to her recognition of the "hero" and to her desire to be loved by him.[118] The protagonist's actions, on the other hand, are fed by his emotional and intellectual attachment to family and patria, as well as the loving and "moving" memories of Soledad. Thus, "sentimental" and "patriotic" ways of reading are brought together in national romances. The eventual marriage, therefore, besides being a union, with national consequences, between two idealized characters, also implies the coming together of two ways of reading (or dealing with) the world under a national goal.

Another way, perhaps more subtle, in which romances mediate between male and female perspectives and representations is by "feminizing" male protagonists.[119] While Sab is an extreme case in the degree of his sentimentality, most of the heroes of national romances are, indeed, "romantic." They exhibit a rich and often conflictive internal life, including the feelings, affections, and emotions, but also the virtues Gómez de Avellaneda attributes to "superior souls." They sometimes read (and write) sentimental literature, and occasionally share the same exaggerated sensibility of many female and very few male characters. Given the patriotic demands of the genre, however, it is crucial that sentimentality does not inhibit action, as in Sab's case and others, but rather, that it motivates it. In either situation, national romances contribute to the creation of modern individuals, individuals whose subjectivities exhibit a deep sentimentality as the foundation for their feelings and actions. Whereas Nancy Amstrong argues that this type of gendered subjectivity arises thanks to the reading and writing of "literature for women,"[120] I would suggest that in Latin America, national romances include and articulate the sentimentality of "female" domestic fiction with the romantic depth provided by "male" subjective poetry and other discourses. Furthermore, they open these two dimensions of modern

118. "[Enrique] Me contaba sus campañas y yo derramaba lágrimas de ternura al oírselas referir. '¡Qué hermoso debe ser el ser amada por un héroe!'" In Mitre, *Soledad,* 64.

119. Sommer affirms that patriotic but "feminized" heroes are better able to "create intimate bonds" with similarly idealized young women, in *Foundational Fictions,* 16.

120. Nancy Armstrong states that "a modern, gendered form of subjectivity developed first as a feminine discourse in certain literarure for women before it provided the semiotic of nineteenth-century poetry and psychological theory," in *Desire and Domestic Fiction: A Political History of the Novel* (New York: Oxford University Press, 1987), 14.

subjectivity to the national. By merging "feelings and the public good" (Altamirano), virtues and society, they invoke the "feminine" for nationalist ends, or they inscribe it, as an affective dimension, at the core of the nation.

Blest Gana's *Martín Rivas* (1862) is particularly aware of these (socially constructed) gender roles and reading practices and is partially troubled by them. Leonor, the female protagonist, while a reader of romantic novels,[121] is portrayed as being more rational than sentimental. Additionally, she challenges female passivity, and breaks the role of the *ángel del hogar* (the ideal women who, in a nationalist context, educates citizens from the confines of her home) when she acts in a public arena to rescue her lover from jail and send him into the safety of temporary exile. On the other hand, reading romantic literature and folletines defines how two of the other main female characters feel, talk, write, and act.[122] Like Sab, doña Francisca's poetic imagination, fostered by reading poetry and novels, is curtailed by her reality.[123] Similarly, Edelmira writes in imitation of the language of "the most romantic folletines," and her protagonist is "the type of hero that avid female readers of novels imagine in their youth."[124] In spite of the narrator's criticism of such romantic excesses, doña Francisca shows an ethical, social, and gender sensitivity, grounded in her readings, that contrasts with her husband's materialism. Likewise, Edelmira possesses an exemplary, albeit lower-class (and thus, subordinate), character.

Unlike what happens in *Sab* or *Soledad,* however, these "female" or "sentimental" ways of reading, and the languages and behaviors they trigger, are repeatedly parodied by the narrator.[125] Nevertheless, when the two (male) protagonists decide to take part in the liberal "revolution" that provides the novel's ideological underpinning, they use an overtly sentimental attitude and language to express their decisions and to guide their actions. The protagonist's "heart" is literally moved (by narratives) to contribute to a national cause.[126] It is worth examining Martín's changes in attitude closely.

121. Blest Gana, *Martín Rivas,* 87.
122. Likewise, Agustín, a frivolous (effeminate?) male character, is described as having a spirit influenced by "romantic drama." Blest Gana, *Martín Rivas,* 247.
123. "La presencia de don Fidel la sacó de su éxtasis poético para arrastrarla a la prosa de la vida." Ibid., 168.
124. Ibid., 181, 291. In real life, as I will note, Gómez de Avellaneda will idealize her (first) fiancé in the same manner.
125. In this sense, Blest Gana's *Martín Rivas* criticizes the romantic excesses of earlier national romances and sentimental literature.
126. Rafael San Luis's vocabulary is more obvious, in spite of his own denials: "No es una novela estupenda lo que voy a contarte. Es la historia de mi corazón"; "Mi nueva

First, he articulates the two gendered ways of "reading" or dealing with the world that I outlined when he states: "[I]nstead of crying our [romantic] disillusions like women, we can dedicate ourselves to a [political/patriotic] cause worthy of men."[127] Secondly, it is clear that listening to political arguments and speeches determined his new course of action. Before making his decision, he "hears heated speeches against the Government's policies"; furthermore, his "soul" is "awakened" by listening to Rafael's "passionate" narrative.[128] Once again, even a novel weary of sentimental readings cannot avoid the use of sentimental language and shows an affective response to political/patriotic storytelling. In other words, the "patriotic readings" (mostly aural) of national romances incorporate very similar types of seduction as those prevalent in sentimental reading practices but for different, this time national, goals.

From Fictional to Life Readings

The last issue I want to explore, however briefly, is whether reading romances or listening to nationalist discourses and patriotic stories actually changed people's (and not just fictional characters') lives. As much more research is needed in this area, I will tentatively suggest that yes, they did. Besides highlighting the role of sentimental novels in the constitution of modern subjectivities, I will note that autobiographies and other nonfictional forms of life writing repeat the same type of reading scenes and practices of national romances, with real-life implications and, often, nation-building consequences. Tzventan Todorov's insight into the similarities in the reading construction of fictional and nonfictional materials is particularly relevant here.[129] Some variants of this phenomenon can be found in texts as di-

---

querida—dijo—es la política." Rivas's sentimental and patriotic "change of heart" is also significant: "Rivas encontró algún consuelo, *sintiendo latir su corazón* con la idea de contribuir también a la realización de las bellas teorías políticas y sociales que aquellos jóvenes profesaban y pedían para la *patria*" [emphasis added]. Blest Gana, *Martín Rivas*, 143, 377, 379.

127. Ibid., 378.

128. "El fuego de su convicción despertó pronto en el alma de Rivas el germen de las nobles dotes que constituían su organización moral." Ibid., 378.

129. "[T]here does not seem to be a big difference between construction based on a literary text and construction based on a referential but nonliterary text. . . . [T]he construction of characters (from nonliterary material) is analogous to the reader's construction (from the text of a novel)." Todorov, "Reading as Construction," 80–81.

verse as Gómez de Avellaneda's *Autobiografía* (1839), Sarmiento's *Recuerdos de provincia* (1850) and José Santos Vargas's *Diario de un comandante de la independencia americana, 1814–1825.*

Gómez de Avellaneda, in her autobiographical texts and novels, provides a clear model for a sentimental way of reading, one in which books, particularly works of fiction, have a direct impact on life, providing models for knowing the world, the perception of self, and the expression of feelings. Her love letters make it clear that the way she sees herself and other real-life characters is directly influenced by her readings. For instance, she attributes to her fiancé "all the qualities of the heroes of my favorite novels."[130] Furthermore, as it has been widely pointed out, the written (autobiographical) construction of her own self, closely parallels Sab's. Given that the novel was published (two years) after the autobiography was written, in this case the fictional character follows a narrated but real-life model. Thus, the lines between life and fiction are blurred in several aspects of this Cuban writer's texts and experiences. Instead of summarily attributing these parallels to Gómez de Avellaneda's "romantic life" or personality, I would posit that they exist because similar "reading" and interpretive strategies are used to understand their worlds and the people in them by fictional and historical "characters" and by readers and writers of both types of narratives. As Todorov summarily puts it, "'Fiction' is not constructed any differently from 'reality.'"[131]

Sarmiento, on the other hand, provides a model for writing a life in terms of nation building. Genealogy, history, and autobiography are totally interconnected in his narrative.[132] The major events in his life are, at the same time, national events. A life that, according to the author, is modeled after

130. "Más tarde, la lectura de novelas, poesías y comedias, llegó a ser nuestra pasión dominante. . . . [N]uestro mayor placer era estar encerradas en el cuarto de los libros, leyendo nuestras novelas favoritas y llorando las desgracias de aquellos héroes imaginarios, a quienes tanto queríamos. . . . Mi familia me trató de casamiento. . . . Por otra parte, yo no conocía el amor sino en las novelas que leía, y me persuadí desde luego que amaba locamente a mi futuro. Como apenas le trataba y no le conocía casi nada, estaba a mi elección darle el carácter que más me acomodase. Por descontado me persuadí, que el suyo era noble, grande, generoso y sublime. Prodigóle mi fecunda imaginación ideales perfecciones, y vi en él reunidas todas las cualidades de los héroes de mis novelas favoritas." In Gómez de Avellaneda, *Autobiografía* ([1839] Madrid: Castalia, 1989), 145–146.

131. Todorov, "Reading as Construction," 81.

132. "A la historia de la familia se sucede, como teatro de acción y atmósfera, la historia de la patria. A mi progenie, me sucedo yo." Sarmiento, *Recuerdos de provincia,* 254.

his readings of other lives, including Benjamin Franklin's, a "sublime model."[133] Echoing a tradition well established in Latin American novels (starting with *El Periquillo*), Sarmiento argues that these models help readers become good citizens. In addition, by also proposing as a model his own efforts to "make for himself a place in American letters and politics," and his own life story as inseparable from his country's, he nationalizes the reading of exemplary lives.[134] Thus, he articulates a "patriotic" way of reading, where the audience is inspired to act on behalf of the nation upon reading a life's history. National romances follow the same strategy: they make their characters act upon "reading" or listening to life stories (fictional or historical) or political discourses and expect their readers to do the same.

On the other hand, when Sarmiento states that after reading the North American patriot's life, he "felt like Franklin," and that all children who read it will also "be tempted to be a Franklincito," he is basically alluding to a rhetorical strategy based on strong reader identification with a textual model, which is very common in sentimental readings. In some cases, "passive" sentimental readers live vicariously through the lives and adventures of their favorite heroes or heroines. In other cases, however, a situation more often contemplated by national romances and clearly at work in Sarmiento's autobiography, readers are moved "to be" or act like those fictional or historical characters. Given that Sarmiento and the intellectuals who wrote the poetics of the novel foresaw this type of reading as a common response of a large part of the public, including children and young people, they were concerned about the "lives" represented in the texts of the period, and attempted to provide patriotic "models of perfection," like Franklin or himself, in Sarmiento's text; Lanza and Enrique, in Mitre's; or Martín Rivas in Blest Gana's.

Recuerdos de provincia and national romances construct selves in closely related ways. Sarmiento and Rivas, for instance, are constituted in

133. Ibid., 357.
134. "La vida de Franklin fue para mí lo que las vidas de Plutarco para él. . . . Yo me sentía Franklin; ¿y por qué no? Era yo pobrísimo como él, estudioso como él, y dándome maña y siguiendo sus huellas podría un día llegar a formarme como él, ser doctor *ad honorem* como él, y hacerme un lugar en las letras y en la política americana. La vida de Franklin debiera formar parte de los libros de las escuelas primarias. Alienta tanto su ejemplo, está tan al alcance de todos la carrera que él recorría, que no habría muchacho un poco bien inclinado que no se tentase a ser un Franklincito, por aquella bella tendencia del espíritu humano a imitar los modelos de la perfección que concibe." In Sarmiento, *Recuerdos,* 279.

similar terms: they are both "self-made men," defined by their intellectual talents and, ultimately, their own actions. They ground their moral rectitude and virtue as citizens in their families and an internal core. Blest Gana describes that inner self as a person's "moral organization,"[135] and Sarmiento appears to refer to the same idea when he speaks of a child's "good inclinations," or his own "natural instinct" and the direction in which it led him.[136] Both authors describe an individual's "core" as a person's seemingly immutable identity, but they also suggest that, as something likely to be interpellated by ideology or seduced by storytelling, it is subject to change. This is basically the romantic subjectivity to which nationalist and political discourses, fictional or not, appeal.

Sentimental and patriotic ways of reading come together in several different ways in national romances such as *Soledad* and *Martín Rivas,* and in autobiographies such as *Recuerdos de provincia.* More surprisingly, they also seem to merge in Vargas's *Diario de un comandante de la independencia americana.* This "diario histórico" is of particular interest because it reproduces reading scenes similar to the ones I just explored in romantic literature in a popular (semiliterate and mostly oral) context in the *republiquetas* or guerrilla phase of the wars of independence.[137] As he tells the story, in 1814, at the age of eighteen, Vargas is literally talked and seduced into joining the patria by his brother:

> Entre esta y otras conversaciones siempre me platicaba a que fuese yo de la opinión a la Patria porque él había sido ciego en esta opinión. . . . [Y] ya con la *seducción* de mi hermano a la opinión de la Patria estaba yo *anhelando* en ella, *deseoso* de serlo [del partido de la patria], sin saber las ventajas que pudiera producir tal partido; abracé la opinión tan *deseada* sin saber los resortes cuáles serían para entrar a su servicio, aunque mi hermano no quería que me entropase al principio [my emphasis].[138]

135. Blest Gana, *Martín Rivas,* 378.
136. Sarmiento, *Recuerdos,* 279, 357.
137. The author refers to his "corta educación" and his "ningunas luces." José Santos Vargas, *Diario de un comandante de la independencia americana, 1814–1825* (Mexico City: Siglo XXI, 1982), 8, 16.
138. "In this and other conversations, my brother always tried to convince me to become a patriot because he believed in that fervently. And his *seduction* made me pine to join, *desiring* to be of that party without really knowing its advantages. Thus I *embraced* the party of the Patria party without knowing exactly why" [my emphases]. Vargas, *Diario,* 22. This fragment is part of "Breve vida del que escribió." It is not dated, but was

In the same way that scenes from written love stories may *seduce* the reader, as Altamirano suggests, and novels open a "new world" for Sab, Vargas as a listener is *seduced* by oral stories. Unlike Gómez de Avellaneda's fictional character, however, he was able to respond affirmatively to those interpellations. Like *Soledad*'s Enrique, who responded with "enthusiasm" to similar patriotic stories and decided to join the forces fighting for independence ("se incorpora"), so do Vargas's "yearnings" and "desires" move him to do the same ("se entropa"), namely, to enlist to fight for a yet undefined patria and, additionally, to write about his experiences. In a move that closely resembles the reading theory and practice of national romances, he is basically seduced into (patriotic) action.

In more general terms, patriotic writing and reading have been, since the beginning of the nineteenth century, the principal mechanism for the invention of national heroes as widely recognized myth-like figures. Whereas patriotic discourses and situations bring nationalism into sharp relief, the nation involves much more, and novels, unlike epic poetry, bring the national imagination "down to earth." They add significantly to the diversity of social groups and geographical horizons represented, and following Scott's lessons, make "heroes" out of common people, individually or collectively. At the very least, novels narrate their multiple stories and experiences, whether heroic or quotidian. In addition, they incorporate scenes of oral storytelling and aural reading practices in an attempt to bridge the gap between print and oral cultures. National romances preserve the epic dimension of patriotic poetry in the idealization of their historical contents, but they also portray the rich and diverse social and spatial scenes of "realist" novels. Moreover, they share with autobiographies diverse combinations of sentimental and patriotic ways of reading, suggesting similarities in the role and effects of reading in fiction and in life.[139] Thanks to all these characteristics, sentimental novels provide for an easier readerly identification with the texts' protagonists, symbols, and values. More importantly, they accentuate the affective dimension in all their representations, making

---

likely written in 1851 or 1853, the date of the author's last failed attempts to get his *Diario* published. The *Diario* was eventually published and edited in 1952 and 1982, by Gunnar Mendoza L.

139. The proximity of novels to orality and autobiographies in many of their rhetorical strategies and reading practices, begins to address two of the major criticisms of the narrative and print-based model of the nation (including Anderson's), namely, that it is only relevant to lettered culture, and that as a textual approach is far removed from "real life."

a more productive use of desire and seduction as a means to encourage the recognition and interpretation of the texts' national elements.

Coding and decoding narratives in specific ways is the key issue in writing or reading the human, social, and natural coordinates of the nation. While the readings that I have outlined are by no means the only possible interpretations, they are certainly grounded in some actual readings and in the horizon of expectations informing the production and reception of novels during the period in which they were written. Romances participate in nation-building processes because of their representations of a range of elements portrayed and perceived as national and, moreover, because of their contribution to the invention of modern individuals and sentimental subjectivities that are the targets of nationalist discourses. In the final analysis, the nation can be imagined, composed, and narrated in many ways, and read in many more. National romances appeal to readers' sensitivities and emotions in order to "seduce" them into action and feelings of collective identity. As part of their legacy, sentimental imaginings, vocabulary, and ways of reading, as well as an encompassing affective dimension, are still central to the sense of belonging to a nation.

6

The Nation in Ruins: Archaeology and the Rise of the Nation

Sara Castro-Klarén

Hasta ti Machu Picchu
Alta ciudad de piedras escalares
por fín morada del que lo terrestre
no escondió en las dormidas vestituras.
En ti, como en las lineas paralelas
la cuna del relámpago y el hombre
se mecían en el viento de espinas
Madre de piedra, espuma de los cóndores
Alto arrecife de la aurora humana
Pala perdida en la primera arena
Esta fue morada, éste el sitio

—Pablo Neruda, "Alturas de Macchu Picchu"[1]

Present resemblances enable us to resuscitate dead recollections

—Marcel Proust, *La Prisonnière*[2]

1. "High city of scaling stones, dwelling place of what the earth did not hide in her slumbering vestiments, in you, as in those parallel lines, the cradle of lightning and men rocked in the thorny wind. Mother of stone, foam of condors, high reef of the human dawn, shovel lost in the early sand, this was the dwelling, this, the place." Pablo Neruda, *Canto General*. Taken from Anderson Imbert, *Literatura Hispanoamericana: Antología e introducción histórica* (New York: Holt, Rinehart and Winston, 1960), 686.

2. Quoted in Richard Terdiman, *Present Past: Modernity and the Memory Crisis* (Ithaca, NY: Cornell University Press, 1993), 3.

The Riddles of Imagined Communities

The idea and ideology of the nation have recently been the subject of intense inquiry. Space restrictions prevent me from reviewing that body of literature. Suffice it to say that the two most prominent arguments to play a role here are the idea of the invention of tradition as advanced by Eric Hobsbawm and Terence Ranger, and Benedict Anderson's thesis on the determining relationship between the growth of print and the spread of nationalism in the New World, Europe, and elsewhere. Anderson has stressed the idea that "nation-ness, as well as nationalism, are cultural artifacts of a particular kind."[3] He adds that the particular ways in which they came into being account for the profound emotional charge associated with their sense of legitimacy.[4] These artifacts, he argues, once created at the end of the eighteenth century in the New World, "became modular, capable of being transplanted with various degrees of self-consciousness, to a great variety of social terrains."[5] On the whole, Anderson's major contribution to the discussion on nationalism devolves on the brilliant design of his concept of "imagined community," an idea that easily travels from one terrain of analysis to another. For that reason it is worth quoting here at length and especially because it in fact was already advanced by Ernest Renan in his (1882) definition of nation as cultural artifact.[5] For Anderson, the "nation is an imagined political community—and imagined as both inherently limited and sovereign."[6] It is imagined "because the members of the even smallest nation will never know most of their fellow members . . . and yet in the mind of each lives the image of their community."[7] Anderson is keen on stressing that nationalism is "not the awakening of nations to self-consciousness: it invents nations where they do not exist."[8] By inventing, Anderson means creating in the sense of making.

However, his chapter on Latin American independence movements registers a number of unresolved problems that Anderson himself calls "rid-

---

3. See Eric Hobsbawm and Terence Ranger, eds., *The Invention of Tradition* (New York: Cambridge University Press, 1983). See also Benedict Anderson, *Imagined Communities: Reflections on the Origin and Spread of Nationalism* (London: Verso, 1983).

4. Anderson, *Imagined Communities,* 4.

5. Ibid.

6. Ibid., 6.

7. Ibid.

8. Ibid.

dles."[9] The riddles are the result of the fact that his theory cannot account for the multiple specificities at play in the processes of independence in Latin America. Despite Anderson's attention to the picaresque novels by José Joaquín Fernández de Lizardi, all published after 1826 and still unavailable in English translation, and his attention to the Creoles' frustration with their exclusion from high office in the colonial administration, it is clear that neither his thesis on the spread of print—in the form of novels and newspapers—nor his elaboration of the "modal journey of pilgrimage"[10] provide a sufficient explanation for the homegrown nationalisms of the Latin American independence movements.

Anderson has little to say on the question of local intellectuals and homegrown discourses of independence in print and iconography as well as other modes of encoding and circulating memory. It is indeed remarkable to see that in the case of Mexico he places his focus on the post-1810 picaresque novels of Lizardi while the whole question of the Virgin of Guadalupe and the low-level clergy that headed the movement for Mexican independence is left out. As Jacques Lafaye has shown, the cult of the Virgin of Guadalupe and its indissoluble link to Mexican national consciousness was not built on, and neither did its spread rest on, the dissemination of print.[11] Likewise, Anderson ignores the historical work of the Jesuit Francisco Javier Clavijero (1731—1787) and his attempt to anchor the Mexican nation in a history of its antiquities. The thesis of "imagined communities" leaves out also and almost by necessity what Carlos Fuentes refers to as "the sacrifice of the poor parish priests who led the uprising of Indians and other rural people, armed with clubs and picks, [that] left independence hanging on an agreement among fighters."[12]

How Anderson deals with Mexico is simply an example that can be multiplied in regard to many other, equally important, discursive specificities. When these are brought into play in the consideration of nation building in Latin America they present a serious challenge to Anderson's modular traveling thesis. Latin American nation building and the nationalisms of the independence period require more complex explanations, themselves based

9. Ibid., 50.

10. Ibid., 57.

11. See Jacques Lafaye, *Quetzalcóatl and Guadalupe: The Formation of Mexican National Consciousness, 1531–1813* (Chicago: University of Chicago Press, 1976).

12. Carlos Fuentes, *Los cinco soles de México: Memoria de un milenio* (Barcelona: Seix Barral, 2000), 132.

on detailed analysis of the crisscrossing of many more discrete discourses and historical forces than just newspapers and novels or Creole inability to journey up the bureaucratic ladder of colonial institutions.

In this essay I explore certain key continuities and breaks in well-established local knowledges and memory systems that exceed the limits of print in the Andes and Mexico. The conjunction of established local knowledges with the appearance of new knowledges, especially archaeology in the national imagination of Mexico and the Andes, provide fertile ground for the examination of the deployment of particular historical forces active in the rise of nations out of the evolving colonial grid.

I focus here on three significant moments in the making of the nation as a cultural artifact linked to a "people" who claim immemorial occupation of the land. These moments in Mexico and Peru have been chosen because the materiality of culture that constitutes them exceeds the bounds of print media, especially novels. For example, the body of knowledge that enables and constrains the Tupac Amaru II rebellion relies on memorial art based on iconography, dance, dress, and ritual. The daily viewing of and interrogation posed by the ancient ruins in the case of Mexico led Clavijero in the late eighteenth century and Eduardo Mariano Rivero in the early nineteenth century in Peru to the exploration, drawing, and writing of the ruins left by the Aztecs, Incas, and Mochicas. In these cases, the study of archaeology stretches the time line of the nation and creates immemorial "ancestors" for the post-colonial nation. In these two instances archaeology allows a mapping of the nation that reconfigures territory by privileging forgotten or even forbidden sites of memory.

In examining the rise of archaeology in helping modern, post-colonial nations "root" themselves to the land, I do not intend to establish empirical relations of cause and effect, for my concern is with discursive formations and my approach is genealogical. It is important to emphasize here that genealogy, in as much as it points to discontinuity, destroys the illusion of linear development. But genealogy also allows the identification of deeper hidden continuities that are the product of sequences of transformations and combinations. The three moments discussed here do indeed exhibit sequences of transformations in the deployment of deviations, incomplete reversals, and reappearances. A genealogical approach to the rise of archaeology in the nascent post-colonial polities does not, as Michel Foucault would put it, "pretend to go back in time to restore an unbroken continuity that operates beyond the dispersion of forgotten things."[13] On the contrary, Foucault states that genealogy, as it follows the complex course of descent, maintains "passing events in their proper dispersion."[14]

In what follows I keep in mind Walter Benjamin's sense of the writing of history from the urgency created by the crisis of the present. I think that Benjamin's emphasis on a perspective informed by the sense of a present crisis illuminates not only the task of the archaeologist "then" but also the endeavor of those who examine the past today. Writing history in order "to seize hold of a memory as it flashes up at a moment of danger," is different from the impossible articulation of the past as it "really was."[15]

If indeed we can only write the past from the sense of one's own present, when examining the discourses that construct the nation in Latin America, it is important today not to lose sight of the recent challenges made to European historiography, especially with regard to the Hegelian single and universal time line. Foucault's challenge to the idea of history that assumes a living world "actually" moving on a single plane of homogeneous space and time is particularly useful here, for if there is a heterogeneous history sustained by parallel, asymmetrical, contradictory, and yet contemporary epistemologies, that indeed is the case of post-conquest Andes. After the conquest, linear Christian time neither meshed nor absorbed Andean concepts of space-time (*pacha*). Moreover, the colonial world as a remote outpost of the center and its self-ascribed homogeneous time produced its own "backward" time location. Questioning the assumption of a homogenous historical and lived space-time is even more relevant here, for such homogeneity is claimed by Anderson to be the result of the spread of print and the subsequent construction of imagined communities. I therefore look into the fractures and limits that mark the differences between subsequent or par-

---

13. Michel Foucault, *Language, Counter-Memory, Practice: Selected Essays and Interviews,* ed. Donald F. Bouchard, trans. Donald F. Bouchard and Sherry Simon (Ithaca, NY: Cornell University Press, 1977), 146.

14. Ibid.

15. See Walter Benjamin, "Theses on the Philosophy of History" in *Illuminations,* ed. Hannah Arendt, trans. Harry Zohn (New York: Schocken Books, 1969). In this famous essay, Benjamin writes: "To articulate the past historically does not mean to recognize it 'the way it really was' (Ranke). It means to seize hold of a memory as it flashes up in a moment of danger. Historical materialism wishes to retain that image of the past which unexpectedly appears to man singled out by history at a moment of danger. The danger affects both the content of the tradition and its receivers . . . [who are] convinced that even the dead will not be safe from the enemy if he wins" (255).

allel ideas of nationhood founded each in turn on sign systems other than writing and the spread of print. On the whole, my chief concern here is the deployment of memory and its often labyrinthine paths in the making of history and nation. I take history to mean both the lived experience entwined in the appearance of events and the writing or recording of the event by a series of mnemonic devices.

Mapping the Nation

In *History and Memory* ([1977] 1992), writing before Anderson advanced his arguments on the New World origin of nationalist discourses, Jacques Le Goff states that the idea of the nation dates back to the French Revolution.[16] He decidedly differs from Federico Chabord for whom the idea of the nation dates back to the Middle Ages. In this regard, Anderson's distinction between the nation as an imagined community and the nation-state is as pertinent as it is illuminating. Jonathan Boyarin makes a useful distinction between an ethnic nation and the nation-state. The ethnic nation or the medieval idea of nation is a concept grounded on a genealogically defined people who hold on to a memory of common origins or common birth. In this sense, the idea of nation is closely linked to the Latin *nasci* from which it derives,[17] but it does not mean an imagined community in Anderson's sense of the term.

Le Goff's notion of the nation as a new divinity or as sacred fatherland establishes a profound link with the writing and reading of history, for it is in the practices of memorialization of the dead and the shape and features ascribed to the father's land where the nation both appears and is sustained.[18] However, the link between the practices that memorialize the

---

16. See Jacques Le Goff, *History and Memory,* trans. Steven Randall and Elizabeth Claman (New York: Columbia University Press, 1992), 151. Le Goff's collected essays on the topic of history and memory first appeared in Italy in 1977 under the title *Storia e Memoria.* His arguments on the origins of the modern nation did of course not benefit from Anderson's arguments as to the New World origin of nationalism and nation. Anderson's critique of the prevailing and determining Eurocentricism present in almost of the literature on nationalism and nation is indeed well taken.

17. See Jonathan Boyarin, "Space, Time and the Politics of Memory," in *Remapping Memory or the Politics of Timespace,* ed. Jonathan Boyarin (Minneapolis: University of Minnesota Press, 1999), 1–38.

18. Le Goff notes that until the nineteenth century history was not regularly taught in schools in France. Aristotle had excluded it from the sciences and medieval universi-

dead—writing of history, erection of statues, tombs, public ritual, poetry and novels, and museums—and the territory designated as the "fatherland" have not always been self-evident.

Renan launched a radical questioning of the constitutive series of ideas that had come to compose the nation: shared immemorial occupation of a territory, common religion, language, traditions, and race. Renan delivered his influential lecture, "What is a Nation?" at the Sorbonne in 1882. He bluntly asked: "Upon what criterion . . . should one base . . . national right? By what sign shall we know it? From what tangible fact can one derive it?"[19]

It is worth reviewing Renan's concerns here, for all the principles that he considers not to be the proper foundations of the nation pertain to ideas that prove crucial to claims for "national" autonomy in the colonial situation. For instance, Renan's preoccupation with national legitimacies is not restricted to the legal question. He is also concerned with problems of unity and homogeneity in and of the population. At the core of the legal problem lies the question of permanent occupation of the land, to wit, the most obvious tangible sign. Renan puzzles over the republican challenge to the idea of right by dynastic (conquest) rule. If after the French Revolution, dynasties can be deemed illegitimate and therefore dynastic rule can no longer provide the basis for neither right nor unity, does the "permanent" occupation of a territory by a given "race" confer on the people "primordial right"? Renan considers the substitution of the divine right of kings for what he calls the "ethnographic principle" a "grave error,"[20] for it could eventually destroy European civilization. The principle of the "primordial right of races" could give legitimacy to the autonomy claims of numerous ethnic groups, who were at the time already subsumed under existing European nation-states. Instead of tangible evidence of territorial occupation, he opts for a vague and somewhat mystical culturalist model in which there

---

ties did likewise. With the French Revolution, the teaching and writing of history received a new impetus. It was taught in primary and secondary schools, as well as at the university level. The nineteenth century ensured the diffusion of historical culture among the masses (Le Goff, *History and Memory,* 152). See also Anderson on Jules Michelet and the emplotment of French national history (*Imagined Communities,* 197–199). Of course the key text here is Hayden White, *Metahistory: The Historical Imagination in the Nineteenth Century* (Baltimore: Johns Hopkins University Press, 1973).

19. See Ernest Renan, "What is a Nation?" trans. Martin Thom, in *Nation and Narration,* ed. Homi Bhabha (New York: Routledge, 1990), 8–22.

20. Ibid., 13.

are universal "things," such as reason, truth, and beauty, which are beyond anthropological specificities.[21]

Surprisingly, Renan also tries to dismantle the link between nation and language. As if abiding by the opening statement of his essay—nations are forged as much by the operation of forgetting as they are by the work of memory—the French historian states that France "has never sought to earn unity of language by coercive measures."[22] In this statement Renan forgets the ongoing process of turning peasants into Frenchmen.[23] However, what Renan has in mind for his critique on the language—nation sequence is the work of comparative philology and its links to archaeology, which together bring back the ethnographic principle. If languages are to be regarded as signs of race, Renan reasons, then linguistic theory carries within it the same disabling dangers as the ethnographic claims. He reasons that neither the specificity of language nor religion nor the idea of "the people's" occupation of the territory in question is sufficiently safe grounds on which to establish the claims of the nation.[24]

21. Ibid., 25.

22. Ibid., 16.

23. See Eugene Weber, *Peasants into Frenchmen: The Modernization of Rural France, 1870–1914* (London: Chatto & Windus, 1979). Homi Bhabha points out that Renan's thesis on forgetting does not apply uniformly. Subaltern groups are invited to carry out the heavier part of the forgetting. Such forgetting leads to a homogenization of memory and the writing of history. This is especially relevant in colonial situations in which power asymmetries constitute the foundation of the lived world. "Non-hegemonic sectors of society are obliged to forget" (311). See Homi Bhabha, "DissemiNation: Time, Narrative, and the Margins of the Modern Nation," in *Nation and Narration,* ed. Homi Bhabha (New York: Routledge, 1990), 291–323.

24. Anthony D. Smith shows that upon inventing the nation, European intelligentsias in the late eighteenth and the nineteenth centuries had to breathe life into the past to create a truly living past. This life-like construction was not achieved by simple antiquarianism. Smith points to the key role played by modern, scientific disciplines—philology, anthropology, history, sociology, folklore, and archaeology—in the translation of the "idealized images of the ethnic past into tactile realities" (180). Smith makes a distinction between the work of "returning intelligentsias" and "secular intelligentsias." It would seem that Renan's rejection of the ethnic principle and the foundational work of philology arise, in part, as a critique of the Romantic interest in ruins and landscape prevalent in the desire to build ethnic nations in Europe as well as the interest in archaeology and philology that followed in the wake of the Napoleonic invasion of Egypt. Smith observes "how this desire for physical tangibility and verisimilitude invaded European intellectual and aesthetic consciousness" (181). This resulted in "a growing awareness of the differences between heritages and pasts that had previously been conflated. From the 1760s a controversy raged between partisans of the 'Roman past' . . . and the purer, linear Greek aesthetic heritage" (181). Philology and even lexicogra-

Renan thus posits the nation as an almost mystical amalgam of "body and soul." Anticipating Anderson, Renan claims that the glue that binds the community is the "sentimental side."[25] Nationality's affect is capable of uniting the soil, as the field of struggle and labor, with the soul, that element that only the spirit (memory?) can furnish. In the end for Renan, "man is everything," that is to say culture, in the formation of this sacred bond of nationality. The nation is a *spiritual principle,* the outcome of the "profound complications of history."[26] Eliding his early emphasis on the forgetting that goes on in the making of memory, the constituting principle of nationality turns out to be the shared possession of a rich legacy of memories and the desire to live together.[27]

Thus, if the nation is constituted not by territory commonly held, nor by shared language or religion, but rather by the possession of common memories about the past, and its being is predicated on the profound imbeddedness of the complications of history, it follows that the nation cannot be improvised and "new" nations cannot exist. The nation, in fact, is the lived (reiterated) memory of the past and it relies on the deployment of the arts or memorializing the dead as Le Goff has pointed out.

For colonial peoples facing the task of establishing a discourse capable of legitimizing not only self-rule, but also the repossession of the territory lost to the colonizing powers, the complications of history and the reiterated memory of the past things are not so simple. Renan's views pose a challenge rather than a possibility. A reiterated memory of the past is a task of deliberate construction in a colonial and post-colonial situation. The same can be said for elucidating the complications of history. Renan's two claims assume an always already shared and homogeneous "history" and "memory," which are in part induced by forgetting. But the given of a colonial situation is that the memory of the past is disputed, contradictory, multiple, and contestatory. Thus, the very issues that Renan wishes to banish from the discussion on the construction of nations and nationalism—primordial right to territorial occupation, ethnographic principle, linkage between language—nation and "race"—are to be found playing key roles in the dis-

---

phy were "pressed into service by the 'returning intelligentsia' with its vision of a didactic past and of history as a salvation-drama" (181). See Smith, *The Ethnic Origins of Nations* (Oxford: Blackwell, 1986).

25. Renan, "What is a Nation?" 18.

26. Ibid., 19.

27. Ibid.

course on the nation in post-colonial situations. Here archaeology provides the discursive space where these issues unfold as the "new," but rather old, post-colonial nations rise from the ruins of conquest.

Imperialism, Nation, and Archaeology

Implicit in both Le Goff's and Renan's idea of the nation is the operation of mapping a narrative (history) onto a territory (fatherland). This narrative anchored in concepts of origin, agency, population self-identity, and memory of dead ancestors and heroes, takes hold in a territory that is delimited as the scenario of lived space.[28] Conceived as a "real place," the space in which we live, the set of social relations that bounds us, the nation becomes the stage on which a people hold on to a tradition and deploy a force onto the past in order to establish cultural boundaries. The modern concept of nation, which is predicated on a single line of homogeneous time, responds to the notion of a "sharply bounded, continuously occupied space, controlled by a single sovereign state, comprising a set of autonomous and yet essentially identical individuals."[29]

Boyarin points out that eighteenth-century views on "space" and "time" as cognitive categories are fueled by the West's colonialist project of "mapping the world."[30] This project holds time as a dynamic and energy-loaded (history) arrow that traverses "dead" and static space.[31] This very emphasis on geography is taken up by colonized peoples as they embark on the struggle for emancipation. Demarcating the ground of the nation, stamping the lived spaces with the time of origin and durability of the colonized

28. "Lived space" is a term introduced by Henri Lefevre to mean a socially created spatiality. Lived space is not far from Foucault's sense of "real place," that is, the space in which we live, the set of social relations, the heterogeneous spaces of sites and relations, the heterotopias that constitute every society. See Edward Soja, "History; Geography; Modernity," in *The Cultural Studies Reader*, ed. Simon During (New York: Routledge, 1993), 142–143.

29. See Boyarin, "Space, Time and the Politics of Memory," 2. Gramsci observed that "in France the meaning of the 'national' already includes a more politically elaborated notion of the 'popular' because it is related to the concept of 'sovereignty': national and sovereignty has, or had, the same value.'" See Antonio Gramsci, *Selections from Cultural Writings,* ed. D. Forgacs and G. Nowell-Smith (London: Lawrence and Wishart, 1985), 208.

30. Boyarin, "Space, Time and the Politics of Memory, " 6.

31. Ibid., 6–7.

ground, demanded that the nationalist claims reconnoiter the possibility and potential of geographic discourses.

For Boyarin, when collective consciousness was articulated in the context of a struggle against European imperialism, colonials adopted the notion that collective identity—and hence both loyalty and legitimate exercise of power—was determined by spatial relations. "By the end of the nineteenth century, then, the contest was for control of space rather than its definition."[32]

If geographic expeditions, with the scientist-explorer at the center, produced the "known" world for Europe and its "others" at the end of the eighteenth century and throughout the nineteenth century, archaeology and its close links to comparative linguistics, re-mapped the globe with a countervailing wind. The force of archaeology acted counter to the spatial dissemination of navigation in the hands of exploration. Geographic mapping of territories allowed colonials to stake foundational grounds on which to build the house of the future nation.

However, the future alone is never enough. For the future to acquire direction and become the shared will to "live together" as Renan put it, a shared past is a necessary and indispensable condition. Archaeology proved crucial for colonial peoples engaged in the endeavor of "inventing" a nation, and indeed, in deploying the ethnographic principle as a positive force on which to base their claims to legitimate struggles for self-rule. Archaeology had the capacity to literally "dig" the people into the ground and thus establish an inalienable link to the past as lived space. In doing so it also proves that the colonizer does not belong.

Perhaps even more important than the material link to the land, for the peoples "without history" archaeology enables the conversion of collective memory into tradition and maybe even into history.[33] Tradition—the transmission of collective memory from generation to generation—in the sight of archaeological monuments can attempt to close the generational gap, the rupture between father and son, which makes of tradition not the lesser of the arts of memory. Tradition in the sight of archaeology comes closer to the production of the smooth and homogeneous time line of history. In *The Ethnic Origin of Nations* (1986), speaking of the European deployment of archaeology in the nineteenth century, Anthony D. Smith writes: "Archeol-

32. Ibid., 9.
33. Let us not forget that the keeping of written records of the past has been, since Herodotus's expedition among the Scythians, the West's requirement for parity with its "others."

ogy has been perhaps the most useful of disciplines in recovering communal pasts. . . . The material remains uncovered bring home to us, as only tactile objects can, the physical immediacy of former eras and archaic peoples, lending vivid substance to the records of chronicles and epics."[34] For the (modern), post-colonial nation, archaeology—sites in place—spatializes on the surface of a re-reconnoitered and rationalized territory, clearly demarcated by linguistic and immemorial boundaries, the place of the communal past and present.

But nothing in the vagaries of mapping the world or the rise of nationalism is actually that simple. While the globe was being both expanded and contracted by faster and better means of communication, it was also being "compressed and controlled by the growth of capitalism."[35] The new knowledges brought along by explorers and scientists such as Alexander von Humboldt and Charles Darwin, in the case of Spanish America had the effect of setting forth a number of local knowledges and forces that, in time, would partially shift intellectual production and control to the formerly colonial (objects) subjects.

The processes involved in the production of power–knowledge were not always unidirectional, that is to say, from Europe to America. As in the case of Garcilaso de la Vega, El Inca, the undisputed founder of nationalist ideology in the Andes and perhaps for all of Spanish America,[36] colonial subjects proved capable of managing the imperial power–knowledge machine in order to contest oppressive discourses and identities spewed out of the colonizing archive. Before Humboldt brought to Europe's attention the importance and grandeur of Inca and Aztec engineering and architecture, the Jesuit Francisco Xavier Clavijero (1731–1787), taking up Carlos de Sigüenza y Gongora's (1645–1700) earlier interests in Aztec antiquities, wrote his *Historia antigua de Mexico* (1780). For Clavijero, Aztec codices, maps, sculpture, and ruins were not just eloquent historical sources but the living presence of the past. It is interesting to note, however, that while Humboldt's visit to Peru in 1802 fueled an already existing interest in ruins and the pre-Conquest past, the text that constitutes Humboldt's own guide

34. Anthony D. Smith, *The Ethnic Origin of Nations* (Oxford: Blackwell, 1986), 180–181.

35. See David Harvey, *The Condition of Postmodernity: An Enquiry into the Origins of Cultural Change* (Oxford and Cambridge, MA: Blackwell, 1989), 240.

36. See David Brading, *The First America: The Spanish Monarchy, Creole Patriots and the Liberal State, 1492–1867* (New York and Cambridge: Cambridge University Press, 1991), 255–273 and 483–491.

as he makes his way down the *cordillera* from Quito to Lima is none other than the *Comentarios reales* by Garcilaso de la Vega, El Inca.[37] Nevertheless, and despite his secondary interest in the Amerindian past, Humboldt's visits and descriptions of ruins in Mexico and Peru validated and promoted the incipient curiosity in local intellectual circles.[38]

Andean Sites of Memory

In this section, I examine and compare the making of the so-called proto-nationalist project of Tupac Amaru II with the rise of national history and its link to archaeology in the two decades immediately before independence. I argue that the difference between the terms of the Andean utopia expressed in the Tupac Amaru II movement and the later archaeological vision of the nation as inalienable territory entails a paradigm shift. Such a shift is, on the one hand, grounded on the specificity of the lived local Andean knowledges and, on the other, on its finely attuned and yet dissonant concordance with a growing sense of the past as "other" during the long nineteenth century.

The deployment of the sites of memory serves me as a pivot around which I will seek to establish the shift. In the case of the national construction entailed in the Tupac Amaru II movement, I find memory practices embodied in the lived organic discourse that ties the present to the past as the living memory that guides everyday practices. The past as present is immediately perceptible; it is in sight of the whole Andean collectivity and fills the coordinates of the lived space. That is why the ideal of restoration is possible. The social memory of the past registers a sense of presentness. It is the living past that enables subjects to engage in testimonies that preserve memory as a seamless web with the lived world. Memory, after the defeat of Tupac Amaru II and the cruel and inhuman punishment imposed on his followers, momentarily orients thinking on the nation toward the future exclusively insofar as memory of the past enters into the silence of trauma and

37. See Estuardo Núñez and George Petersen, eds., *Alexander von Humboldt en el Peru: Diario de viajes y otros escritos* (Lima: Banco Central de Reserva del Peru, 2002), 69–71, 106, 127, 192–198.

38. See Alejandro de Humboldt, *Cartas Americanas* (Caracas: Ayacucho, 1980). See chapter 4, "The Age of Reason," in Ignacio Bernal, *A History of Mexican Archaeology:The Vanished Civilizations of Middle America* (London and New York: Thames and Hudson, 1980); and Deborah Poole, *Vision, Race, and Modernity: A Visual Economy of the Andean Image World* (Princeton, NJ: Princeton University Press, 1997).

the full crisis of independence. Contemporary Andean historians register this slicing of the lived space of the past with a significant silence in the making of the nation's history. That resounding silence was brought about by the strict censorship imposed by the Spanish authorities after the execution of Tupac Amaru II.[39] The national subject would seem to lack a place from where to speak the self in either time or space. According to Raúl Porras Barrenechea, the writing of national history during the early decades of the republic was given almost no attention. The message of the aboriginal cultures, Porras said, seem now far away, and indeed postponed indefinitely. And the republican present did not seem important. The nation's history was not taught either in schools nor at the universities.[40] Not until the appearance of *Paisajes peruanos* (1912) by José de la Riva Aguero did the nation emerge as a continuous space-time construct. In this regard it is not insignificant that the first "history" of the Peruvian past is authored by a foreigner. William Prescott's *History of the Conquest of Peru* (1847) remains unrivaled until the end of the nineteenth century. The silence of history will find in antiquarian collections, field trips, and emotional but unsystematic explorations of ruins the point of enunciation for a new discourse on the nation as past and present and the link between the dead and the living.

The deployment of memory and the constitution of the past/present during the Age of Andean Insurrection (1720–1790) has been studied and clarified in the work of pathbreaking ethnohistorians.[41] Both José Gabriel Condorcanqui (1738–1781), better known as Tupac Amaru II, and Juan Santos Atahualpa (1710–1756), based their claims to authority and leadership on the idea of direct descent from the Incas (ethnographic nation). The underlying assumption was that the rebels would restore the cosmological as well as the social, economic, political, and affective order of the past. The contract between the rebel "Incas" and their followers, be they the Cuzco aristocracy or the peasantry at large, came about on the basis of a shared,

39. In *Fuentes historicas peruanas* (Lima: Instituto Raúl Porras Barrenechea, 1963), Raúl Porras Barrenechea writes, "Se dió poca importancia a la historia nacional en las primeras décadas de la república. Rotas las tradiciones que nos unían con España, lejano y pospuesto el mensaje de las culturas primitivas se concedió poca importancia al presente republicano. . . . La historia no ocupa un puesto en la inquietud cultural ni en los programas de los colegios y universidades" (473).

40. Porras Barrenechea, *Fuentes historicas peruanas,* 473.

41. See Alberto Flores Galindo, ed., *Tupac Amaru II–1780* (Lima: Retablo de Papel, 1976); and Manuel Burga, *Nacimiento de una utopia: Muerte y resurrección de los Incas* (Lima: Instituto de Apoyo Agrario, 1988). See also Alberto Flores Galindo, *Buscando un Inca* (Lima: Instituto de Apoyo Agrario, 1987).

living memory. The sense of place, the space of lived social relations, the heterotopic[42] character of Andean memory constituted the conditions of possibility for the restorative ambition of the neo-Inca projects.[43]

For John Rowe the "going back" in the dressing fashion of the *curacas* (indigenous leaders) indicates, in a thesis contrary to the claims made by the *Invention of Tradition,* that "es notable la autenticidad del estilo Inca de los trajes" and that "la tradición inca [permanecía] auténtica y viva."[44] Manuel Burga has documented the sites of memory—ritual processions, clothing, insignia, food, language, altars, and theater—deployed by the neo-Inca revival of the Andean elites.[45] These were visual spaces that competed with alphabetic memory, for they also bore the capacity to retain and disseminate the narrative of Inca ancestry well beyond the limits of print media. Around the middle of the eighteenth century "a veritable cult of Inca antiquity flourished in the old Inca capital. Public ceremonies, *curacas* dressed as Incas, flags, conch shells and symbols of the sun"[46] were regularly displayed in view of a public that comprised all sectors of society, including the Spanish clergy which, for reasons of their own, chose to look the other way.

Inspiration for neo-Inca revivalism is attributed almost unanimously[47] to the re-publication and wide circulation of Garcilaso de la Vega's *Comentarios reales* (1609) in 1722. While in this case one could cite the power of

42. On heterotopia, see Michel Foucault, "Of Other Spaces," *Diacritics* 16 (1986): 22–27.

43. John Rowe argues that after three generations of Jesuit education the *curacas* had forgotten Inca religion (21). However, "donde se nota más la fuerza de la tradición cultural inca es en el traje. . . . En estos cuadros se nota algo sorprendente; se ha dado un paso atrás en la adopción de las modas europeas y se muestran los nobles incas con vestidos más tradicionales que los que aparecen en los dibujos de Guamán Poma" (22). Rowe, "El movimiento nacional Inca del siglo XVIII," in *Tupac Amaru II–1780,* ed. Alberto Flores Galindo (Lima: Retablo de Papel, 1976), 11–53). See also Flores Galindo, "Túpac Amaru y la sublevación de 1780," in *Tupac Amaru II–1780.*

44. Ibid., 23.

45. Manuel Burga, *Nacimiento de una utopía: Muerte y resurrección de los Incas* (Lima: Instituto de Apoyo Agrario, 1987).

46. Peter Klarén, *Peru: Society and Nationhood in the Andes* (New York: Oxford University Press, 2000), 116.

47. See Brading, *The First America;* Rowe, "El movimiento nacional Inca del siglo XVIII"; Flores Galindo, *Buscando un Inca;* Burga, *Nacimiento de una utopia;* Scarlett O'Phelan-Godoy, "Túpac Amaru y las sublevaciones del siglo XVIII," in *Túpac Amaru II–1780,* ed. Alberto Flores Galindo (Lima: Retablo de Papel, 1976); Klarén, *Peru,* chapter 4; and Ward Stavig, *The World of Túpac Amaru: Conflict, Community and Identity in Colonial Peru,* (Lincoln: University of Nebraska Press, 1999).

print, reading and orally disseminating the multiple contents and rhetorics of Garcilaso's lengthy and complex book are vastly different from the effects of newspapers, and the serialization of novels and pamphlets. The reading of Garcilaso proved "incendiary" among the Indian gentry.[48] Tupac Amaru II carried the book with him as he traveled the Andes with his mule trains. It is thus not farfetched to imagine the easy passage and mixing of the contents and effects of the *Comentarios reales* into the mainly oral and visual culture of the period.

In fact, the bishop of Cuzco, Juan Manuel de Moscoso y Peralta, directly attributed the force and restorative clarity of the rebellion to the reading of the forbidden book. The bishop reasoned that "if the *Comentarios* of Garcilaso had not been the reading and instruction of the insurgent[,] . . . Tupac Amaru would not have embarked on the detestable audacity of his rebellion."[49] But the moment of revelation for the bishop was not yet over. In his letter to the *visitador* (magistrate) Antonio de Areche during the siege of Cuzco (1781), the bishop realized that he had been blind to the meanings of the cultural space he had been "sharing" with the Andeans under his tutelage. The bishop had not been decoding the Andean colonial sites of memory: dress, food, Quechua theater, ritual dance, and even landscape and architecture, which for a reading- and writing-centered sense of culture and communication must have seemed nothing other than silent objects not worth an intellectual's attention.

Incendiary as the *Comentarios* may have been, the book alone could not have created the possibilities for insurgency. It is actually its convergence with the constant sight of Inca portraits and costumes that kept alive the Inca past that enabled the insurgents to imagine the past as a golden age. In retrospect, Bishop Moscoso grew more and more disturbed at the Spaniards' oversight. It was a blunder to allow the Indians to make and publicly display their fabled ancestors in no less a place than the Jesuit Colegio de San Francisco de Borja, for "the Indians are a species of rational beings who are more impressed by what they see than by what they are told."[50]

It would seem that the bishop of Cuzco, even in his retrospective wisdom, forgot the events of the Taqui Oncoy,[51] as well as the campaigns for the extirpation of idolatries that consumed the Andes in the fires of evange-

48. Brading, *The First America,* 490.
49. Ibid., 491.
50. Ibid.
51. See Luis Millones, ed., *El retorno de las huacas: estudios y documentos del siglo XVI* (Lima: Instituto de Estudios Peruanos, 1990).

lization only a century before his watch. Both the Taqui Oncoy and the con-
fessions made to José de Arriaga by the indigenous priests of the *huacas*
(holy places and entities) in the Lurín valley, better known today as the *Mitos de Huarochiri,*[52] remain as telling documents on the Andean resistance
to the extirpation of local memory. However, the memory of the injury to
the colonial state by the priests and curacas of the sixteenth century proved
to be only too well and alive. The colonial state followed the execution of
Tupac Amaru II and the destruction of his family with the *quintado,* that is,
the execution of every fifth able-bodied male in every *tupamarista* villages.[53] This measure was meant to put an end to all local intellectuals. The
Europeanized and highly educated Indian elite was silenced. Tupac
Amaru's proto-nationalist and counterhegemonic insurgency came to an
end with the physical disappearance of the bodies of the curacas who, by
rule of descent, constituted a site of memory and thus provided, like the
king's body in France, a link with the past of the nation as a set of indivis-
ible biological and cultural relations in space and time.[54]

In a more present-oriented study, Flores Galindo in *Buscando un Inca*
(1987) examines (1) the survival of the millennial (oral) narrative tradition
of the Incarrí and the ritual dances, which themselves relate the past in conjunction with an understanding of the present world of each community, and
(2) the ritualization of food, drink, and dress as expressive vehicles of subjective identities. I would add that at stake in this massive display of ritual is
the production of time and space as a set of bridges over repeated fractures.
These are strategies that enable Indians, from their own knowledges and
practices, to "think" the "right" to occupy and use the land. While this memorialization of tradition does not make use of the alphabet and as a whole has
been deemed "oral," upon closer reflection it is obvious that it is neither oral
nor subterranean as Flores Galindo characterized it.[55] It is in fact a visibility
coded in signs and systems of signification that go well beyond the power of
alphabetic memory sites such as books, novels, and newspapers.

52. José María Argueda and Pierre Duviols, *Mitos de Huarochiri: Narración
Quechua recojida por Francisco de Avila,* bilingual ed., trans. José María Arguedas
([1598?] Lima: Instituto de Estudios Peruanos, 1966).

53. Klarén, *Peru,* 191.

54. Despite the fact that the nineteenth century is also a very long century in the Andes, it is beyond the scope of this essay to examine the sites of memory in the more than
100 Indian rebellions of the Andean insurrection period, and the many others that were
to follow into the twentieth century. See Flores Galindo, *Buscando un Inca.*

55. Ibid., 90, 93.

With the exception of the narrative of Incarrí, all other sites of memory examined by Flores Galindo and Burga represent forceful visual and aural forms of encoding memory and subjectivity that, at any time, can be deciphered and re-encoded into linguistic constructs of different kinds and genres. Ritual dance does indeed tell stories but its deployment is not by linguistic means until another form of cognition interpellates it. It involves codification of body movements and costumes (color and design) in conjunction with music (sound and rhythm) that acquire meaning as they come together in a dynamic combination, and publicly displayed on a specific day of the calendar that organizes the passage of time for the community of interpreters. The linguistic dimension accompanying ritual dance is of course in Quechua, itself a constant presence linking the past to the present. The same can be said of all other performances, including dress, food, and medicine. All such performances represent a coherent overlapping of many cultural codes, which when decoded via language, represent powerful passages between past and present.

In contrast to print culture, these spatio-temporal passages involve the theatricalization of belief and practice. Like Inca and post-Inca *tablas* or *quicllas* (paintings on cloth or wood) and plays, they encode a memory that requires an ever renewed and flexible community of interpreters who can at once produce the same text and adapt it to the changing re-interpretative conditions. However, these visual (plus linguistic) representations of the past cannot in any way be considered subterranean as Flores Galindo stated, for they need the light of day and the participation of the entire interpretative community to ensure their validity and survival. On the contrary, it is print culture with its demand for the individual and silent operation of the interpretative act that is more likely to produce a subterranean world of knowledge and feeling. The nonalphabetic public Andean traditions that converged in the Tupac Amaru II rebellion produced visibility in Foucaultian terms.

The force of the event was dispersed with the quintado and re-absorbed into the practices of everyday (Quechua) life, but it, like the Inca or the Incarrí, did not disappear. Food and dress rituals continued. Dances and commemorations repeated themselves with the regularity of the seasons. Above all, the land, dotted as it was with *chacras* (cultivated fields), *apus* (great lord, tutelary mountain), and huacas remained as "silent" but signifying sites in which the connection with the past was re-elaborated. The heterotopic character of Andean space-time was not smoothed over by the defeat of Tupac Amaru II, but it did pull apart the convergence of memory sites that made the rebellion thinkable.

Local Knowledges and Paradigm Shifts

After the execution of Tupac Amaru in 1782, the "national" project centered in Cuzco had spent all its force and the idea of the nation reappeared with the Amantes del País in Lima. The young Creoles witnessed with disquiet a new twist in the colonizing process. The age of scientific exploration was re-positioning the space-time they inhabited. From a place valued for its mineral wealth, Peru was now seen in the metropolis as a place replete with the data necessary for completing the global mapping of the world undertaken by a swiftly modernizing Europe. Under the Enlightenment's new knowledge requirements and its new conception of the past, the colonials' incipient vision of the past suffered yet another complication and entered more decidedly than ever into new zones of uncertainty and contradiction from those already capitalized in Garcilaso's struggle with historiography.

Neither the cooperation nor the permission of the Creole elite were necessary for the new science to enter (in Edward Said's sense) the land.[56] In fact, visits to Lima by the new explorers and scientists left the Creoles with the distinct impression that they were "behind" in the homogenous space-time that Anderson posits as the horizon for the "Creole pioneers." Their knowledge warehouse regarding their "own" land appeared indeed empty and the place where they would fill it was not the local environment but rather where the scientists came from. Intellectually and emotionally underequipped to begin to reconnoiter the multiple dimensions of the inherited space-time of which they understood little, they began their own voyage in the opposite direction. New knowledges—geography, physics, botany, and mineralogy—were the goods sought by the Lima elite.

It is well known that the Enlightenment encouraged an "aliento nacionalista" (nationalist enthusiasm). Enlightenment intellectuals' interest in geography, fauna, and flora inspired an interest in the past in members of the learned society Amantes del País, among others. According to Porras Barrenechea, *El Mercurio Peruano* "is concerned with uncovering the spiritual past of Peru."[57] In 1816, the viceroy Rodríguez de Mendoza puzzles over the absence of historical and geographical knowledge. Ignoring or forgetting the orders issued by Charles V prohibiting the writing of history and of the Indians' "antiguallas," the viceroy interpellates no one and everyone at the same time when he asks: "And what reason might there be to ignore

56. See Edward W. Said, *Orientalism* (New York: Vintage Books, 1979).
57. Porras Barrenechea, *Fuentes historicas peruanas,* 473.

the geography and history of the land beneath our feet?"[58] It seems also that the viceroy's questions gloss over the fact that the expulsion of the Jesuits in 1767 resulted in a "loss of management and entrepreneurial efficiency [intimately connected] to the Jesuits' establishment of teachers colleges, schools and universities in Lima and Cuzco"[59] as well as an incipient but strong interest in the writing of local "American" histories.

Mexico: A Case in Point

The most salient loss in geography and history was of course the departure of the exiled Jesuit Clavijero (1731–1787), who had begun to write *Historia Antigua de Mexico* (1780) while still in Mexico and expecting to be appointed to the newly created chair in antiquities at the Real Pontificia Universidad.[60] Clavijero laments the loss of the sources that Sigüenza y Góngora (1645–1700) had so lovingly accumulated on Mexican antiquity. The Jesuit sees himself following in the footsteps of the foundational gestures of the first "Mexicanist."[61] Like Sigüenza y Góngora, and also in emulation of Garcilaso, but in contrast with the Amantes del País, Clavijero states that his "desire is to advance the claims of both strands of inheritance."[62] For Clavijero, Mexico's glory and possible nationhood meant the relation of the ancient past (Aztec) to the present (post-colonial).

In this regard, Ignacio Bernal points out that "Mexican patriotism saw itself as a cultural and not a political matter." Anticipating Renan, for Sigüenza y Góngora, Clavijero, and the Nahuatl scholar Augustín de Vetancourt, culture and nation were not only equivalent but in fact depended on each other.[63] For them, as in the case of the Cuzco elite, the sites of culture/nation were the original Indian records, books (codices), "maps," sculptures, calendar stones, temples, pyramids, and "myths" and accounts

58. Ibid.
59. Klarén, *Peru,* 101.
60. See Bernal, *A History of Mexican Archaeology,* 14.
61. The "sociedades económicas de amigos del pais" which proved crucial to the development of Spanish American intellectuals at the time of the Enlightenment owe their origin, partly, to the stress that Padre Benito Jerónimo Feijóo (1676–1764) placed on experience and direct observation in learning (Bernal, *A History of Mexican Archaeology,* 72).
62. Ibid., 52.
63. Ibid., 54.

of the past. The fortuitous but consequential presence of Leonardo Boturini, who arrived in Mexico in 1736, contributed strongly, if strangely, to further the equivalence between nation and culture.

Boturini's affection for and obsession with Sigüenza's papers and collection of antiquities led to the catastrophic confiscation of the collection by the Spanish authorities in Mexico. The collection continued to suffer important losses even later in Spain where Boturini had sought refuge for and with what he salvaged as he fled persecution by the colonial authorities in Mexico. His *Idea de una Nueva Historia General de la America Septentrional* (1746), largely based on Giambatista Vico's ideas on history, reopened the question of the origins of the American Indians and the problems involved in thinking about history in universal (homogeneous space-time) terms.[64] Although Boturini's work met with something less than success, it prompted Clavijero's sense of urgency about his own project. It clarified the need for the institutionalization of the study of the Mexican past, conceived as a line that led directly to the origins of the Amerindian peoples. Bernal notes that when the hearing of Boturini's case regarding his unauthorized stay in Mexico and the possession of parts of the confiscated collection was over in Spain, the Consejo de Indias recommended the establishment of an Academia de la Historia de Mexico in the capital of New Spain.[65]

No such thought ever crossed the minds of the Spanish authorities who put down the Tupac Amaru II rebellion, despite the fact that many of the measures taken in the aftermath of the rebellion implicitly and explicitly recognized the culturalist nature of the nationalist thinking today recognized as "ahead" of its time. Perhaps the fact that Boturini was an Italian working with Vico's ideas and the fact that he seemed to be dealing mainly with alphabetic encoding of memory records weighed on the minds of the Spanish authorities and caused them to think of Boturini's history as an enterprise of their own. Perhaps even more important in the reception of Boturini's work by the Spanish authorities was the fact that the French Revolution had not yet occurred.

At any rate, the Amantes del País in Peru did not accept in silence the

---

64. It is well known that Boturini's idea of history as a time construct derived from Vico's (1668–1744) *Scienza Nova* (1725), which in turn was based on the study of Roman law. Following Vico's division of the temporal line, Boturini envisions three breaks as a way of organizing his knowledge of Mexico's past: a divine world (the time of the gods), a heroic world (the time of heroes), and a time of humans. Bernal, *History of Mexican Archaeology,* 59.

65. Bernal, *History of Mexican Archaeology,* 61.

racist and anti-American views of the Enlightenment. Like Clavijero, in trying to bring forth the evidence that would sustain their claims regarding the
intelligence and accomplishment of Amerindians, the Amantes del País
wrote in 1791 an entire issue of the *Mercurio Peruano* dedicated to Peruvian antiquities, ruins, and monuments.[66] They took special notice of Cor-
nelius de Pauw, a young Edinburgh botanist responsible for editing the first
edition of the *Encyclopedia Britannica,* and the generally negative judgments on the Peruvian and pre-Columbian past described therein.

Bernal points out that many of the Jesuits exiled in Rome, informed by
their many years of residence in Ibero-America, were infuriated by the thesis on American inferiority developed by the major intellectual figures of
the time (David Hume, George-Louis Leclerc Buffon, and Georg Hegel,
among others). Clavijero wrote especially to counter the work of the ency-
clopedist de Pauw in his *Recherches Philosophiques sur les Américaine*
(1768).[67] Because Clavijero was in Italy, he based his work mainly on papers and Aztec paintings. But he could not emphasize strongly enough the
importance of ruins and monuments for history writing as well as the need
to preserve them as the chief evidence of the nation's glorious past. Thus
the connection of the nation to ruins of the past was already established by
Clavijero.

The Emergence of an Archaeospace

It is significant to remember that the first history of Mexico appears before
the wars of independence, while in the case of Peru the nation will have to
wait for an entire century before thinking about the past achieves an intellectual coherence that permits the emergence of a line, jagged and broken
as it may be, that traces causes and effects. The past, as the time of dead ancestors, will first appear in the discourse of the nation as the work of archaeology. The nation then slowly emerges as an archaeospace that both
marks and erases the distance from the past. A new archaeospace is born
where the landmarks bear names such as Pachacamac, Chavin, Tiahuanacu,
and Chan-Chan.[68]

66. Porras Barrenechea, *Fuentes historicas peruanas,* 57.
67. Bernal, *History of Mexican Archaeology,* 68–74.
68. Archaeology has recently been the object of a postmodern critique. Finding
meaning in the past is no longer a simple and transparent objective act of knowledge for
archaeologists. The interpretation of material culture is now being carefully examined

One could argue that the defeat of the proto-nationalist project had a paralyzing effect on thinking the nation. As in the case of the French Revolution, the Tupac Amaru II rebellion produced a breach with the immediate past that in some ways began to be perceived as "other." In France, as the country began to change from a rural society into a place of urban dwellers, a "massive disruption of traditional forms of memory . . . [occurred, and] the past begins to look like a foreign country."[69] The institution of memory and thus the question of history became a critical preoccupation. Intellectuals began an inquiry into what was to be called the "modern" as distinct from the past. No greater contrast could be drawn than with the bleak historical scene in Peru in which the sequence of two great breaks with the past produced the incontestable silence of the nineteenth century.

At issue is the concept of the past. If memory is the key agent in the construction of the past, the would-be historian in Peru encountered immediately the disquieting lack of transparency of the written and nonalphabetic records of the past. The facts of conquest made the recording of memory a problematic modality for access to the past. Instead of establishing records, narratives, and subjects, memory in the plural seems to breed controversy, alternative knowledges, and disputed accounts. Something more solid and less plurivocal and contestable than the accounts of the Spanish chroniclers is needed in order to provide the foundations on which the house of the nation can be built.

It is widely acknowledged that the father of modern, scientific archaeology in Peru was the German scholar Max Uhle whose long residence and

---

in its practices and history. Henrietta Moore examines the sensitive link between archaeology and origins and points to the fact that "narratives in archeology and anthropology often mislead, and they mislead because they present themselves as concerned with beginnings." She warns that "our stories of the past must end with the present . . . our representations of the past are shaped not by what we know to be true of the past, but by what we believe to be true of the past." Moore, "The Problems of Origins: Poststructuralism and Beyond," in *Interpreting Archaeology: Finding Meaning in the Past,* ed. Ian Hodder (London and New York: Routledge, 1995), 51. I have already pointed out that I was going to treat the many approaches to the construction of the past that the writing of history entails in a Benjaminian way, in as much as the past is always approached from the urgency of the present. Moore's concerns dove tail with my own genealogical approach. In this regard, Ian Hodder's questions on context and the reading of material culture as a text are also important for any study dealing with archaeology and its hermeneutical power. See Ian Hodder, *Reading the Past: Current Approaches to Interpretation in Archaeology* (Cambridge and New York: Cambridge University Press, 1991).

69. See Terdiman, *Present Past,* 5.

undisputed authority in and on Peru was encapsulated in the fact that between 1906 and 1912 he was the director of the Museo Histórico de Lima.[70]
Uhle's scientific studies (measurements of monuments and sites in combination with stratigraphic excavation and regional chronology)[71] of ruins and
other archaeological monuments is not without important precedents. In
fact, it is almost impossible to separate the history of archaeology in Peru
during the first half of the nineteenth century from the history of scientific
travel and exploration.

In his search for historical sources, Porras Barrenechea lists only one
prominent local collector of antiquities: the opulent Lima businessman Pedro Bravo de Lagunas. Another person mentioned by Porras is Llano Zap-
ata who apparently wrote a memoir in which he described "restos incaicos
de templos, acueductos y caminos."[72] As a landscape configured by ruins,
as a territory of interest because of its connection to antiquities, or as an archaeospace, Peru begins to make brief but repeated appearances in the trav-
elogues of scientists and explorers. In these texts the past is not only "other,"
due to its remoteness in time, but it is also other because of its remoteness
in spatial distance from Europe and its cultural distance from both the past
and modern times in European space-time. The ruins stand out in their
grandeur but their allure is underscored precisely by the neglect and even
remoteness with which the local intellectuals regard them. "Hieratic" and
"hermetic" are the preferred adjectives intended to describe the monuments.
Upon a closer look, it is clear that both "hieratic" and "hermetic" speak
more accurately of scientists' sense of their own incapacity to read the monument than of the monument's own semiotic status. However, this very
sense of labored or impossible interpretation is what makes depicting the
ruins irresistible especially to the explorer who includes in his retinue a
good draftsman, as Humboldt did.

The French traveler and botanist José Dombey (in Peru between 1778
and 1785) left perhaps the most lasting impression among Peruvians.[73]

---

70. Porras Barrenechea, *Fuentes historicas peruanas,* 73.

71. See Paul G. Bahn, *The Cambridge Illustrated History of Archaeology* (Cambridge and New York: Cambridge University Press, 1996), 195–196.

72. Porras Barrenechea, *Fuentes historicas peruanas,* 57.

73. Pascal Riviale, *Los viajeros franceses en busca del Peru antiguo (1821–1914)*
(Lima: Instituto Francés de Estudios Andinos, 2000). Writing from a French point of
view, Riviale says that the first eyewitness information about Peru to arrive in France
was the product of the commercial route opened by the merchants of Saint-Malo in the
early eighteenth century. This was followed by reports of educated travelers such as

Dombey was the first "scientist" to venture beyond Lima. In *Imagen francesa del Peru: Siglos XVI–XIX,* Pablo Macera[74] indicates that most of Dombey's originals were lost in the fire that he set to his papers after returning to France. Nevertheless, it is known that he kept a botanical and archaeological diary. He visited and measured Pachacamac, and upon his return he took some fine Paracas textiles and 400 *huacos* (ceramics buried in pre-Columbian tombs) intended as gifts for Louis XIV.[75] Macera says that "hasta Dombey la arqueología no existía en el Perú."[76]

Humboldt's arrival in 1802, his admiration for the "simplicity, symmetry, solidity and consistency" of Inca architecture[77] closes the eighteenth century's views on archaeology, leaving one puzzling message to the incipient groupings of intellectuals in Peru.[78] Despite the disparaging views

---

Feuillée in 1714, Frézier in 1716, and Le Gentil in 1727. He adds that "Las instrucciones 'etnográficas' remitidas por el Abad Barthelemy al botánico Joseph Dombay constituyen una interesante ilustración de las modificaciones sobrevenidas tanto en la percepción que se tenía del Perú y de las fuentes documentales útiles como en la manera de enfocar éstas" (24).

74. See Pablo Macera, *Imagen francesa del Peru: Siglos XVI–XIX* (Lima: Instituto Nacional de Cultura, 1976). According to Macera, until the publication of the results of Charles-Marie La Condamine's expedition (1751), most of what the French knew about Peru was derived from the *Comentarios reales.* Slowly ideas derived from the Spanish chronicler began to be displaced by the knowledge amassed by French explorers in America (30–34). Dombey's works follow in the footsteps of La Condamine, although it is important to remember here that most of them are lost (41). Nevertheless, he is the first naturalist who traveled to the interior of Peru and also the first to attempt a close examination of Pachacamac (44–45).

75. Macera writes that while in Peru, Dombey was attacked by members of the Spanish Ruiz y Pavón expedition with the intent to rob him of his research. The botanist Ortega coveted Dombey's botanical collection and in fact modeled the *Flora Peruviana* on the method and classification grid developed by Dombey. Upon returning to France in 1785 at the age of forty-three, Dombey's health was ruined. "Calvo, con escorbuto, sin dientes, resentido con su gobierno y con la corte de Madrid, se retiró a Lyon casi loco y en un momento de desesperación quemó los originales de la obra que pensaba dedicar a Luis XVI." Macera, *Imagen francesa del Peru,* 59.

76. Macera, *Imagen francesa del Peru,* 59.

77. Porras Barrenechea, *Fuentes historicas peruanas,* 58. Humboldt attributed all architecture, roads, and aqueducts in Peru to the Incas. His imagination did not encompass the existence of other highly sophisticated pre-Inca cultures.

78. In 1839 the French scientist Alcide d'Orbigny (1802–1857) published his *L'Homme Américaine* in which he proposed a new classification of Amerindian "races." The American physiologist Samuel George Morton had just published his *Crania Americana* (1839). Based on cranial measurements taken from his worldwide skull collection, Morton concluded that there was not a single human species but several, each with

expressed by the encyclopedists, the remnants of the pre-Columbian past
were a focus of interest and even admiration for those who actually visited
Peru and directly experienced the scope and features of the territory.[79] If archaeological preoccupations were the province of the travelers, digging was
still in the hands of the *huaqueros* (robbers of pre-Columbian tombs), with
the notable exception of a "peruano aireado en Europa,"[80] Mariano Eduardo
Rivero. Both Porras and Estuardo Núñez consider Rivero "el precursor de
nuestra moderna ciencia arqueológica" (the forerunner of our modern archaeological science).[81] This Peruvian, "aired out in Europe" (i.e., Rivero
spent time studying and living in Europe), is on Porras's list of sources used
in writing the *History of Peru,* but virtually nothing is available on the life
or work of Rivero.

Narrating the Nation's Archaeospace

The story of the book Rivero wrote is not only interesting but germane to
the matter at hand, for it encapsulates the guiding idea of this chapter: the
redefinition of the idea of the nation after the Tupac Amaru II rebellion in
light of the establishment of an inextricable time line between the nation
and an archaeospace made possible in "modern" Peru by the new science
of archaeology.

The life and work of Rivero appears indelibly intertwined with the life
and research of Johann Jacob von Tschudi (1818–1889), the Swiss scholar
who arrived in Peru in 1838 with a degree in medicine, but ended up making a major contribution in Quechua linguistics and archaeology. Like
Dombey, Tschudi was also a naturalist who devoted equal attention to the

---

a separate origin. D'Orbigny, basing his arguments on data collected during his stay in
Bolivia (1830–1833), proved Morton incorrect. These two studies opened the nineteenth
century's debates on the origin and diversity of the Amerindian peoples. Despite the fact
that d'Orbigny spent only a couple of months in Peru and was unable to visit any major
archaeological site, the long-standing debate of the origin of Amerindian peoples is very
much in Rivero's mind and research. In his book he gives a detailed account of the latest episodes in the debate and contests any view that posits separate origins. For more
on d'Orbigny, see Riviale's *Los viajeros franceses,* 22–54.

79. In *Fuentes históricas peruanas,* Porras ratified this state of affairs: "[D]urante la
primera etapa republicana la curiosidad arqueológica es tan solo patrimonio de los huaqueros, [y] algunos coleccionistas empíricos" (53).

80. Ibid., 58.

81. Ibid., 59.

fauna, flora, geography, and the language of the native people. Despite the fact the Tschudi's major work would eventually result in a study of Quechua and especially of its literary forms and the *Apu Ollantay,*[82] at the time of his arrival in Peru most explorers and travelers still believed in a clear distinction between "nature" and "history." The "native" people and their costumes and other remnants of their past belonged to the *nature* side of the divide. Even language and city building, two instances of collective and individual consciousness, failed to be included on the *history* side. Such a division continued the logic inaugurated with the Conquest, based as it was on the denial of coevalness. The challenge for Rivero, Tschudi's good friend, guide, and colleague, was to find the knowledge apparatus that would allow him to reverse the ideological assumptions imbedded in the naturalist's episteme. Thus far, ruins had testified not to the past as present but rather to the past as distinct and disconnected from the present.[83] The task of linking the glorious but ruined past to the rising nation fell not to history (documentary and archival) but rather to archaeology (visible, tactile, and measurable, and nonalphabetic). The immediate and unmediated presence of the ruins, like the fauna and flora, appeared ready to be taken by the naked eye or by instruments newly designed by science, all of which mimicked the visual structures of perception of the eye, unfettered by the letter.

Rivero was born in Arequipa and studied in Europe during the first quarter of the nineteenth century.[84] His field of study was mineralogy. It is fair to surmise that his education in Europe was probably aimed at the acquisi-

82. *Apu Ollantay* was a popular Quechua drama in the eighteenth century. First performed for Tupac Amaru II in 1780, it is written in the pre-conquest Wanka traditional composition style of enacting historical deeds. The play tells the story of the warrior Ollantay, his illicit love for an Inca princess and subsequent rebellion and punishment. After the Tupac Amaru II rebellion, the Spanish authorities banned the secular Quechua language theater. Suppression of this drama tradition offers proof of the force that such theater retained for the indigenous people's sense of identity. For further discussion of the origins and history of Quechua drama in the Andes, see Roberto González Echevarría and Enrique Pupo-Walker, eds., *The Cambridge History of Latin American Literature,* vol. 1 (Cambridge: Cambridge University Press, 1996), 55,262, 406.

83. The challenge remained throughout the nineteenth century and continued into the twentieth century. In the case of d'Orbigny, whose work showed France that Peru was much more than fauna and flora, his views of the people and society were nevertheless disparaging and negative. "Con las opiniones políticas de d'Orbigny . . . el Perú descendía a la categoría de una tribu en contraste con su pasado histórico y sus recursos naturales. Las dos imágenes no parecían coincidir." Macera, *Imagen francesa del Peru,* 116.

84. Porras Barrenechea, *Fuentes históricas peruanas,* 62.

tion of up-to-date knowledges in mining and chemistry. In 1826, the year when Bolívar departed from Peru, Rivero was named the first director of the Museo Nacional by the Liberator himself. The mining engineer was obviously well connected in the upper ranks of Peruvians fighting for control of the state, for he was chosen to lead one of the most self-referential institutions and key sites of memory in the nation-state.

Rivero's interest in antiquities was obviously shared by an influential sector of the elite. Two years after his inauguration (1828), he wrote an article on Peruvian antiquities. It eventually became the book-length study that he published with Tschudi's help in Vienna. *Antigüedades peruanas* (1851) was published under an ambiguous authorial connection with Tschudi.[85] It was the first book authored by a Peruvian to be published with a very large number of color plates on the many mummies, cranial remains, textiles, huacos, maps, and monuments studied in the text. According to Porras, the rather lengthy book "awakened curiosity concerning archaeology . . . and is the point of departure for all such investigations undertaken in the nineteenth century."[86] The book has often been attributed to Tschudi, but Porras confidently states: "[T]he true author of this synthesis of Peruvian historical and archaeological knowledge at the middle of the nineteenth century is Rivero."[87] Tschudi himself, in the prologue, endorsed the book without reservations and gave all the credit to Rivero.[88]

One of the most important changes to arise with scientific travel literature was the appearance of a sort of double vision, as the pages of the books

---

85. Estuardo Núñez, in *Viajes y viajeros extranjeros por el Perú* (Lima: Conacyt, 1989), says that Tschudi is "uno de los mas típicos viajeros románticos que asoman por el Perú" (325). But he does not detail the reason why, for him, Tschudi's work is "romantic" other than to speak of his delight in life and his sense of adventure. Núñez does make a distinction between the "romantic traveler" and the later scientific explorers (325). However, Núñez states that the *Antigüedades peruanas* is indeed the first work of scientific archaeology on Peru (329), and that Tschudi understands the entire work to be Rivero's with the exception of the chapters on language, which is, of course, what Tschudi himself says in the introduction to the *Antigüedades*.

86. Porras Barrenechea, *Fuentes historicas peruanas*, 61.

87. Ibid., 60.

88. Tschudi himself is credited with having initiated serious philological work on the Quechua language and its textual realizations. Núñez writes that "frente al poco rigor filológico de Markham [Clement Robert Markham (1830–1916)], Tschudi señaló el rumbo en la investigación filológica del drama." Núñez, *Viajes y viajeros extranjeros por el Perú*, 332. Shortly before his death, Tschudi published in Leipzig a collection of his works on the Quechua language, which includes essays on "historia cultural y lingüística del Peru antiguo" (332).

grew richly illustrated with black and white sketches and color plates. Rivero was familiar not only with the work of scientific travelers to Peru such as Dombey and Charles Marie de La Condamine, he was also a student of the work of other botanists and ethnographers who made extensive use of illustrations. In addition, he was aware of the new scientific methods and technologies introduced by Humboldt. The impact of Humboldt's method and descriptive vision can be better assessed in light of the systematic publication of his beautifully and abundantly illustrated 35 volumes published between 1807 and 1839 in Paris. Drawings, sketches, and plates figure as key elements in the configuration of knowledges that Rivero sought to bring together in his *Antigüedades.*

Antigüedades peruanas presents the object of cognition in the conjunction of written words with graphics. The "reader"/viewer takes in the linguistic description informed by the graphic "illustration." The travelogue aspects of Rivero's book coordinates what the author sees with his own eyes with what the reader sees on the page. This doubly mediated seeing nevertheless inscribes the value of the direct experience of the present onto the world as if it were a totally new perspective. The travelogue of the scientist relies also on the conceit of the new. Rivero takes advantage of the idea that scientific traveling configures a totally "new" America as it is apprehended by new methods and perspectives. Macera argues that the modern and scientific thrust of the explorer bolsters his claims to knowledge and authority with the powerful innovation of the graphic impact of maps, charts, and views of the land, the fauna, the flora, volcanoes, and human types on the land. Rivero's rendition of ruins, skulls, ceramics, and people on the land profit from the "visual methodology" inaugurated by Humboldt.[89]

The traveler archaeologist joins to his scientific descriptions the emotional experience of the encounter with the object of his desire. The thrill of being for the first time in front of an "unknown" landscape is brought back by the traveler to share with his audience. The historical operation of the travelogue is to produce at once, as Michel de Certeau showed in the case

89. Although centered on the "vision" of "race," Deborah Poole's discussion of the traveler's gaze lays the groundwork for future studies on the intersection of archaeology and other topics in nation building and imaging. See especially chapter 3, "An Economy of Vision," in *Vision, Race, and Modernity.* In reference to Humboldt, Poole remarks that "[i]t was his interest in migration that fueled Humboldt's study of New World archaeology, for it was in the mute stones and hieroglyphs of the Andean and Mexican archaeology that he hoped to read America's 'racial' history" (76).

of Jean de Léry,[90] the ruin as a virtual object immediately available to the pleasures of the reader and at the same time mark the difference and distance between the reader's experience in his chair and the object in real time and space, out there, in America. The travelogue creates a flat surface in which the objects appear in the memory dimensions and dynamics of the traveler.

However, in the case of Rivero, the objects remain in the immediacy of the land, "the land beneath our feet," as Viceroy Rodríguez indicated. The distance produced by the travelogue as genre is narrowed in the case of a national narrative such as *Antigüedades peruanas* (1851). The writing/ sketching dynamics of the travelogue and of the "news of the empire" thus play only a minimal part in the work Rivero wrote in conversation with Tschudi. The Swiss scholar, it is important to say here, by reason of his contact with Quechua as a living language, also altered his initial plans and ended up moving Quechua to the side of ethnohistory in the nature/history divide.[91] Rivero's chief interests and perspectives are actually historical, for the archaeospace of Peru that he develops is more concerned with the age of the object than with the characteristics of the space. Thus, Rivero's work on "antiquities" establishes the indissoluble link between history and archaeology, between the "hieratic" monuments and the discourse that renders them into an ongoing history. To this effect, he writes:

> Among all the sciences which are involved in the study of history, none exceeds in importance archeology, or the knowledge of the monuments and antiquities; a science which, has proceeded to tear the veil which covered the past ages, synthetically to reconstruct the events of remote periods, and to supply the scarcity and total absence of chronicle and tradition.[92]

I have not been able to secure the Spanish edition of *Antigüedades peruanas*. However, I was surprised to learn that less than two years after its publication in Vienna and the solemn presentation that Rivero made of it to the Peruvian Congress, an English-language edition was already circulating in

90. Michel de Certeau, *The Writing of History,* trans. Tom Conley (New York: Columbia University Press, 1988), 209–243.

91. Back in Vienna and especially during the later part of his life, Tschudi continued to correspond with his "Amigo entrañable de la juventud, Mariano Eduardo Rivero." See Núñez, *Viajes y viajeros al Peru,* 328.

92. Mariano Eduardo Rivero and John James von Tschudi, *Peruvian Antiquities,* trans. Francis L. Hawks (New York: George Putman & Co. 1853), 1.

the United States. German and French translations also appeared the same year.[93] The English translation carries a reduced number of plates and none in color.[94] Although most of the sketches appear as part of the last chapter, which is dedicated to the description of ancient monuments, on the page opposite the title page is a long, complex view of the sizeable architectural remains and landscape of the "Palace or temple of the island of Coati, in Lake Titicaca." The sacred island in Lake Titicaca is one of the presumed places of origins of the Incas.

According to Francis L. Hawks, the English translator, the immediate translation and publication of the book was undertaken in view of the popularity achieved by Prescott's *History of the Conquest of Peru*. Rivero's book is also judged to offer "much that did not fall within the design of [Prescott's] admirable work."[95] Indeed Rivero's organization of knowledge reveals a plan to incorporate the apparatus and discourse of the new sciences into a thorough and vast investigation. He had two aims in mind: first, the reexamination of the Spanish chroniclers in search of (hard) data, and second, to bring to bear on the subject the latest developments in Europe and the United States in anthropological (physical and cultural), archaeological, and linguistic studies.

Perhaps ahead of his time, Rivero's foundational project calls for a comparative method. "We are not of the number of those blind admirers of the ancient Peruvian culture. . . . [Neither do we consider] the narratives of the old Spanish chroniclers . . . mere fables.[96] His is then a research project that does indeed live up to the "conscientious comparison of these narratives with the remains of Peruvian antiquity."[97] Although he is one of the first Americanists to plough systematically through the writings of José de Acosta, Cieza de León, Fray Marcos de Niza, Fernando de Montesinos, and many others, as well as the archival records used by Prescott, Rivero relies heavily if not on the data, certainly on the vision of Garcilaso de la Vega, El Inca. Rivero deals with what he calls Garcilaso's "partiality,"[98] and he warns the reader to take Garcilaso with a grain of salt. However, when it comes to

93. Núñez, *Viajes y viajeros al Peru,* 338.
94. The translator Francis L. Hawks indicates that the Spanish original has fifty-eight large plates, "most of them colored and all beautifully executed." Rivero and Tschudi, *Peruvian Antiquities,* xi.
95. Ibid., Introduction, n.p.
96. Ibid., xiii.
97. Ibid.
98. Ibid., 47–49.

what Renan later would call the "spirit of the nation," Rivero cannot resist the seduction structured by Garcilaso's voice, style, elegant nostalgia, and subtly contestatory historiography.

If Garcilaso's effort to somehow merge[99] Andean knowledges with Renaissance epistemologies and historiography was monumental and almost superhuman, the task Rivero set for himself was in a way even more daunting. Rivero faces the infinite expansion of European knowledge operating together with the ever fading Andean knowledges and memory. Much of Rivero's book is taken up, like the *Comentarios reales,* with correcting the myriad old and new accounts and inventions of the origin of the Amerindian peoples, the origin and chronology of the Incas, and so on. Like Garcilaso he corrects by showing the contradiction active in the knowledges characterized by the "fabulous" and often dehumanizing accounts of the people and their culture. He also marshals the contemporary scientific evidence available—cranial measurements, observation and description of mummy bundles, temporal estimates on the antiquity of the ruins, and comparative studies of Old World religions and linguistics. Unlike Garcilaso, who longed to return to Peru so that he could have better sources and the privilege of firsthand observation and collecting, Rivero had at his disposal two key fields of memory and depositories of information: language and ruins.

Tschudi claims authorship for chapter 5 of the *Antigüedades,* the chapter dedicated to the Quechua language and literary compositions. It is clear that both men, unlike Renan, recognize the intimate relation of language to the historiographical operation and most especially to the archaeological project. They find it strange that "even those who have studied the archeology of [Peru and Bolivia] have passed by the study of the idioms spoken by their independent and powerful inhabitants in earlier times. Without doubt language is the chief archeological element, the sole monument of reconstruction [for] the entire essence of a people."[100]

In his preface, Rivero considers that the study of history is important to the present of the republic inasmuch as it can be instructive of how past societies "prepare a people for the enjoyment of national liberty."[101] In other words, the study of ancient Peru is neither part of a Romantic curiosity nor

---

99. See Sara Castro-Klarén, "Mimicry Revisited: Latin America, Post-colonial Theory and the Location of Knowledge," in *El debate de la postcolonialidad en latinoamerica,* ed. Alfonso de Toro and Fernando de Toro (Frankfurt and Main: Vervuert, 1999), 137–164.

100. Rivero and Tschudi, *Peruvian Antiquities,* 93.

101. Ibid., 1.

is it an addition to the cult of exoticism. If "modern" nations grounded the possibility of a future on the idea of the rational exercise of liberty (by its very nature, ephemeral), then the government envisioned and practiced by the Incas—on the very same land on which the Peruvian nation-state struggled to define itself—had something relevant to say. Like Garcilaso and the Tupac Amaru II rebellion before him, Rivero understands that "the code which governed the Ancient Peruvian nation, dictated by its founder, Manco Capac . . . laid the foundations of that public happiness, of which for some centuries his descendants have been deprived."[102]

Rivero adds that his plan is to study the beneficial institutions "on the very spot where they existed," to examine their archeological monuments, "to obtain an exact knowledge of the language, laws, science, religion and customs." All of this is to be done by complementing archival and library knowledges with travel and firsthand material observation, for he has traversed "the land of the Incas."[103]

The Ethnographic Territorial Nation

Rivero's discourse articulates three key notions in the discourse of the nation: ethnographic priority and descent, territorial permanence, and originary language. Rivero, contrary to Renan, affirms the primacy of these three components in the making of nation. These are the very notions that Renan took up some forty years later in "What Is a Nation?" and which remain alive in today's discussion of the making of imagined communities. In *Antigüedades peruanas,* by way of establishing the scientific permanence of the ruins, Rivero performs an inverse historical operation to Renan's and Anderson's reading of the invention of the nation. Like Garcilaso, he *joins together* what the Conquest and European historiography had set apart. The present geography of Peru, mediated by archaeology, is indeed claimed as the same land (landscape) as the one crafted and transformed by the Incas. Temporal distance is thus narrowed or even sutured together so as to produce the "same" space, continuous in time. Therefore, human events happened on the "same" territory and the people today are indeed the descendants of the Inca empire. Today's people long for, and in fact have embarked

102. Ibid.
103. Ibid., x.

on a search for public happiness (the rational exercise of liberty), under the banner of a nation-state that actually did exist in the past.

While Rivero's line of descent is clear, from the Incas to the current nation-state, the identity of the descendants appears at best ambiguous and blurred precisely because he wants to produce a national subject beyond the existing distinctions among Indians, mestizos, and criollos. He also wants to produce a subject beyond the anthropological debate on cranial measurements and diverse human origins. It is not ease to determine if Rivero also labors under the contradiction encapsulated in "Incas sí, indios no" as was later the case with the aristocratic historian José de la Riva Agüero (1885–1944). Descriptions of the Incas' crafts of religion, architecture, road building, medicine, and other knowledges and arts do not stay confined to the past in Rivero's narrative, for he brings in ethnographic findings to illuminate the remnants of the past. His present observations and considerations on language, theater, and poetry are used to round out or penetrate our understanding of the past. Archaeology—the observation, dating, assessment, and interpretation of ruins—is the one branch of knowledge and modality of presentation of the past that overwhelms the past/present divide by which the "modern" republic is unquestionably turned into the "land of the Incas." The archaeological perspective transforms the nation's territory into a field of memory. Andean topography acquires a new disposition. Its borders and delineations reflect the location and size of the cultural areas identified around the chief ruins of temples, administrative centers, cities, roads, and aqueducts. Tiahuanaco, Huanuco Viejo, Pachacamac, Chan-Chan, Chavin, and Paramonga constitute the new lexicon that names the archaeospace of the nation.

Conclusions

Fortunately for Rivero's foundational enterprise—raising the nation from the ruins of the past—language, line of descent, territory, tradition, and archaeospace were available to him as both empirical experience and epistemological categories. Despite Renan's disqualifiers, these categories continue to be the foundational blocks of the nation's narrative. Memory, as in the case of Garcilaso, weaves a myriad of fables that connects and intertwines linkages between territory and human occupation in time and space. The telling of narratives yields the "spirit" of the nation.

However, the spirit of the nation, that indispensable "extra," arises in

Peru at the confluence of myriad lines and sites of memory and forgetting. It is clear that the Tupac Amaru II movement had kept and dynamized a memory and narrative of the nation well outside the bonds of print and the print culture of the Creole elites. Nevertheless, the rebellion's memory and its modes of inscription left in its wake a sense of the (ethnographic) nation as a place and people connected with the pre-Conquest past that is still present in ruins and language. Archaeology throughout the nineteenth and twentieth centuries enlarged the territory of the archaeospace that first appeared in book form by Rivero. With the growth of the archaeospace of the nation, the time gap between past and present narrows. And thus the Chilean poet Pablo Neruda feels at ease claiming Macchu Picchu as the cradle for all "American" past and present "nations." Finally, in 1990 the Peruvian archaeologist Luis Lumbreras in his epilogue to the secondary school manual *Visión Arqueológica del Perú Milenario* can confidently write on the relationships among humanity, land, and knowledge: "The earth grew in our hands and our wisdom. . . . We learned the secrets that made us great, with much labor, and our sages [*amautas*] carefully kept them. Every peasant filled his hands with history."[104] Lumbreras's understanding of the relationship between archaeology and the nation's present and future articulates the space where the national subject appears consolidated in a plural "nosotros"—the descendants of the pre-Conquest Andeans—and "nuestros" that Rivero could only posit as a utopian subject on and in the "land of the Incas." That subject stands the test of time, for it is the object of the safekeeping of the amautas now reconfigured, by the power of archaeology, into the ancestors of a long, if often broken, line of intellectuals thinking the nation in ways and manners that exceed the narrow epistemology of the written word and its printed dissemination.

104. Luis Lumbreras, *Visión arqueológica del Perú milenario* (Lima: Milla Batres, 1990), 323.

7

An Amnesic Nation: The Erasure of Indigenous Pasts by Uruguayan Expert Knowledges

Gustavo Verdesio

A study of foundational narratives in Latin America must be aware of the origin of the concept "nation." As is well known, the concept originated in Europe,[1] and it presents the nation as a continuous narrative of progress and narcissistic self-generation[2] as an act of self-realization performed by a homogeneous society. As with all constructs, nations are cultural artifacts and, in order to understand them, "we need to consider carefully *how they have come into historical being, in what ways their meanings have changed over time,* and why, today, they command such profound emotional legitimacy" [my emphasis].[3] In the case of Uruguay, it is very clear that the way in which

1. Hugh Seton-Watson, *Nations and States* (Boulder, CO: Westview Press, 1977), 220.
2. Homi K. Bhabha, "Introduction: Narrating the Nation," in Bhabha, *Nation and Narration* (London and New York: Routledge, 1990), 1.
3. Benedict Anderson, *Imagined Communities* (London: Verso, 1983), 13–14. Anthony Birch also believes the nation is a construct: "[N]ations are relatively recent and relatively artificial creations." Birch, *Nationalism and National Integration* (London: Unwin Hyman, 1989), 8.

the nation came into historical being was a consequence of the adoption of strategies and values originated in what is known as the West. This situation, which is not exclusively Uruguayan, is taken into account by Seton-Watson's distinction between old and new nations:

It is, however, important to distinguish between two categories of nations, which we will call the "old" and the "new." The old are those that acquired national identity or national consciousness before the doctrine of nationalism was formulated. The new include those for whom two processes developed simultaneously: the formation of national consciousness and the creation of nationalistic movements. Both processes were the work of small, educated political elites.[4]

The new Latin American republics had to confront the problem of not being a nation in the same sense that the European ones were; hence, the need to generate a national history, a national culture, and an official educational system, all necessary resources for the creation of national consciousness.[5] The situation of those new nations was perceived a few decades

4. Seton-Watson, *Nations and States,* 6–7. Joshua Fishman's distinction between state-nation (characterized by the preexistence of the state from which the creation of a nation is fostered) and nation-state (where the nation exists before the state) relates to the one offered by Seton-Watson, but the latter emphasizes the emergence of national consciousness while the former focuses on the chronological precedence of one notion over the other. Fishman, *Language and Nationalism: Two Integrative Essays* (Rowley, MA: Newbury House, 1973), 24–28.

5. Boyd C. Shafer, *Faces of Nationalism* (New York: Harcourt Brace Jovanovich), 195–218; Johann Gottlieb Fichte, *The Characteristics of the Present Age,* trans. William Smith (London: John Chapman, 1849), 220. About the role of ideological apparatuses, see the following passage by Angel Rama: "Convenciones no escritas que integran el modo operativo de las clases dirigentes (a cuyas necesidades responden) y que incluso no necesitan ejercerse coercitivamente, sino que se trasmiten por la pedagogía oficial, por el dominio de los sistemas de expresión y comunicación, por una especie de moral pública intangible" (Nonwritten conventions that integrate the operative mode of the ruling classes [to whose needs they respond] that do not need to be coercively enforced but are, instead, transmitted by the official pedagogy, by the control over the means of expression and communication and by a kind of intangible public moral). Rama, "La púdica dama 'literatura,'" in *Antología del ensayo uruguayo contemporáneo,* vol. 2, ed. Carlos Real de Azúa (Montevideo: Universidad de la República, 1964), 616. About the attempts to create a national consciousness from cultural institutions, see Hernán Vidal, *Literatura hispanoamericana e ideología liberal: surgimiento y crisis* (Buenos Aires: Hispamérica, 1976), 29–30. For a study of this phenomenon in Uruguay, see Abril Trigo, *Caudillo, estado, nación: literatura, historia e ideología en el Uruguay* (Gaithersburg, MD: Ediciones Hispamérica, 1990), 37–38.

ago by Mariano Picón Salas, who noticed that because "estas formas de nacionalismo no tenían la larga gestación milenaria que en Europa, había que
forzar, por ello, sus motivaciones espirituales" (those forms of nationalism
did not have the long, millenarian gestation they had in Europe, it was necessary to create, in a farfetched way, their spiritual motivations).[6] In
Uruguay, too, several observers became aware of this situation. Bernardo P.
Berro[7] was one of the writers who perceived that in Uruguay the effect (i.e.,
the state) was declared before the existence of the cause (i.e., the nation).
Another writer, Angel Floro Costa, interpreted national independence as a
gift to the new state that forced it to elaborate national myths in order to
forge a national past.[8] The last example that I will offer here is the following statement in 1855 by Manuel Herrera y Obes:

> For having inverted the natural order; for having started from what
> should have been the ending of a process; for having persisted in an un-
> derstandable error; for the effort to have written constitutions, made up
> in a couple of long, sleepless nights, without any knowledge of the char-
> acteristic physiognomy of the Peoples for whom they were being writ-
> ten . . . the States of Spanish America are now in the miserable condition
> in which they live.[9]

In this chapter, I examine some of the discursive strategies put into practice
by the Uruguayan state and its political and intellectual elites in the second

6. Mariano Picón Salas, "Unidad y nacionalismo en la historia hispano-ameri-
cana," in *Dependencia e independencia en la historia hispanoamericana (Antología)*
(Caracas: Consejo Nacional de la Cultura, Centro de estudios latinoamericanos "Rómulo Gallegos," 1977), 159.
7. Bernardo Prudencio Berro, "Programa de política," in *Escritos selectos,* vol. 111
of *Colección de clásicos uruguayos,* ed. Juan E. Pivel Devoto (Montevideo: Biblioteca
Artigas, 1966), 246–247.
8. Angel Floro Costa, *Nirvana* (Montevideo: Dornaleche y Reyes, 1899), 151.
9. Por haber invertido el orden natural: por haber empezado, por dónde devió [sic]
acabarse: por haber persistido en el error, muy disculpable de nuestros padres: por el em-
peño de tener, antes de todo, constituciones escritas, fabricadas, en una o dos noches de
vigilia, sin conocimiento de la fisonomía característica de los Pueblos para quienes se
daban . . . es que los Estados de la América Española se encuentran en la miserable condición en que viven." Cited in Juan Pivel Devoto, *Historia de los partidos políticos en el
Uruguay,* vol. 1 (Montevideo: C. García & Cía., 1942), 227. According to Alberto
Methol Ferré, modern Uruguay is not even a nation but a state; what exists, though, is a
Latin American nation of which Uruguay is only a part. Methol Ferré, "Dos odiseas
americanas," in *Antología del ensayo uruguayo contemporáneo,* vol. 2, ed. Carlos Real
de Azúa (Montevideo: Universidad de la República, 1964), 637.

half of the nineteenth century. I pay special attention to strategies elaborated by practitioners of some of the expert knowledges (i.e., disciplines, especially historiography and archaeology) and by the political elites and public figures of that era, in order to point out some coincidences among them. Those coincidences led to the proposal, by most of the authors studied here, of a very Europeanized notion of nation that excludes any contributions coming from non-European ethnic groups or cultures. The absence of one of those "others" of the West, the Amerindian, in the narratives of the Uruguayan nation, is the main topic of this chapter.

Let us start by briefly commenting on the Uruguayan political situation in the 1870s. At that time, political parties had failed in their role as providers of cohesion to the nation. Consequently, the "militarism era" began. The main actor of this period was Colonel Lorenzo Latorre, who, through diverse means, "established [state] authority, promulgated the legal codes, unified the country administratively, and gave the state definitive internal configuration by dividing its territory in different sections that are still current" (instauró la autoridad, promulgó los códigos, unificó administrativamente al país, le dio definitiva configuración interna con las subdivisiones territoriales que perduran hasta hoy).[10] Methol Ferré goes a little further and declares Latorre to be the founder of the Uruguayan state.[11] A similar view can be found in Roberto Ares Pons, who believes that Latorre "realizó el Estado" (made the state), through both the elimination of one of the main obstacles to its crystallization (the gaucho) and by preparing, through legal and coercive measures, the country for the adoption of capitalism as the dominant form of production.[12]

The promulgation of several fundamental legal codes and laws, the fencing of the countryside (which helped demarcate more clearly the limits of private property), and the indiscriminate (and sometimes brutal) use of force for the enforcement of the law and the restoration of "order" (the order desired by the oligarchy, to be more precise) justifies the consideration of Latorre as the strongman who made it possible for Uruguay to become a "safe" country, that is, a country that was then able to enter the capitalist world (or,

10. Juan Pivel Devoto, "Prólogo," in *La independencia nacional*, vol. 145 of *Colección de clásicos uruguayos* (Montevideo: Biblioteca Artigas, 1975), xxxix.
11. Methol Ferré, "Dos odiseas americanas," 37. According to Carlos Real de Azúa, the state had been imagined/conceptualized since 1830 from an enlightened perspective. Real de Azúa, *El patriciado uruguayo* (Montevideo: Asir, 1961), 77.
12. Roberto Ares Pons, *Uruguay: ¿Provincia o nación?* ([1961]Buenos Aires: Coyoacán, 1967), 36–41.

if one prefers, it was possible then for the capitalist world to enter Uruguay). Latorre is responsible, in other words, for the entrance of Uruguay into the ranks of modern states.

Yet, Latorre knew that the mere legal framework was not enough for consolidation of the state. Because he was aware of this, he did not hesitate in giving his total support to José Pedro Varela, a principled intellectual who had a project for the reform of the educational system. Colonel Latorre's support of Varela's reform made it possible for Uruguay to develop one of the most powerful and pervasive state apparatuses for the reproduction of ideology: an official education in the hands of the state.[13] This complex combination of means for domination and control ("disciplinamiento" is the term used by José Pedro Barrán) characterizes the situation of the Uruguayan state in the 1870s that Barrán describes as follows:

> The state underwent modernization and its coercive power became effective and real, at the same time that it monopolized brute force since 1876; the train gave mobility to government troops and fostered the Montevideanization of the country, understood as an irradiation of the values of modernity from the capital city to the countryside—the last refuge of the "barbaric" sensibility. . . . The public school system, the Church and the police promoted the values that the economic transformations required if what was intended by the citizens was to continue to live within the community and not outside it: efficacy, work, study and the seriousness of life.[14]

13. According to Boyd C. Shafer, popular education is one of the most effective means for the consolidation of the state. Shafer, *Faces of Nationalism* (New York: Harcourt Brace Jovanovich, 1972), 195–201. It is also one of the methods of control of the discursive production Michel Foucault talks about. Foucault, *L'ordre du discours* (Paris: Gallimard, 1971), 10.

14. "El estado se modernizó y volvió efectivo y real su poder de coacción, a la vez que monopolizó la fuerza física, desde 1876; el ferrocarril dio movilidad a las tropas del Gobierno central y alentó también la montevideanización del país, entendida aquí como irradiación de los valores de la modernidad desde la capital a la campaña, el último refugio de la sensibilidad 'bárbara.' . . . Escuela, Iglesia y Policía fomentaron, en realidad, y para poner límites a sus influencias, lo que las transformaciones económicas imponían si se quería seguir viviendo dentro de la comunidad y no como marginados: la eficacia, el trabajo, el estudio, la seriedad de la vida." José Pedro Barrán, *El Disciplinamiento (1860–1920),* vol. 2 of *Historia de la sensibilidad en el Uruguay* (Montevideo: Ediciones de la Banda Oriental, 1991), 18–19.

From the state, then, the ideals of respectability, virility, and decorum that characterized the bourgeois, nationalistic European doctrines, were promoted.[15] Interestingly, those ideals were incarnated in the man who gave the first step in Uruguay toward the construction of the nation through the state: Colonel Latorre. Deviations from that behavioral model no longer had a place in the nation. And one of the cultures that was left without a place in the national project was that of the gauchos, whom Latorre attempted to destroy as a social group or subculture. In the framework of the national narrative predominant in Uruguay in the second half of the nineteenth century, the gauchos needed to be eliminated because, among other reasons, they were the inheritors of indigenous barbarism. In actuality, theirs was the only culture that flourished outside the boundaries of urban centers (the Amerindians had already been eliminated by 1831–1832), and as such, they were the last obstacles to progress understood in Western terms.

Unlike other extinct indigenous groups, the Charrúa who inhabited Uruguay and the Argentine coast, did not vanish due to slavery and abusive labor exploitation at the hands of the European colonizers: the Charrúa lacked an agricultural system that allowed the development of the *encomienda* arrangement which flourished in other parts of the continent. And because there were no traces of the exploitation of precious metals by the local Amerindians, mining activities did not develop either. Besides, unlike more prestigious (by European standards) aborigines (such as Andean or Mesoamerican ones), they did not live in cities (they were either nomadic or semi-nomadic groups), which prevented them from having close contact with the invaders. This means that they were not as exposed (at least in the first decades of contact) as other Amerindians (who lived a sedentary life in a fixed territory) to the new bacteria brought by the Europeans. The Charrúa disappeared suddenly, victims of a cowardly betrayal.

In Uruguay, one of the first measures enforced by the first independent national government was, in 1831, to ambush the extant Charrúas who inhabited the territory. The lifestyle of the Charrúa was, in the opinion of the Creole elites, incompatible with the capitalist system and the notion of private property. For this reason, Fructuoso Rivera, the first constitutional president

15. About the close relationship between respectability (and its consequences of virility, homophobia, decorum, and austerity) and the bourgeoisie (and its creations, including nationalism, capitalism, and so on), see George L. Mosse, "Introduction: Nationalism and Respectability," in Mosse, *Nationalism and Sexuality* (New York: Howard Fertig, 1985). Some of these ideals coincide with aspects that, according to Barrán, define the "civilized" sensibility. Barrán, *El Disciplinamiento,* 11–21, 34–53.

of the República Oriental del Uruguay, organized a barbecue of gigantic proportions in order to ambush the Charrúas. The Charrúas were invited to leave their weapons outside so that they could enjoy the abundant succulent beef and the alcoholic beverages in a pacific mood. Once the aborigines were inebriated, Rivera's men proceeded to assassinate them. Although this massacre was orchestrated by the president of the republic, it would be a little naive to make him the sole responsible agent of such a cowardly action. As Daniel Vidart rightly points out, Rivera was only the trigger of a firearm that had been loaded for a long time.[16] Nobody spoke out to condemn the genocide of that indigenous culture. The Creole establishment erased the event from the national memory and set out to thoroughly forget the crime that had been perpetrated. In fact, the genocide of the Charrúa people was, until very recently, a forbidden topic in Uruguay. In actuality, prohibitions against speaking about it were not really necessary, as the descendants of the perpetrators led by the president of the republic did not wish to think about it.

This tendency to forget an ignominious past may explain the predominant lack of interest in both the colonial past and the indigenous history shown by practitioners of expert knowledges in Uruguay. Maybe there are other reasons for that obliviousness. Whatever the case, the fact is that in the debates that took place between José Pedro Varela and Carlos María Ramírez during the political period dominated by Colonel Latorre (the 1870s) on the viability of Uruguay as a country, the discussion never included the Amerindians (mostly of Guaraní descent) who were still present in the territory after the extermination of the Charrúas. In those debates, the country was always imagined as a European nation, without any consideration whatsoever of the possible indigenous (or any other non-European) contributions to its historical evolution. It is opportune to quote a brief passage where Varela proposes, in the face of the nation's internal anarchy, ignorance, and lack of government and external military weakness vis-à-vis its powerful neighbors Argentina and Brazil, a possible solution, based on the example given by Switzerland: "In our opinion, then, small nations are only viable when they are surrounded by big nations, if they are always an example of liberty, happiness, and wisdom; that is, if they are always happier, freer and more educated than the nations that surround them."[17] That

16. Daniel Vidart, *El mundo de los Charrúas* (Montevideo: Ediciones de la Banda Oriental, 1996), 93.

17. "A nuestro juicio, pues, las pequeñas nacionalidades sólo son viables, hallándose rodeadas por grandes naciones, siempre que den ejemplo de libertad, de felicidad y de

happiness, that freedom and that wisdom must be the consequence, according to Varela, of education:

> The stability of small nations is, then, intimately linked to the freedom they enjoy, to the morality they have, and to the happiness of all of the members of their communities; and all those conditions are closely, indissolubly tied to the education of the people . . . the stability of the oriental [Uruguayan] nationality is, in the last instance, a matter of education.[18]

The notion of education that Varela is propounding does not include the propagation of indigenous values and knowledges. On the contrary, he believed that those cultures (which did not exist as such in Uruguay in the 1870s, although individuals with indigenous biological heritage were still present in the territory) were decrepit[19] and that, therefore, they were a burden for the new republic, a residue from the past. His idea of education was mostly based on Western values, of which Switzerland was for him the best incarnation.[20] It is, then, through a "civilizing," occidentalizing education that producing a more complex and elevated social order would be possible.

If the reader is thinking that in the Uruguayan society of the second half of the nineteenth century only the political elites were oblivious to the indigenous cultural legacy, he or she would be wrong. The literati, for example, represented the nation in a similar fashion. Let us see, then, what kind of presence the Amerindian had in the history of Uruguayan literature. I am not going to provide here a systematic study of that presence, but rather an attempt to briefly comment on two paradigmatic texts regarding the representation of aborigines in Uruguayan literature. Suffice it to say that, in general, the Charrúas have appeared very seldom in the works of Uruguayan narrative and poetry. One of the texts that I am going to comment on here, the late Romantic poem *Tabaré* (1886), by Juan Zorrilla de San Martín, is

---

sabiduría; es decir, siempre que sean más felices, más libres, y más ilustradas que las naciones que los rodean." José Pedro Varela, "De nuestro estado actual y sus causas," in *El destino nacional y la universidad,* vol. 67 of *Colección de clásicos uruguayos,* ed. Arturo Ardao (Montevideo: Biblioteca Artigas, 1965), 161.

18. "La estabilidad de las pequeñas nacionalidades está, pues, íntimamente ligada con la libertad de que se goza, con la moralidad que se tiene, con la felicidad de todos los miembros de la comunidad; y estas condiciones todas, se hallan estrechas, indisolublemente unidas a la instrucción del pueblo . . . la estabilidad de la nacionalidad oriental, es en último término una cuestión de educación." Ibid., 162.

19. Ibid., 140.

20. Ibid., 159–162.

one of the few works of literature that included characters representing that ethnic group. The poem narrates the misadventures of the eponymous hero, who is the mestizo son of a Spanish mother (a captive) and a Charrúa father. One of the consequences of his mixed heritage is that his looks are indigenous over all, but his eyes are blue. However, his Charrúa condition is not only revealed by his phenotype, but also, and most importantly, by his education and lifestyle, which he acquires in the *tolderías* (the temporary dwellings of the Amerindians) of his father's people. This melancholic Amerindian (whose love for a Spanish woman whose name is, significantly, Blanca—meaning "white" in Spanish—leads him to his death) is the representative of an ethnic group that, according to Zorrilla de San Martín, was destined to disappear. In his poem, then, the Amerindians are a breed that, due to their incapacity to adapt to "civilized" life and progress, were doomed to disappear from the face of the earth. As can be seen, the poet's opinion does not differ much from that of the political elites who massacred the real Charrúa in 1831.

What Zorrilla de San Martín does, then, is to elevate the Charrúa to the level of an icon a few decades after their extermination. As Angel Rama has pointed out with respect to gauchesca poetry, once the social/cultural group that bothered the lettered city (i.e., the Europeanized Creole elites who ruled the young republics) disappears (be it gaucho or Amerindian), it can be more or less harmlessly incorporated into the national cultural tradition. In other words, only after they are exterminated can they be represented. This appropriation of an indigenous past is not the only possible attitude in Uruguayan intellectual history. There is another one that is, in actuality, more common: to completely ignore the indigenous other.

In the model for Latin American (and therefore Uruguayan) culture proposed by José Enrique Rodó, another important name in Uruguayan literature, the Amerindian is completely absent. In his *Ariel,* the Shakespearean eponymous character incarnates Greco-Roman culture, a culture that must be the model for and inspiration for the peoples of Latin America. Nothing is said there, however, about the role of indigenous or African heritage on the continent. Reading Rodó's book, one would think all Latin American countries had solved the "problema del indio" or that such a problem never existed. Some may try to explain that significant absence in Rodó's text by reminding us that when he wrote, the Amerindians did not exist as an organized culture in Uruguay and, therefore, it is understandable that he did not mention them. It is true that one's thinking is strongly influenced by time and place, but that alone does not explain why, only a few years after the publication of a text like "Nuestra América," by José Martí, where the importance of the indigenous contribution to the culture and civilization of the continent is clearly stated, Rodó chooses to pretend the Amerindians simply did not exist. Interestingly enough, in spite of that omission, the intellectuals from the rest of Latin America (where Amerindians were still numerous and socially and culturally organized) embraced Rodó's ideas—known as Arielismo—for many years. These two paradigmatic texts show us two possible ways to deal with the Amerindians in the history of Uruguayan literature: either to ignore them as if they did not exist or to represent them in a way that their extinction appears as something inevitable and, in the last instance, necessary.

In the field of historiography the panorama is not much better. There are very few academic works about the pre-Columbian era in the territory. The same can be said about the colonial period. Perhaps the exceptions are a book by Juan Pivel Devoto[21] and some of the work by José Pedro Barrán. However, even in these exceptional cases, colonial means "beginnings of the nineteenth century" or, in the best of cases, "turn of the eighteenth century." In this way, if a foreign observer desired to write a history of the cultural and social evolution in the territory of present-day Uruguay, he or she would conclude that, according to the available bibliography, the colonial past and the pre-Columbian era were almost nonexistent. And if they existed, their importance was almost nil.

The few nineteenth-century Uruguayan historians who dealt with aboriginal pasts followed what was said by the chroniclers of the colonial period. Therefore, it should not come as a surprise that they repeated, almost verbatim, the representations of the Amerindians produced by the colonial authors.[22] Juan Manuel de la Sota, the first historian of the Uruguayan territory (his book was published in 1841), was no exception to that rule: he based his account of Amerindian pasts on colonial sources that he seldom contradicted.[23] De la Sota's motivation was, like that of many other historians, political: he wanted to find historical antecedents that

21. Juan Pivel Devoto, *Raíces coloniales de la revolución Oriental de 1811* ([1952] Montevideo: Medina, 1957).

22. For a study of three centuries of colonial chroniclers' representations of the Amerindians, see Gustavo Verdesio, *Forgotten Conquests: Re-reading New World History from the Margins* (Philadelphia: Temple University Press, 2001).

23. Juan Pivel Devoto, "Prólogo," in Juan Manuel de la Sota, *Historia del territorio Oriental del Uruguay,* 2 vols. (Montevideo: Biblioteca Artigas, 1965), 1:x–xi.

would support the republic's territorial rights.[24] Aware of his role as a reproducer of state ideology, de la Sota intended to contribute to the building of the young republic's historical consciousness by discovering in the facts of the past the reasons for its existence in the present.[25] That is why he decided to write, in contrast with what was common practice at that time, a history of the territory known as the República Oriental del Uruguay in 1841 instead of a history of the region known as Paraguay or Río de la Plata.[26]

The image of the Amerindians produced by de la Sota has, as I mentioned above, many similarities to the ones produced by colonial authors. For example, he accepts the version that says that the Amerindians who received the "discoverer" of the Río de la Plata, Juan Díaz de Solís, ate him in 1516.[27] This myth originated in the earliest chroniclers and it has been repeated endlessly to this day.[28] Primary and secondary school students hear the systematic repetition of that myth for years, which explains why most Uruguayans today imagine the scene of the "discovery" as a cannibalistic banquet—a banquet whose existence is still a moot question.[29] Yet, the anthropophagus myth is not the only one de la Sota takes from colonial chroniclers: he also reproduces some of their evaluations about the Amerindians' characteristics. For example, he says that they were cruel, barbaric, and ferocious.[30] He also says that the Charrúa, whom he calls "the Spartans of America," lived in a state of barbarism.[31] Although he accepts the version that presents them as the cannibals who ate Solís, he believes that banquet was an exception and not a cultural habit.[32] He adds that they were exterminated by the first constitutional president of the republic, Fructuoso Rivera, in 1831, but he omits to say *how* that happened.[33] This silence about

24. Ibid., viii–ix.
25. Ibid., ix.
26. Juan Manuel de la Sota, *Historia del territorio Oriental del Uruguay,* 2 vols. (Montevideo: Biblioteca Artigas, 1965), 1:6.
27. Ibid., 1:14.
28. For a study of the discursive history that produced the official history of the "discovery" of the Río de la Plata, see Verdesio, *Forgotten Conquests,* chapter 1.
29. For a discussion of the myth of cannibalism in the "discovery" of the Río de la Plata, see Gustavo Verdesio, "Las representaciones territoriales del Uruguay colonial: Hacia una hermenéutica pluritópica," *Revista de Crítica Literaria Latinoamericana* 23, no. 46 (1997): 135–161.
30. De la Sota, *Historia del territorio Oriental del Uruguay,* 1:21.
31. Ibid., 24.
32. Ibid.
33. Ibid., 22.

the cowardly stratagem that ended the Charrúa is, as I have already observed, the most common attitude vis-à-vis the unnamable: the genocide of one of the Amerindian groups that populated the territory.

There exists among the earliest writers, then, a tendency to reproduce the representations of the Amerindians offered by colonial chroniclers. That is why the aborigines are often considered as a problematic element of the territory, much like an element of nature. Francisco Bauzá, for example, begins the introduction of his book with a portrait of the territory encountered by the first explorers that presents it as a "comarca de indios salvajes" (land of savage Indians).[34] His description of those Amerindians is an already familiar one: they lived in a primitive rusticity and were frugal and brave[35]; their language was as poor as their attire.[36] What he does not reproduce is the myth of Charrúa anthropophagy. On the contrary, he dedicates several pages to prove that they were not cannibals.[37]

Bauzá informs us that, as a people who mastered techniques to polish stones, they could be portrayed as living in the Neolithic.[38] This characterization allows him to locate the Amerindians in a universal continuum: [A]ll peoples have gone through an identical period. . . . [T]he Neolithic period has been an indispensable condition of human social organization, a necessary precedent in the development of progress.[39] In this way, in a portrayal that is frequent among Western scholars, the Amerindians appear as beings in a developmental stage inferior to the one shown by Western society. What Bauzá does is to take an occidental interpretational model of the human past as the standard against which the development of the Amerindians is evaluated. In that model of human evolution there are stages that succeed each other toward a civilizational ideal. The Amerindians of Uruguay do not fare very well in that model, because it places them in a stage of evolution previous to the one reached by modern-day Western civilization. In this way, even though they were contemporaries of the Europeans who wrote about them, they were relegated to the past of hu-

---

34. Francisco Bauzá, *Historia de la dominación española en el Uruguay,* vol. 1 (Montevideo: Barreiro y Ramos, 1895), 3.

35. Ibid., 143.

36. Ibid., 146.

37. Ibid., 186–189.

38. Ibid., 185.

39. "[T]odos los pueblos han cruzado por un periodo idéntico. . . . [E]l periodo Neolítico ha sido una condición imprescindible de la organización social de la humanidad, un precedente necesario al desarrollo del progreso." Ibid., 186.

mankind. This attitude, called "denial of coevalness" by Johannes Fabian,[40] is very well illustrated by Bauzá.

One the most interesting aspects of Bauzá's book is that he talks, for the first time in a history book on Uruguay, about the Amerindians who populated the territory before the arrival of the first European explorers. Unlike de la Sota, who limited himself to commenting on the deeds of the latter, Bauzá mentions the culture of the mound builders.[41] He compares, due to the similarities found in the architecture of the earthen monuments, the Uruguayan mounds to the ones built in North America. The mounds found in Uruguay are testimony, according to Bauzá, to a migration of the original mound builders (in North America) toward Central and South America.[42] The traces left by the original mound builders in Uruguay had only started to arouse interest among scholars at the time of the publication of his book.[43]

Those traces, represented by the "cerritos" or mounds found in San Luis (present-day Rocha Department) and in Soriano Department, are described by Bauzá in some detail: he informs us about the kind of soil used for their construction, what kind of interments they contain, what other objects were found in them, and so on.[44] This evidence, according to the historian, leads to the conclusion that the Amerindians who built those mounds were part of a more ancient and more primitive civilization than that of the aborigines found at the time of contact.[45] His evaluation of that civilization is based on a model that judges cultures from their ruins and vestiges, which are testimonies to what they were able to do with matter:

> The degree of culture achieved by an indigenous culture is demonstrated by the manipulation of matter that the traces from the past show. Thus, the great nations now extinct left wonderful ruins within which the traces of scientific and artistic work that informed their plans and purified their national genius can be noticed; conversely, the poverty of an incipient civilization can be seen in the traces left by uneducated nations.[46]

40. Johannes Fabian, *Time and the Other: How Anthropology Makes Its Object* (New York: Columbia University Press, 1983).
41. Bauzá, *Historia de la dominación española en el Uruguay,* 131.
42. Ibid., 132.
43. Ibid., 133.
44. Ibid., 134.
45. Ibid.
46. "El surco de lo pasado se estratifica a la materia que les rodea, demostrando por la transformación manual de ella, el grado de cultura que alcanzaron. Así, de las grandes

An important detail is that the incipient nations he talks about are such because, like all the civilizations developed in America, they are newer than those developed in the Old World.[47] However, differences between indigenous societies exist: the Mexican and Andean cities at the time of Moctezuma and Atahualpa prove that their civilizations were superior to that shown, for example, by the ruins left by the mound builders.[48] Yet, "despite their superiority over their predecessors, the Americans were very backward culturally, in terms of progress at the time of the conquest" (no obstante esta superioridad sobre sus antecesores, estaban los americanos harto atrasados a la época de la conquista).[49] Bauzá's model, then, presents indigenous cultures (even the ones Western society considered as the most "advanced") as primitive, as belonging to a past stage in the evolution of humankind. Among the most primitive ones were those who inhabited the territory of Uruguay at the time of European contact, and in particular, the Charrúa, "whose rustic simplicity could be considered as the last link of a chain" (cuya grosera simplicidad podía tomarse por el último eslabón de una cadena).[50] In this portrayal of human culture before the arrival of the Spaniards, the aborigines, as can be seen, are not presented as admirable beings.

Perhaps this is one of the elements that could help us understand the lack of interest in the indigenous past of Uruguay shown by the paucity of studies on that topic. I am referring to the prevalent evaluation (similar to Bauzá's) of aboriginal cultures as ones that did not reach a level of social development measurable in occidental terms. People in 1895 and today admire the "great civilizations" of the continent because the occidental ideological framework is determined by a teleological and evolutionary criterion. To put it another way, what may make the three great cultures so attractive to people educated in Western culture is their high level of social development in occidental terms. Our way of understanding history as a teleological progression, as an evolution toward a certain goal or ideal, does not differ much from Bauzá's and makes the Inca, Aztec, and Maya cultures resemble more so than other indigenous groups the evolutionary ideal that

---

naciones hoy desaparecidas, dan testimonio de ruinas maravillosas en cuyo seno se distinguen las huellas del trabajo científico y artístico que informó los planes y depuró el gusto del genio nacional; notándose por lo contrario en las huellas dejadas por las naciones incultas, toda la pobreza de una civilización incipiente." Ibid., 135–136.

47. Ibid., 136.
48. Ibid., 137.
49. Ibid.
50. Ibid.

predominates in Western societies. They had a state (central government), good administrative organization, armies, division of labor, and so on. The other indigenous cultures, those not organized around a state, are considered less interesting and, therefore, inferior.

Amerindians like the Charrúa pose a problem to writers who, like Bauzá, are aware of the importance of the colonial past for the development of a nation after independence.[51] By opening the door to the colonial period, they are also opening it to the indigenous past and its role in the historical development of colonial times. That past, as discussed previously, did not seem to be something Uruguayan historians were very proud of. For this reason, writers like Pablo Blanco Acevedo, who admitted the relevance of the colonial epoch for the understanding of the development of the Uruguayan nation, preferred to limit his research endeavors to the study of the colonial city.[52] Bauzá, instead, accepts the challenge and, no matter how primitive the indigenous cultures were in his opinion, acknowledges their role in the history of human society in the territory. Yet, this acknowledgment does not change his occidentalized view of the nation, thanks to the disappearance of the Charrúa in 1831–1832, who were the incarnation of the most important threat ("barbarism") to a "civilizational" project that resembled the one articulated by Domingo F. Sarmiento in Argentina. With the disappearance of the Charrúa, their contribution to the national narrative could be ignored—it would be argued that they left no significant traces—and it became possible to present them as ancestral ghosts who lived in a barbaric era. This representation of the Charrúa is similar to the one Sarmiento offers about the Huarpes, Amerindians from his native San Luis (Argentina), who appear as a breed that left very few vestiges of their existence on the planet.[53] The few legacies of the Huarpes to the San Luis of Sarmiento's time were, from his perspective, negative, and thus had to be eliminated. Huarpe barbarisms were a hindrance to the imposition of the social order Sarmiento promoted: that of the lettered city that Rama[54] talks about. This is the same lettered city from which Zorrilla de San Martín po-

---

51. Ibid., 7.

52. Pablo Blanco Acevedo, *El gobierno colonial en el Uruguay y los orígenes de la nacionalidad,* vol. 149 of *Colección de clásicos uruguayos,* vol. 1 (Montevideo: Biblioteca Artigas, 1975), xxvi.

53. Domingo F. Sarmiento, *Recuerdos de provincia* (Barcelona: Editorial Ramón Sopena, 1968), 18.

54. Angel Rama, *La cuidad letrada* (Hanover, NH: Ediciones del Norte, 1984).

sitioned himself when he offered a similar evaluation of the role of the Charrúa in the history of the territory.

The contempt shown by the aforementioned authors for the Amerindians of "historical time" can be understood in the light of the evolutionary ideas held by the authors read thus far: the Amerindians from Uruguay, like the Huarpes described by Sarmiento, did not leave many traces of their life on earth and, most importantly, they did not produce a spectacular architecture like the one found in Mesoamerica and the Andes. As Robert Silverberg states for the United States, it is understandable that the colonists and their descendants did not like the idea of living in a land populated "by naked wandering savages."[55] Yet, during the continual expansion of Western culture to the west of the North American territory, those same colonists encountered abundant earthen constructions covered by vegetation. Those monuments became, for the colonists of the eighteenth and nineteenth centuries, the raw material for the creation of myths about the territory they inhabited.[56] The spectacular nature of some of the mounds they saw led them to suppose that their builders were members of a an extinct race, because the Amerindians they confronted were, in their eyes, so barbaric and unsophisticated that they could not possibly have been credited with the authorship of works that required so much effort and organization.[57] That extinct race could not, for many an author, have an indigenous origin: the mound builders must have been the descendants of outstanding civilizations from the Old World, such as the ones originated in Phoenicia, Israel, or Persia, among others.[58] A possible explanation of this refusal to attribute Amerindian authorship to the mounds can be found, according to Silverberg, in the consideration of that attitude as part of a political campaign against the aborigines: they were, after all, a big obstacle for the expansion of Western civilization in North America.[59] Roger G. Kennedy also explains U.S. writers' attitude toward indigenous pasts in terms of the interests of an expanding Western civilizational project: "Hastily and unrepentantly, Jeffersonians and Jacksonians thrust the Indians aside by means which might lie easier on the conscience if those displaced were thought to have neither

55. Robert Silverberg, *The Mound Builders* ([1970] Athens: Ohio University Press, 1986), 10.
56. Ibid.
57. Ibid., 11.
58. Ibid., 15.
59. Ibid., 117.

history, art nor religion worthy of the respect of the displacers."[60] In the Uruguay of the 1880s (the decade during which the first archaeological works on the local past start to emerge), that kind of narrative was not absolutely necessary, due to the previous elimination of Amerindian cultures that gave occidental culture a free ride in that territory.

The attribution of mounds to superior cultures from the Old World did not take place in Uruguay, as we already saw in the text by Bauzá, who was left totally unimpressed by the local mound builders, to the extent that he thought of them as a group that reached a civilizational stage lower than the one attributed to the Amerindians encountered by the first explorers. A possible explanation of the different interpretations of the mounds by authors in Uruguay and the United States is that the mounds which ignited the imagination of the latter were the ones produced by the cultures known as Adena and Hopewell, that flourished, according to Silverberg,[61] between 800 B.C. (or 400 B.C., according to other authors[62]) and A.D. 500, and architectonic prodigies like Cahokia, built by the cultures belonging to the Mississippian tradition (that begins, approximately, in the seventh century of the current era). Those North American cultures built enormous mounds and very complex embankments that extended, in some cases, for kilometers and sometimes reached impressive heights. Conversely, the mounds found in Uruguay look more like the earthen structures of the archaic period in the United States (7000 B.C. to 1000 B.C.), which are less spectacular (with the exception, perhaps, of places like Poverty Point, in Louisiana) than those (like Cahokia) belonging to the Mississippian tradition. The mounds of the North American archaic period, like those built in Uruguayan territory, did not excite the imagination of scholars who, educated in a culture that saw those earthen structures from an evolutionary perspective, found them of very little interest.

In the second half of the nineteenth century, the Uruguayan literati, politicians, and historians were not the only ones who managed to forget or minimize the contributions of the Amerindians to the history of human life in the territory: the practitioners of an incipient discipline, archaeology, also offered a negative image of the Amerindians. As seen already, Bauzá made

60. Roger G. Kennedy, *Hidden Cities: The Discovery and Loss of Ancient North American Civilization* (New York: Penguin, 1994), 223.
61. Silverberg, *Mound Builders,* 181.
62. For example, Kennedy, *Hidden Cities,* 15.

use of archaeological data for the elaboration of an evolutionary model in which there was very little room left for the Charrúa and other indigenous groups of both pre-Columbian and contact times. Let us now see what an archaeologist (probably the first one to emerge in Uruguay), José H. Figueira, says in 1892 about the former: "Nothing is known about their history before the conquest" (Nada se sabe acerca de su historia en tiempos anteriores a la conquista),[63] an acknowledgment that forces him to resort (like Bauzá) to what the colonial chroniclers said about them.

According to Figueira, the Charrúa had neither law[64] nor religion, and only a very vague notion of the supernatural.[65] Their ideas, their spiritual life, and the strength of their intellect were almost exclusively at service of subsistence.[66] They were, besides, inimical to civilization, a tendency that explains why their way of life changed so little during the three centuries of the colonial period.[67] In order to halt their criminal activities, "fue menester destruirlos" (it was necessary to destroy them).[68] Figueira is the first author who both talks about the ambush that ended with the Charrúa and justifies it.[69] This hypothesis, which presents the extinction of the Charrúas as inevitable due to their lack of preparation for "civilized" life, is the same that we saw in Zorrilla de San Martín, who was a contemporary of Figueira. Yet, not only the Charrúa appear as barbaric in Figueira's text: the other indigenous groups who populated the northern shore of the Río de la Plata are presented as savages not suitable for "civilized" life.[70] This is a sign, according to the same author, of inferiority typical of the most backward races,[71] whose members' mental capabilities did not develop beyond the stage of childhood.[72]

This view of the Amerindian of "historical time" harmonizes with an image of the nation that does not leave any room for the cultures that do not adapt to an occidental civilizational criterion. It is not surprising, therefore,

63. José H. Figueira, *Los primitivos habitantes del Uruguay* (Montevideo: Dornaleche y Reyes, 1892), 14.
64. Ibid., 22.
65. Ibid., 25.
66. Ibid., 28.
67. Ibid., 33.
68. Ibid.
69. Ibid.
70. Ibid., 43.
71. Ibid.
72. Ibid.

to find this perspective articulated by the founder of Uruguayan archaeology, who was not only defending the ideas of the dominant group that he was a part of, but also was a practitioner of an incipient discipline that from the beginning was related to nation building. According to Margarita Díaz-Andreu and Timothy Champion, nationalism had a great influence on the interpretations produced by archaeological research and on the development of the discipline as such. Moreover, the emergence of nationalism "stimulated the very creation of archaeology as a science and informed not only the organization of archaeological knowledge but also its very infrastructure. Without the existence of nationalism, archaeology or the study of the past might never have advanced beyond the status of a hobby or a pastime."[73] This relationship between nations and archaeology is based on the fact that the existence of the former "implies the existence of a past which, for their own good and that of the individuals who belong to them, should be known and propagated."[74] In this way, the institutions and disciplines (the expert knowledges) endeavored to justify the territory in which the nation developed.[75] The nation, then, was the base and the objective of the research agenda of the disciplines.[76] And it should be remembered that those same disciplines, according to Santiago Castro-Gómez, have legitimized all the political, aesthetic, and economic Latin American projects since the nineteenth century.[77]

Archaeology as a discipline has played an important role, according to Victor A. Buchli, in the realm of social reproduction.[78] Archaeology and the nation, then, go hand in hand and, when the latter consolidates, the laws that regulate national heritage and the museums system start to emerge.[79] In this sense, it is useful to remember the role that states played (and still play) in the definition of what past and what objects must be preserved. For exam-

73. Margarita Díaz-Andreu and Timothy Champion, "Nationalism and Archaeology in Europe: An Introduction," in *Nationalism and Archaeology in Europe,* ed. Díaz-Andreu and Champion (London: UCL Press, 1996), 3.

74. Ibid.

75. Ibid.

76. Ibid.

77. Santiago Castro-Gómez, "Latinoamericanismo, modernidad, globalización: Prolegómenos a una crítica poscolonial de la razón," in *Teorías sin disciplina: Latinoamericanismo, poscolonialidad y globalización en debate,* ed. Santiago Castro-Gómez y Eduardo Mendieta (Porrúa, Mexico: Universidad de San Francisco, 1998), 196.

78. Victor A. Buchli, "Interpreting Material Culture: The Trouble with Text," in *Interpreting Archaeology: Finding Meaning in the Past,* ed. Ian Hodder, Michael Shanks, et al. (London and New York: Routledge, 1995), 182.

79. Díaz-Andreu and Champion, "Nationalism and Archaeology in Europe," 6.

ple, museums regulate, to some degree, the survival of the past.[80] Having said that, it should be pointed out that countries with a long nationalistic tradition, such as England, did not pay special attention to the preservation of the monuments of the past until the 1882 regulation.[81]

If a concern for the regulation of heritage occurred so late in an old European nation, it should not surprise us that in a brand-new republic like Uruguay (whose independence was declared in 1830) the state had been remiss in encouraging the systematic development of archaeology at the end of the nineteenth century. However, despite the lack of state support, archaeology started to develop in the 1880s. Of course, its findings tended to reinforce the national narratives, as we saw in the cases of Figueira and Bauzá (especially in the latter's comments on the ethnic groups of pre-Columbian times), but the state did not support those efforts directly until much later. Perhaps due to the lack of official support, the first person who studied Amerindian antiquities in Uruguay (and published a text in 1877 that was reproduced in his important book *La antigüedad del hombre en el Plata*), was Florentino Ameghino, an Argentine archaeologist.[82]

Ameghino's book was inspired by a feeling that was, in the last instance, nationalistic: in its 650 pages, he intended to prove the coexistence of human beings and the megafauna of the Quaternary period.[83] If he could prove his hypothesis, the presence of *Homo sapiens* in the territory of present-day Argentina would be much older than believed at that time. Although it is true that his assertions are shared by archaeologists today, the fact is that his objective was still a nationalistic one: to exalt the image of humans from the pampas before a surprised (but appreciative) European academic audience.

Let us move now to what Ameghino said about the lands of Uruguay, which were of interest to him because they belonged to the same region whose human history he was attempting to clarify. One of the things he wrote about the *paraderos* (sites) he visited is that they showed a great number of stones that must have been transported from distant sites, which could only mean that those paraderos were Charrúa lithic workshops.[84] When he found mortars at those sites, he concluded that the Charrúa must have been

80. Ian Hodder, *The Archaeological Process: An Introduction* (Oxford: Blackwell, 1999), 15.

81. Grahame Clark, "Archaeology and the State," *Antiquity* 8, no. 32 (1934): 414.

82. Florentino Ameghino, *La antigüedad del hombre en el Plata,* 2 vols. ([1880] Buenos Aires: La Cultura Argentina, 1918).

83. Ibid., 1:9, passim.

84. Ibid., 215.

agriculturalists, despite the total absence of information about that social practice in then-available ethnohistoric sources.[85] Another assertion he made is that the aforementioned Amerindians were cannibals, thus repeating one of the long-lived myths of colonial times.[86] He concluded also that Rivera exterminated them but, as usual, he did not mention the circumstances under which that extermination occurred.[87]

Ameghino also discussed the inhabitants of the territory in prehistoric times. He claimed that he had not found incontrovertible evidence that demonstrated the coexistence of Quaternary-era megafauna and human beings in Uruguayan territory, prior to 1880, the year his book was published. In that year, however, he was able to produce evidence that suggested, in his opinion, such coexistence: a silex dart point found near the fossil remains of a Panochtus, a Quaternary-era animal.[88] Thus, the antiquity he proposed for humans in the pampas was confirmed by investigations conducted in another part of the region (Uruguay), which strengthened his hypothesis for the early appearance of humans in the Río de la Plata.

Another prehistoric culture that Ameghino talks about was the one that allegedly built the Palacio de Porongos, the homonymous place located in present-day Flores Department. Although he could not visit the site personally, he reproduced an article about it written in 1876 by Mario Ísola,[89] an Italian aficionado who resided in Uruguay. In Ísola's text, the anthropic origin of the cave called Palacio was taken for granted. This assumption made the cave a true mystery, according to Ísola, whose impressions are reproduced in Ameghino's book:

> The only vestiges left by the indigenous races that wandered in our territory at the time of the conquest do not suggest the least architectonic manifestation. Consequently, in order to explain the existence of a building that represents great efforts and certain level of intelligence it is necessary to go back in time and imagine a race superior to those [found at the time of the conquest] who have left only stone balls as testimony to their existence.[90]

85. Ibid., 228.
86. Ibid., 264.
87. Ibid., 260.
88. Ibid., 2:291.
89. Mario Ísola, "Cerro de las Cuentas," in José Joaquín Figueira, *Contribución al estudio de los aborígenes del Uruguay: "Los Charrúas" de Pedro Stagnero y "Cerro de las Cuentas" por Mario Ísola* (Montevideo: N.p., 1957), 37–40.
90. "Los únicos vestigios de las razas indígenas que vagaban por nuestro territorio

The proofs offered by Ísola are not very persuasive, though. For example, a piece of evidence that he interprets in favor of the anthropic origin of the cave is a series of pointy agathas that do not belong to that site but are located at a distance of two leagues.[91] The weakness of the proofs he offers was already evident a few decades after the publication of Ísola's piece, as can be seen in the second edition of Orestes Araújo's *Diccionario geográfico,* under the entry "Palacio, Gruta del."[92] There, the author presents the two possible hypotheses about the origin of the grotto: it was either a natural formation or made by humans.[93] The author of the dictionary seems to favor the first one.[94]

One of the most interesting aspects of Ísola's article is his derogatory characterization of the Amerindians at the time of Contact: it is so pejorative that it is impossible for him to imagine them as the cave builders. This leads him to propose an ancient superior race as the one responsible for the making of the cave. In this respect (i.e., the assessment of prehistoric cultures), his views are different from those held by Bauzá a few years later (in 1895) about the mound builders in Uruguay. As discussed above, Bauzá, unlike several North American authors, thought that the prehistoric mound builders belonged to a race inferior to the ones that populated the Americas at the time of Contact. However, it is evident that Ísola is thinking of yet another prehistoric culture, one that would have, allegedly, built the cave known as the Palacio. Apparently, the occidental civilization that dominated the territory at the time of publication of Ísola's article could not view the Amerindians of historical time as civilized predecessors, but was prone to admire and respect a fictional culture that was able to build the Palacio cave. The criterion for the evaluation of that culture coincides with Bauzá's: the value of civilizations should be measured by what they were able to do with matter.

---

al tiempo de la conquista no dan motivo alguno a suponer la menor manifestación arquitectónica y de consiguiente para explicarse el hecho de existir un edificio que representa grandes esfuerzos y cierta inteligencia, es necesario retroceder siglos e imaginarse una superioridad de raza relativamente a aquellos que apenas han dejado como testimonio de su existencia, toscas bolas de piedra usadas como armas arrojadizas." Ameghino, *La antigüedad del hombre en el Plata,* 1:257.

91. Ibid.

92. Orestes Araújo, *Diccionario geográfico del Uruguay,* 2d ed. (Montevideo: Tipo-Litografía Moderna, 1912), 336–337.

93. Ibid., 337.

94. Ibid.

Ísola's opinions on the relation between Amerindian pasts and the occidental civilization that developed in the second half of the nineteenth century in Uruguay can be better understood upon consideration of his other activities at that time. He was a professional chemist and, therefore, qualified as a practitioner of one of the expert knowledges of modernity. Among his professional achievements, the foundation of the first natural gas production and refining plant in South America shows his relationship to public works understood as civilizational.[95] In addition, his relationship with public figures and statesmen (i.e., with protagonists of the national narrative) is shown by his embalming the bodies of caudillo General Venancio Flores; author of the constitution, Joaquín Suárez; and Bishop Jacinto Vera.[96] His close ties to the nation are also revealed in his participation in mining activities, one of the most important forms of natural resource exploitation in the national territory.[97]

However, despite his ties to the nation and its protagonists, his archaeological activities were not financed by state funds; for instance, his expeditions to the Palacio and to the Cerro de las Cuentas were funded by himself. That *cerro* (hill), known by the abundance of colored beads that it contained, is at the root of certain myths created by rural dwellers,[98] who thus used the material culture left by the Amerindians as the raw material for their rural Creole oral culture. In order to find out what gave origin to those myths, the chemist made an expedition to the site, after which he concluded that the famous beads were nothing but glass beads of Spanish origin obtained by the Amerindians by trade at the time of contact.[99]

The approaches prevalent in Uruguayan archaeology at the end of the nineteenth century are, in Leonel Cabrera's opinion, rather naive.[100] Its practitioners paid little attention to the stratigraphy of the sites and tended to associate the material record to the ethnic groups in the area at the time of Conquest.[101] That predominant attitude (that of the antiquarian or col-

95. José Joaquín Figueira, *Contribución al estudio de los aborígenes del Uruguay: "Los Charrúas" de Pedro Stagnero y "Cerro de las Cuentas" por Mario Ísola* (Montevideo: N.p., 1957), 28.

96. Ibid., 31.

97. Ibid., 33.

98. Ísola, "Cerro de las Cuentas," 38.

99. Ibid., 39–40.

100. Leonel Cabrera, *Panorama retrospectivo y situación actual de la arqueología uruguaya* (Montevideo: Universidad de la República, 1988), 8.

101. Ibid.

lector) would change only at the second half of the twentieth century, according to Cabrera.[102] That is why it is not unusual to find people without specific training in archaeology, such as Julio Piquet, a poet and writer who accompanied José H. Figueira on an expedition to the Cerro Tupambay (also known as Tupambaé) in 1881. In a report that Piquet published in 1882 in the newspaper *La Razón,* he wrote that the Charrúa (who were thought to be the builders of the tombs located atop the Cerro) were barbaric, cruel, vengeful, and cannibals.[103] In the same report, he also mentioned the battle that ended the Charrúas.[104] Of course, this battle never happened; instead, the Charrúa were exterminated in an ambush. In another article published in the same newspaper, Piquet wrote that Figueira believed that the tombs located on the cerro were built by the Charrúa,[105] despite the fact that the expeditionaries opened between six and eight tombs without being able to find any human remains.[106] Given these results, Piquet asked himself what the nature of those little mounds was. The response he came up with was that they were not necessarily tombs but commemorative mounds.[107] According to Piquet, they were certainly built by the Charrúa, because who else would expend so much time and energy on such a useless endeavor?[108]

The opinions of the first generation of archaeologists did not remain confined to the most refined elite circles, but were transmitted to a wider audience by the state's apparatus of ideological reproduction. For example, Ísola's piece on the Cerro de las Cuentas was reprinted in a primary schoolbook published by Pedro Stagnero, in 1883 and 1885.[109] In that same book there is another reprint of an article authored by Stagnero himself, entitled "Los Charrúas," where he notes that they were cannibals.[110] In didactic fashion, so that the tender minds of the students understand the meaning of

102. Ibid., 10.
103. Julio Piquet, "Tumbas Charrúas," in *Una excursión arqueológica al Cerro Tupambay realizada en los comienzos de 1881,* ed. José Joaquín Figueira (Montevideo: N.p., 1958), 13.
104. Ibid.
105. Julio Piquet, "¡Al Tupambay! Una excursión arqueológica," in *Una excursión arqueológica al Cerro Tupambay realizada en los comienzos de 1881,* ed. José Joaquín Figueira (Montevideo: N.p., 1958), 14.
106. Ibid., 16.
107. Ibid., 16–18.
108. Ibid., 18.
109. José Joaquín Figueira, *Una excursión arqueológica al Cerro Tupambay realizada en los comienzos de 1881* (Montevideo: N.p., 1958), 19.
110. Ibid., 33.

such practices, he explains: "Antropófagos quiere decir hombres que comen carne humana" (Cannibals means people who eat human flesh).[111] He also informed his young readers that the Charrúa were a very ignorant people,[112] ate their prisoners,[113] and were very superstitious.[114]

This representation of the local Amerindians, especially those of the time of Contact (of the prehistoric ones very little was known, as José H. Figueira confessed), has been repeated ad nauseam. Its effects on the Uruguayan social imaginary are, predictably, devastating: citizens ignore the indigenous past and, as a consequence, the contributions of the aborigines to humankind are completely forgotten. Maybe because of this lack of knowledge of the indigenous past, in combination with the entrance of Uruguay to the regional market known as Mercosur in the 1990s, which had an impact on national narratives, we are witnessing today the unprecedented interest by vast segments of the population in indigenous issues. The problem with this is that the aforementioned issues are not being treated or discussed in a rational way.

In Western culture, most people with a basic education construct their worldview and their pasts with the help of scientific and mythological elements.[115] In contemporary Uruguay, the mythological element clearly predominates. That is why the success of Danilo Antón's books (a geologist turned historian), which create a dubious and idealized indigenous past, does not come as a surprise. Antón has published three books on these issues: *Uruguaypirí,*[116] in which he explores the non-European roots of the country; *Piriguazú,*[117] in which he revises the parallel histories of the diverse ethnic groups that populated the Río de la Plata region in pre-Columbian times; and *El pueblo jaguar,*[118] a history of the Charrúa nation. Antón's methods are not the most sound from an ethnohistoric perspective but, beyond his sometimes unfounded hypotheses, his agenda is interesting in that it seems to adequately interpret certain needs of his reading public: the search for roots and non-European traditions in a country that has al-

111. Ibid.
112. Ibid., 34.
113. Ibid., 35.
114. Ibid.
115. Miroslav Hroch, "Epilogue," in *Nationalism and Archaeology in Europe,* ed. Margarita Díaz-Andreu and Timothy Champion (London: UCL Press, 1996), 296.
116. Danilo Antón, *Uruguaypirí* (Montevideo: Rosebud Ediciones, 1994).
117. Antón, *Piriguazú* (Montevideo: Rosebud Ediciones, 1995).
118. Antón, *El pueblo jaguar* (Montevideo: Piriguazú Ediciones, 1998).

ways been proud of its Europeanization. His attempt at recuperating the cultural capital of Amerindian groups ignored by the West is an example of this and, it is opportune to remark, a necessary operation.[119]

Yet, his work can be criticized in many respects. For example, he opens himself to criticism when he states that all Amerindians knew how to practice agriculture, or when he finds a relationship between the extinct mound builders and a nonexistent ethnic group, the Arachanes.[120] The problem today in Uruguay is that some of the people who write from a more legitimate locus than Antón's, the discipline archaeology, work with a perspective that is hardly more acceptable. This grim intellectual situation should not be surprising, because almost the totality of the archaeological research conducted in Uruguay has been traditionally influenced, until very recently, by a very ideologized perspective. Until 1986, archaeologists used an implicit hierarchical framework for the evaluation of Amerindian civilizations that posits occidental culture as the highest civilizational development possible. All other cultures are measured as relatively "advanced" or "backward," depending on how close or how far they "place" in comparison to Western culture.[121]

This is why some old guard anthropologists, in reaction to the new information and hypotheses advanced by the archaeologists who began excavating in Rocha Department in 1986, have publicly contested those investigations. The most notorious case is Daniel Vidart's *"Los cerritos de los indios,"* a book in which he claims that the attention paid to the new excavations is exaggerated.[122] His resentment vis-à-vis the paradigm shift is noticeable throughout the rest of his book, where he makes a few dubious claims. One of them is that the most recent investigations do not contribute any new insights to the prehistoric panorama of the region—something Renzo Pi Hugarte agrees with, although he does not bother to explain why.[123] Vidart, for his part, attributes ridiculous assertions to his younger

119. See Antón, *Piriguazú,* 47, 68.

120. I could quote more of Antón's arguable affirmations, but I refer the reader instead to another article where I analyze them. Gustavo Verdesio, "El retorno del indio olvidado o los usos del pasado indígena en el imaginario uruguayo," *Revista Canadiense de Estudios Hispánicos* 36, nos. 1–2 (2001–2002): 63–82.

121. José M. López Mazz and Roberto Bracco, "Las sociedades prehistóricas: viejas y nuevas aproximaciones," *Anales del VI.º encuentro nacional y IV.º regional de historia* 1, no. 1 (1989): 109.

122. Daniel Vidart, *"Los cerritos de los indios" del este uruguayo* (Montevideo: Ediciones de la Banda Oriental, 1996), 5.

123. Renzo Pi Hugarte, *Los indios del Uruguay* (Madrid: Mapfre, 1993), 46.

colleagues: the existence of slaves in mound builder society and an estimated population of 300,000.[124] It should be pointed out that the archaeologists accused by Vidart never wrote such nonsense (he takes his information from a couple of notes written by journalists who do not know very
much about the subject).

Vidart also says that the only contribution of the new excavations to the
understanding of the mound builders is the discovery of a pumpkin seed,
because all other objects had already been unearthed in excavations previous to 1986.[125] It should be pointed out that the exhumation of objects does
not tell us anything about the past without the aid of a framework provided
by a chronology and an archaeological context that could help us explain
the raw data: the mere extraction of undated objects and their conservation
on shelves and display windows in a museum do not say much about the
cultural context in which they were produced. Such a framework was never
produced until 1986, probably because most of the practitioners of the discipline were enthusiastic amateurs rather than professionals.

Fortunately, present-day archaeologists in Uruguay are not content with
the recollection of stones and bones for display in museums or private
homes. They have attempted, for the first time in Uruguay, to produce a
chronology and a context that could help us understand the mound builders
of Uruguay. Their studies reveal that the resources which nature put at their
disposal were much more generous and abundant than thought before 1986.
The temporary model they are proposing is that of hunter-gatherers who ex-
ploited a territory of high productivity. That productivity is measured by the
return values to human work, that is, the difference between investment and
benefit offered by the exploitation of nature.[126] The exploitation of the territory allowed by that particular environment, together with the high number of mounds found, suggests to the archaeologists a model of a culture
with a highly concentrated population—a model that contradicts the prevalent one.[127] In sum, the prehistoric panorama that archaeologists are proposing now is the following: a highly concentrated population with eco-

124. Vidart, *"Los cerritos de los indios,"* 48, 51, 52, 54.
125. Ibid., 21, 36.
126. José M. López Mazz and Roberto Bracco, "Relación hombre—medio ambi-
ente en las poblaciones prehistóricas de la zona este del Uruguay," in *Archaeology and
Environment in Latin America,* ed. Omar Ortiz-Troncoso and Thomas van der Hammen
(Amsterdam: Universitat van Amsterdam, 1992), 276.
127. Ibid., 277.

nomic strategies that allowed them to invest energy in activities such as mound building that did not have a utilitarian return.[128]

López Mazz and Bracco state that the time that mound building consumes, in combination with the excellent conditions for subsistence offered by the environment, suggests a certain degree of sedentism among the mound builders of Uruguay.[129] Another element that suggests this is the funerary function served by the cerritos, many of which contain individual or multiple interments.[130] The alleged sedentary practices of that group adds yet another disagreement to the traditional portrayal of hunter-gatherers in Uruguay, which presents them as small nomadic groups struggling to survive amidst a hostile environment that provided them with poor natural resources.[131]

Although we still do not know much about the mound builders of Uruguay, it seems that the road opened by the excavations that began in 1986 has more chances to succeed in the unveiling of that culture's past. Unfortunately, the results of the most recent excavations are not, despite Vidart's opinion, as popular as they should be. As a matter of fact, Vidart's books—which have become best-sellers among primary and secondary schoolteachers—are much more popular than his younger colleagues' work. Thanks to this phenomenon, the segment of the Uruguayan public interested in the mound builders has access to it exclusively through Vidart's outdated, almost obscurantist, version. The success enjoyed by Danilo Antón's books deserves similar reflections: his idealized versions of the Amerindians have been republished several times (I consulted *Uruguaypirí*'s sixth edition), and are discussed in newspapers and magazines and during radio and TV broadcasts. Although the attention his work has enjoyed is understandable in light

128. Ibid.

129. Ibid., 278.

130. Jorge Femenías, José M. López, Roberto Bracco, Leonel Cabrera, Carmen Curbelo, Nelsys Fusco, and Elianne Martínez, "Tipos de enterramiento en estructuras monticulares ('cerritos') en la región de la cuenca de la Laguna Merín (R.O.U.)," *Revista do CEPA* 17, no. 20 (1990): 348. "Las sociedades que esos restos funerarios sugieren es de tipo complejo, donde el trabajo comunitario debía tener una organización bastante sofisticada, si juzgamos por el tratamiento diferencial que le daban a los muertos—un elemento que permite conjeturar una sociedad en camino hacia una organización no igualitaria." José López Mazz, "Aproximación al territorio de los 'constructores de cerritos,'" in *Arqueología en el Uruguay: VIII Congreso Nacional de Arqueología Uruguaya*, ed. Mario Consens, José María López Mazz, and María del Carmen Curbelo (Montevideo: N.p., 1995), 71.

131. López Mazz and Bracco, "Las sociedades prehistóricas," 111.

of the longtime silence kept by Uruguayan authors about Amerindian cultures, it is regrettable that this ideologized version of the indigenous past is the one privileged by the public.

In Uruguay, a Europeanized nation, some people are attempting to recover, in different ways and through different means, a lost cultural diversity. However, the mass media and the best-selling authors, as seen here, favor an image of the Amerindians that has as many limitations as the ones produced by nineteenth-century authors. It is only through a rigorous study of both the documentary sources and the most recent archaeological excavations that we will be able to approach the indigenous past in a way that is less uncertain and most respectful of cultural differences. Only in this way will we be able to fill, little by little, the vacuum left by the national narratives concerning the Amerindians of the territory. Only in this way will it be possible for Uruguay to recover the memory of the first dwellers of its territory and stop being, once and for all, an amnesic country.

8

Showcases of Consumption: Historical Panoramas and Universal Expositions

Beatriz González-Stephan

The construction of national identities in nineteenth-century Latin America rested partly on symbolic goods capitalized through a grammar of accumulation fictively emphasizing abundance, density, and antiquity. Hence, we have the production of a cultural heritage, occurring in what we might term a new economy of representation.[1] The Spanish American republics, highly sensitive to their innumerable insufficiencies after the wars of independence, addressed insistent efforts—and considerable resources, as well—to

Translated from Spanish by John Charles Chasteen.

1. See Yvette Sánchez, *Coleccionismo y literatura* (Madrid: Cátedra, 1999). The industrial era, guided by the bourgeoisie, witnessed both the proliferation of material goods and a common urge to accumulate them. See also Jean Baudrillard, *El sistema de los objetos* (Madrid: Siglo XXI Editores, 1988); Colin Campbell, *The Romantic Ethic and the Spirit of Modern Consumerism* (New York: Basil Blackwell, 1987); W. Hamish Frasier, *The Coming of the Mass Market* (Hamden, CN: Archon Books, 1981); and Nick Merriman, *The Bon Marché: Bourgeois Culture, Heritage, and the Public in Britain* (Leicester: Leicester University Press, 1991).

the production of cultural goods. It is scarcely odd, then, that museums, libraries, anthologies, literary histories, and universal expositions should all have been organized by the same narrative thread. Latin America's fables of identity were, in large measure, constituted through these catalogs representing a national space and a national history. A single ordering principle animates them all. They are galleries, showcases of what the nation offers to the ever more demanding international market.[2]

The second half of the nineteenth century saw the development of this new economy of representation in tandem with the global extension of industrial capitalism. The increasing variety of previously unimaginable technological curiosities worked a profound modification on perceptive systems in a short period of time. By means of these new systems, which were especially visual in nature, the material world radiated a new sensuality accessible through the voyeuristic pleasure of the gaze. To inspire desires of possession, the represented products first hypnotized with extravagant visual acrobatics. The new techniques of representation were quickly integrated into the mechanisms of state control and capitalist exchange. Modern societies configured themselves as spaces for the spectacular display and circulation of merchandise.

There were many dimensions to the consolidation of a state apparatus and its consensual validation as the political embodiment of an imagined national community. Architecture feats of engineering, obelisks and triumphal arches, squares and avenues, cafés and race tracks, parades and literary contests, newspapers and operas, waterworks and public lighting—all had their role to play. Political elites became keenly aware of the importance of various gestures within the new economy of representation, not the least of which was the election of political "representatives." The power of appearances, the impact of form, the persuasive uses of style and disguise—all came together in a shadow play where portraits stood for people, statues for heroes, anthems for nations, railroads for progress, and merchandise for work.[3] The new economy of representation affected all sorts of social practices, always under the influence of a bourgeois public and its rising expec-

2. Cf. Hugo Achugar, ed., *La fundación de la palabra: Letra y Nación en América Latina en el Siglo XIX* (Montevideo: Universidad de la República, 1998); and Alvaro Fernández Bravo, "Cánones y colecciones: construcción de patrimonios culturales en el Cono Sur," paper presented at the biannual meeting of the Latin American Studies Association, Chicago, IL, 1998.

3. Cf. Paulette Silva Beauregard, *Una vasta morada de enmascarados. Poesía, cultura, y modernización en Venezuela a finales del siglo XIX* (Caracas: Ediciones de la

tations of consumption, shaking off the perceived monotony of a not-too-distant colonial past. To ensure state control—always the price to be paid for peace and order—the national attention was incessantly directed toward symbols of material progress that were presented with an exhibitionist and celebratory spirit much given to grandiloquence and theatricality. The compulsion to accumulate was directed not only to technological novelties but also to the trivial consumer goods characteristic of the gradually saturated market.

The culture of writing—the privileged realm of the symbol-manipulating elite that Angel Rama called "the lettered city"—gained new outlets with the growth of a reading public, served especially by the proliferation of newspapers, but it competed for prestige with an older culture of spectacle, invigorated in the nineteenth century by new technologies of visual reproduction. Even printed pages themselves, such as the serious texts of historiographical treatises, were increasingly interrupted by illustrations. Daguerreotype images of each republic's illustrious authors could now appear, ranged as in a family album, on the pages that explained their merits in the constitution of a national literature. Newspapers and magazines displayed such modern technology in more widely visible media. In fact, the proliferation of illustrated media depicting the commercial, scientific, and artistic life of the country suggests the need to rethink the meaning of "reading" when it comes to the late nineteenth-century press. A national culture was witnessed visually as much as read in publications that frequently featured their "illustrated" character in the title, such as *La Ilustración, El Zulia Ilustrado,* and so on.[4]

A national culture, therefore, required embodiment in images. Language and literature had to be mediated by new forms of consumption, and images constituted an important form of standardization. Walter Benjamin's work on images might lead us, at this point, to rethink the consumption of the period's literature as a dialogue between the written word and other modal-

---

Casa de Bello, 1993); Angel Rama, *Las máscaras democráticas del modernismo* (Montevideo: Ediciones Arca, 1985).

4. A notable Venezuelan example is *El Album,* which began to publish lithographed portraits of well-known authors (such as Espronceda or Avellaneda) by 1845. This publication was preceded (less notably) by *El Promotor* (1843), and soon followed by *La Ilustración* (1854) and *El Oasis* (1856). In the final third of the nineteenth century, illustrated periodicals became common: *El Renacimiento* (1879), *Museo Venezolano* (1886), *La América Ilustrada y Pintoresca* (1886), *El Zulia Ilustrado* (1888), and *El Cojo Ilustrado* (1892).

ities of modernizing culture, helping us to see literary albums and museums, magazines, and theatrical performances, in the same frame of reference.[5] The juxtaposition of word and image made a record of "progress," displayed the national territory's potential wealth of raw materials awaiting productive exploitation, presented history—the narrative wealth of the past—and represented, in general terms, a sort of primitive accumulation of cultural capital for the national patrimony. Thus did the collector's spirit animate the discourse of albums and expositions, identifying the nation by the exhaustive accretion, organization, and exhibition of its constituent elements.[6]

The search for political legitimacy in Spanish American nations exposed the contradictory nature of modernization on the periphery of the international economy. The bourgeois protagonists of that search had to distinguish themselves from the landed patrician classes of the colonial order, on the one hand, and from the hegemonic pretensions of metropolitan capital, on the other. That they did so through immodest accumulation and exhibition should surprise no one. To present their emerging nations as lands of abundance, replete with possibilities for inclusion in the international market, they concentrated particularly on expositions of raw materials needed by metropolitan industries. But they also displayed sumptuary goods and technological gadgets to indicate their avidity and ability to consume the products of those metropolitan industries. On the other hand, fearing the anonymity of total immersion in an international consumer culture, Latin American bourgeoisies deployed a grandiloquent historical and literary discourse to provide a prestigious past and cultivated present worthy of their refined consumer tastes and their future aspirations as self-appointed representatives of the nation. Here, the strategy of accumulation was applied anew, this time symbolically in anthologies, museums, and dictionaries, all directed to the creation of national traditions and cultural heritage.[7] In so doing, they waved the banner of material progress, and also of spiritual progress, summed up, in good nineteenth-century fashion, by the word "civ-

---

5. Walter Benjamin, *Discursos interrumpidos, I. Filosofía del arte y de la historia* (Madrid: Taurus, 1993) and *Iluminaciones, II. Poesía y capitalismo* (Madrid: Taurus, 1993). See also the productive application of Benjamin's concepts in Celeste Olalquiaga, *The Artificial Kingdom* (New York: Pantheon Books, 1998).

6. For further examples, see Eric J. Hobsbawm, *La era del capital (1848–1875)* (Barcelona: Grijalbo, 1988) and Thomas Richards, *The Commodity Culture of Victorian England: Advertising and Spectacle, 1851–1914* (Stanford, CA: Stanford University Press, 1990).

7. Richards, *Commodity Culture,* 17–72.

ilization." Some of their enterprises (such as commercial galleries and universal expositions) displayed mostly material progress, while others (such as national libraries) heralded their self-interested loyalty to the sublime autonomy of art—their artistic achievements being more likely than their precarious level of material progress to provide satisfactory visions of a distinctive national identity.

Admittedly, the collector's urge had been around since the renaissance, but mostly circumscribed to particular situations. Royalty collected musical instruments and works of art; amateur naturalists collected plants and insects. Not until the nineteenth century, however, with the rise of the bourgeoisie, did collecting become a massive social phenomenon. Only then did collecting cease merely to affirm the personal ego of the collector, and, instead, articulated by specialized knowledge that classified and ordered the collections, become an expression of the will to power, a strategy of state domination within Western societies, and a gradually extending technique of Western hegemony over the rest of the world. Collections of knowledge—inventories and archives of a national culture—exercised this function no less than did collections of goods at a commercial exposition.[8]

Here we find a confluence of practices that sheds considerable light on the active configuration of national cultural patrimonies. The elaboration of national histories and literatures occurred in a manner that reflected not only the collecting and cataloging tendencies just described, but also the same orientation toward spectacle that we find in the period's many universal exhibitions. National historiographies and literary anthologies were permeated by the culture of the market, which one can detect in their serialized presentation organized into various "departments" and showcased for the reader/consumer. The pervasive presence of photography in both expositions and lavish publications of this kind is not at all fortuitous. Thus, when Colombian José María Torres Caicedo attended the International Literary Congress of London in 1879, he made an explicit comparison between his own presentation on the periodization, evolution, and originality of Latin American literature, on the one hand, and the previous year's Universal Exposition in Paris, on the other. Torres Caicedo also presented a long list of writers to show that "Latin America has its own wise men, thinkers, and literati," contrary to what might be assumed by Europeans about "those lit-

8. For a more detailed discussion of this relationship, see Beatriz González Stephan, "Poder y cultura nacional: Estado e historiografía literaria (Venezuela, Siglo XIX)," *Estudios: Revista de investigaciones literarias y culturales* 1 (1993): 47–60.

tle republics."[9] It is worth adding, in this connection, that some years before Torres Caicedo had published three fat volumes of *Biographical Essays and Literary Criticism* (appearing between 1863 and 1868), a sort of "literary historical album" of Latin American men of letters. The volumes presented the continent's literary wares for an audience clearly intended to reach internationally well beyond the borders of the countries they described. As Torres Caicedo pointed out in London, Latin America was rich in fertile soils, in wheat, barley, and corn, in coal, iron, and platinum, but also in literature. He clearly believed that Latin Americans needed to represent their countries with more than the desiccated animals and indigenous feather ornaments that had dominated their contributions to the recent Universal Expositions of London and Paris. He must have suspected that a mostly "anthropological" orientation in Latin American self-representation merely bolstered Europe's already well-demonstrated colonizing vocation in his part of the world.

Not only did collections of raw materials and cultural achievements reveal homologous organizing principles, they also displayed a compensatory complementarity. Latin America had entered the first universal expositions primarily as unelaborated nature. Latin America was meat, coffee, wheat, cacao, copper, wood, salt, guano. The catalog of each exposition described these products—their origin, qualities, and uses—in minute detail. But the space of Latin America on the resulting world map was left empty of social and cultural content.[10] The response, as signaled by Torres Caicedo, was found in collected references to thousands of cultural achievements, an encyclopedic impulse of monumental proportions still capable of astonishing

9. José María Torres Caicedo, "La literatura de la América Latina," *Informe presentado en el Congreso Literario Internacional de Londres en 1879,* reproduced in Arturo Ardao, *Génesis de la idea y el nombre de América Latina* (Caracas: Centro de Estudios Latinoamericanos Rómulo Gallegos, 1980), 221–240.

10. Cf. Alvaro Fernández Bravo, "El museo latino: iconografías de la nacionalidad en las exposiciones universales," paper presented at biannual meeting of Latin American Studies Association, Miami, FL, 2000. Fernández Bravo shows how the Argentine pavilion at an 1889 exposition presented that country one-dimensionally as a slaughterhouse and producer of meat. As a result, Argentina was reduced, in the imaginative landscape of Latin America as viewed from Europe, to an empty pasture rich in productive possibilities, awaiting the labors of European immigrants. For an example of these exposition catalogs, see Adolfo Ernst, *La Exposición Nacional de Venezuela en 1883: Obra escrita de orden del Ilustre Americano Antonio Guzmán Blanco* (Caracas: Imprenta de Opinión Nacional, 1884), and a facsimile republished in Ernst's *Obras completas,* vols. 3–4 (Caracas: Fundación Venezolana para la Salud y la Educación, 1983).

us today. The intended message was clear. The wobbly and only recently consolidated national states of Latin America were staking a claim to rough parity with those at the metropolitan center of the international economy. They had history. They had literature. And they had abundant material goods to exchange. The thick, profusely illustrated catalogs testified to these facts for the benefit of all those who had not been present at the expositions themselves. These catalogs became, in effect, a genre in themselves, as inventories of the merchandise on display, while quantifying, enumerating, imposing uniformity, and fitting Latin American products and ideas into a preexisting rhetoric.

Latin America's first national literary histories were, as already noted, part of this larger phenomenon. They appeared beginning around 1850, but proliferated most intensely during the last two decades of the nineteenth century and the first decade of the twentieth, thus coinciding markedly (and not coincidentally) with the vogue of universal expositions. Some important examples are José María Vergara y Vergara's *Historia de la literatura en la Nueva Granada desde la Conquista hasta la Independencia* (1867), Juan León Mera's *Ojeada histórico-crítica sobre la poesía ecuatoriana* (1868), Miguel Luis Amunátegui's *Alborada poética en Chile* (1892), Agustín Gómez Carrillo's *Reseña histórico-crítica de la literatura guatemalteca* (1893), culminating with Carlos Roxlo's gigantic *Historia crítica de la literatura uruguaya* (1911–1920) and Ricardo Rojas's *Literatura argentina* (1917–1922). These works appeared as part of a general affirmation of the civic imagination, a surge of patriotic fervor associated with the ever more intense participation of Latin America in the international market, a participation that had sharpened the bourgeois taste for the consumption of such relative luxuries as literature.

Following the logic of a culture of spectacle, and right in step with the appearance of these literary histories, Latin American nations made a show of their levels of civilizing progress in Universal Expositions of their own. Chile hosted the first in 1875; Argentina, the second, in 1881; and Venezuela, the third, in 1883. Along with the mentioned publications, the protean space of each exposition presented merchandise-filled shops, art-filled galleries, and historical dioramas arranged to provide a supposedly totalizing view of the national culture just in time for a series of centenary commemorations associated with national independence. The hundredth birthdays of national heroes and celebrations of final victory in decolonizing wars seemed insufficient to this purpose. Newly invented red-letter dates were also required. For example, "Day of the Discovery and of the Race"

holidays in honor of illustrious subsequent rulers (or, in some cases, of those rulers' mothers), even the arrival or departure of any particularly distinguished personage—might become an excuse for countless ostentatious displays of national progress, from elaborate inauguration ceremonies for bridges and telegraph lines to the publication of national dictionaries and the first performances of operas.[11]

The contours of the modern consumer society were taking shape in these closing decades of the nineteenth century. The productive forces of capitalism had begun to reveal their full potential to transform the material world, not only through technological revolutions of various descriptions, but also, and even more sweepingly, by means relentlessly inundating the market with articles for daily use, consumption, and appreciation. Universal expositions and literary histories—the first filled with material products, the second, with aesthetic ones—had multiple functions in this context. At one level, they were indices of what was available. At another, they were ritual practices that taught veneration for the newly available merchandise and instilled desire to possess it, with art and literature figuring as simply one more sort of merchandise. The prospering bourgeoisies of Latin America could "see what they wanted" (a hydraulic pump, a hygienic corset, primary school textbooks, or portraits of national heroes) presented in a manner that foreshadowed the department stores of the mid-twentieth century and the shopping centers of that century's closing decades.[12]

The objects in a late nineteenth-century Universal Exposition had no price tags attached, of course, but their "democratic" availability for acquisition by anyone who could pay nonetheless was inherent in the manner of their presentation. Such expositions channeled the taste of Latin America's emerging middle classes. When they could not afford to buy the materials on display, they could often get facsimiles—cheap mechanically repro-

11. Cf. Horacio Salas, *El Centenario: La Argentina en su hora más gloriosa* (Buenos Aires: Planeta, 1996); Beatriz Sarlo and Carlos Altamirano, "La Argentina del Centenario: Campo intelectual, vida literaria, y temas ideológicos," *Hispamérica* 25–26 (1980): 33–59; Patricia Andrea Dosio, *Una estrategia del poder: La Exposición continental de 1882* (Buenos Aires: Facultad de Filosofía y Letras, 1998); Rafael Ramón Castellanos, *Caracas, 1883: Centenario del Natalicio del Libertador* (Caracas: Academia Nacional de la Historia, 1983).

12. See María Inés Turazzi, *Poses e trejeitos: A fotografia e as exposições na era do espectáculo (1839–1889)* (Rio de Janeiro: FUNARTE, 1995); Timothy Mitchell, "The World as Exhibition," *Journal of Comparative Studies of Society and History* (1985): 217–236; Susan Stewart, *On Longing: Narratives of the Miniature, the Gigantic, the Souvenir, the Collection* (Baltimore: Johns Hopkins University Press, 1984).

duced prints of the exhibited national "masterpieces," for example. The shared semiotics of spectacle, serialization, and systematic compartmentalization common to exhibitions, literary anthologies, and department stores promoted the assimilation of natural resources and poetry to other marketable commodities.

Perhaps it is insufficient to posit a situation of reciprocal appropriation and contamination among various cultural practices. Nonetheless, the writing of literary history certainly gained much of its specificity from the process whereby literary works became commodities. It is instructive to observe the actual contexts in which literature circulated during the later decades of the nineteenth century. In magazines and newspapers that which was "literary" appeared embedded in that which was commercial, scientific, and technological. In these venues, too, literature appeared as one more variety of modern consumer goods. The mechanical reproduction of images, which played an increasing role in periodical publication, as has already been described, contributed to the process by transforming cultural objects into icons that inspired desire, acquisition, and collection. In this respect, newspapers and magazines extended the function of literary albums and exhibition catalogs. All, and each in its own way, contributed to the overall growth of the same grammar of accumulation, operating within the same economy of spectacle. As a result, literary histories could offer a visual canon of the nation's men (or even, in a view cases, women) of letters, a panoramic view of national histories and literatures made possible only by conditions of intellectual production, mechanical *re*production, commercial circulation, and political consolidation—all specific to Latin America in the late nineteenth century.

Let us look now more closely at the Venezuelan case, a quite illustrative one for our purposes. The substantial consolidation of the national state under the long authoritarian government of Gen. Antonio Guzmán Blanco (1870–1888) was followed by the appearance of the first literary histories of Venezuela around the symbolic year 1883, the centenary anniversary of the birth of the Liberator, Simón Bolívar. There was much to occupy the attention of Caraqueños and foreign visitors in that year, in which 62,841 people visited the city's Universal Exposition and at least a few of them perused a showy two-volume *Literatura venezolana* by José Güel y Mercader, as well as Ramón Hernández's book with the same title, both published in homage to the national hero and both on display at the Exposition. So, expositions and literary histories not only operated on similar principles of accumulation, classification, and juxtaposition, they also existed in physical association, one giving access to the other. Thus, the picture galleries of the Exposition led one to the Hall of Fine Arts, containing Güel's book, itself a picture gallery of illustrious Venezuelans. Adolfo Ernst's catalog of the event, *La Exposición Nacional de Venezuela: Obra escrita de orden del Ilustre Americano General Guzmán Blanco* (1884), preserved the association for posterity.[13]

Unlike the foundational narratives that appeared shortly after the creation of independent Latin American republics, expositions and literary histories required the prior existence of more consolidated cultural and political structures. The luxurious binding of the thick volumes with their covers of finely embossed leather itself suggested the collective achievement of a certain level of material opulence. The ordered contents also gave a sense of "having arrived," of representing a cultural capital that would command respect in the eyes of foreigners. They had an air of substance and permanence utterly unlike the great majority of what Latin American printing presses had produced over the course of the nineteenth century: pamphlets, almanacs, administrative forms, and periodicals containing occasional local color sketches, installments of novels, official announcements, an occasional poem, and always plenty of ephemeral politics. The literary histories were no less than the published equivalents of public monuments and statuary, designed to be massive, enduring tributes to the cultural aspirations of the nation.

Perhaps weightiest of all was the *Primer libro venezolano de literatura, ciencias, y bellas artes* (1895), a volume of truly unmanageable bulk, published by Imprenta de El Cojo to show off that press's new printing technology, most particularly the quality and quantity of its photographic illustrations—a full-dress staging of national modernity with its bright catalog of names, faces, works, and dates. Here were the nation's worthiest intellectuals, neatly categorized as mathematicians, dentists, poets, gynecologists, lawyers, geographers, musicians, journalists, painters, pedagogues, orators, and hygienists. Among them—and the volume's presentation made this a progressive point of pride—appeared women who had already contributed to national progress. The various galleries of this enormous tome opened up, like sections of a department store, to present convenient access to its cultural goods. Did the reader cultivate the musical arts? Turning to

13. Rafael Ramón Castellanos, *Caracas, 1883* (Caracas: Academia Nacional de la Historia, 1983). From this point forward, I use "Exposition," with a capital "E," to refer to the Venezuelan Exposition of 1883.

the appropriate department, she or he could find musical notation for stylish waltzes and polkas, and so on. The *Primer libro venezolano de literatura, ciencias, y bellas artes* was, in effect, a catalog, an album, and yes, an exposition, of symbolic capital.

International capitalism, because it commercialized so much of its production using technologies of visual reproduction, was giving a new emphasis to form and appearance. Manipulating appearances through artifice and disguise had never been more profitable. This sharpened appreciation for appearances had significant cultural ramifications. The pleasure and power of observation and visual discernment became more important, more esteemed. Furthermore, the new emphasis on visual consumption, arising primarily in the commercial realm, soon spilled over into the area of civic spectacle, as seen in books such as *Primer libro venezolano de literatura, ciencias, y bellas artes*. Or rather, perhaps one saw precisely the spillover, the commercialization of national achievement, the bourgeois spirit of accumulation applied to objects of civic pride, the logic of mass merchandising that made something—anything at all—once removed from its original context, into a commodity. Such albums seemed to offer readers the chance not only to view, but also somehow to *possess* by viewing. The items they displayed had become available for further appropriation, now quite beyond the commercial realm—as if a steam engine, or a bridge, or painless dentistry, had no use value, but merely existed as talismans of modernity or prestigious *objets d'art*.

The logic at work was the same as applied to museums. Like museums, universal expositions and literary histories likewise integrated cultural "remains" into disciplined, chronological series, making them homogeneous parts of a larger, serialized modernity. Museums also created heterogeneity by selecting their contents for "ex-position," "placing them outside" the order of everyday things, to be viewed as something "exotic," "barbarous," or "primitive." One also thinks of the museum practice of creating historical dioramas, lifelike scenes, sometimes apparently unremarkable, but set apart from immediate reality and therefore invested with transcendental importance. Literary histories and universal expositions did something similar by presenting, "ex-positioning" in the same sense, cultural artifacts or fragmented visions of the past to constitute national histories and literatures apart from quotidian mediocrities.[14] The commemoration of certain aspects

14. These and related cultural processes are explored in Remo Guidieri, *El museo y sus fetiches: Crónica de lo neutro y de la aureola* (Madrid: Tecnos, 1997); Arjun Ap-

of national history functioned the same way. By highlighting the centennial of the birth of Simón Bolívar, for example, commemorative patriotic discourse made the event a landmark of the nation's historical imagination but also *removed* the event from the natural flow of history to place it within a rose-tinted bubble of artificial, state-sponsored remembrance. The spirit of Venezuela's 1883 Universal Exposition, and of the related published national representations under consideration here, was highly normative. To create an image of the nation and its history was also to purge and correct that image. The overall effect was to obscure, rather than to illuminate, history. The articles showcased by the Exposition, when not marked by their sheer novelty (like the many mechanical devices) or by their ahistorical rawness (the case of all the "raw materials," for instance), were historical only in the most didactic and politically loaded sense. Martín Tovar y Tovar's canvases of the wars of independence, created (more than recreated) scenes of patriotic heroism to stir generations of school children. The Liberator's centenary was an apt occasion for the collection and organization of a national cultural canon, but the real historicity of the events surrounding national independence became, if anything, more remote as a result of the commemorative discourse of the Exposition.

The historical representations in the discourse of Venezuela's Universal Exposition of 1883 thus had more to with the present—or even with the future—than with the past. The overwhelming abundance of raw materials at such expositions indicated that Latin American economies were still very far from producing the manufactured goods associated with the level of "civilization" from which the past was supposedly viewed. Books like the *Primer libro venezolano de literatura, ciencias, y bellas artes* presented a colonial and postcolonial past as viewed from a "present" that did not yet really exist. The real present, not buoyed up by (but rather crushed under the weight of) an uneasy and disadvantageous peripheral modernity, imposed the invention of fictive traditions best understood as consumer products. The Venezuelan Universal Exposition of 1883 could serve, in this respect, as a model for many others, bringing together in its crowded halls raw materials and history, "the raw and the cooked."

---

padurai, ed., *The Social Life of Things: Commodities in Cultural Perspective* (Cambridge: Cambridge University Press, 1988); Susan Pearce, *Museums, Objects,* and *Collections: A Cultural Study* (Washington: Smithsonian Institution Press, 1992); Emily Apter and William Pietz, eds., *Fetishism as Cultural Discourse* (Ithaca: Cornell University Press, 1996).

As a showcase of consumption, the Exposition brought together a riotous diversity of materials, from machines for grinding coffee beans to pianos made by the firm Trimer, Hiller, and Rodríguez; from revolvers, coaches, and typewriters, to samples of soap, candles, and tobacco; from silkworm cocoons and stuffed natural history specimens to paperweights emblazoned with the trivialized image of this or than patriotic hero. The showcase displayed to the world's curious gaze signs of both material progress (e.g., sewing machines manufactured in Venezuela by Winkelmann Hermanos) and moral progress (e.g., Tovar y Tovar's oil paintings depicting "The Signing of the Declaration of Venezuelan Independence," "The Battle of Carabobo," and "The Death of Guaicapuro"). Importantly, by bringing these materials together under one roof, by displaying them as various aspects of the same show, the Universal Exposition of 1883 firmly united the various meanings of progress in the minds of those in attendance. By collecting and juxtaposing the motley, decontextualized fragments, the Exposition gave content to the sketchy template of national identity.

To transform fragments of rural reality by means of complex symbolic manipulations into a vision of the past suitable for Latin America's peripheral, urban modernity—here was one of the most conspicuous services provided by men and women of letters to the consolidation of the national state. The result was an illusion whereby novelists or painters brought together pre-Colombian peoples with Simón Bolívar, popular couplets with José Angel Lamas's *Popule Meus,* all part of the national makeover through which nations like Venezuela sought their global market niche, advertised themselves for foreign investment, and attempted to attract European immigration to their shores. The makeover featured "savage" geography, abundant in exportable natural resources, but the savagery of this *tierra incógnita* full of jungles was cushioned by a dose of "culture." History and literature were an essential part of the packaging, as prime mechanisms for the colonization of the imagination. That these undertakings in Latin American have always been so Eurocentric is not accidental.[15]

The special aura of these cultural forms was not only part of the "masqued ball" of neocolonialism. It was also part and parcel of ongoing revolutionary changes in all sorts of symbolic languages, visual and aural. The capacity to agglutinate or consolidate control of territory, populations,

15. Michel de Certeau, *La escritura de la historia* (Mexico City: Universidad Iberoamericana, 1993); Serge Gruzinski, *La colonización del imaginario* (Mexico City: Fondo de Cultura Económica, 1991).

and economic resources depended in part on force, and in part on persuasion. To dynamize all communications media was necessarily part of the architecture of power, and therefore, a prime objective of all the region's emerging national states, as well as a by-product of integration into the international market. Therefore, activities as diverse as the construction of railroads, bridges, telephones, and telegraphs were part of the same overarching process as the development of national histories, the publication of literary albums, and the erection of museums and expositions. Perhaps this process is by now no longer surprising. It is all part of the same cultural logic whereby literary history became part of national showcases of consumption and a step toward industrialization, the same logic whereby universal expositions became an important means of staking claim to a place in "Western civilization" in late nineteenth-century Latin America.

Contributors

Sara Castro-Klarén is professor of Latin American culture and literature and director of the Latin American Studies Program at the Johns Hopkins University. Her books include *Escritura, transgresión, y sujeto en la literatura latinoamericana* (1989) and *Women's Writing in Latin America: An Anthology* (1991). She is currently finishing a book on the trope of cannibalism and its intersection with colonialism in Euro-America.

Sarah C. Chambers is associate professor of history at the University of Minnesota and author of *From Subjects to Citizens: Honor, Gender, and Politics in Arequipa, Peru, 1780–1854* (1999). Her current research focuses on feminine epistolary in nineteenth-century South America and on family, politics, and the state in Chile between 1780 and 1860.

John Charles Chasteen has taught Latin American History at the University of North Carolina at Chapel Hill since 1990. His books include *Heroes on Horseback: A Life and Times of the Last Gaucho Caudillos* (1995); and

National Rhythms, African Roots: The Deep History of Latin American Popular Dance (2004).

Tulio Halperín Donghi is professor emeritus at the University of California at Berkeley. His vast and influential opus includes *The Contemporary History of Latin America* (1993), *Proyecto y construccion de una nacion, 1846–1880* (1995), and *Vida y muerte de la república verdadera* (2000).

Beatriz González-Stephan holds the Lee Hage Jamail Chair in Latin American Literature in the Department of Hispanic Studies at Rice University. Formerly, she was professor of Latin American literature and cultural theory at the Universidad Simón Bolívar in Caracas. Among her books are *Fundaciones: canon, historia y cultura nacional* (2002) and *The Body Politic: Writing the Nation in Nineteenth-Century Venezuela* (in press).

François-Xavier Guerra, whose untimely death occurred in 2002, was professor of history at the University of Paris I. Guerra was author of *Modernidad e independencias: Ensayo sobre las revoluciones hispánicas* (1992) and coeditor, with Antonio Annino and Luis Castro Leiva, of *De los imperios a las naciones: Iberoamérica* (1994).

Andrew J. Kirkendall is associate professor of history at Texas A&M University. He is the author *of Class Mates: Male Student Culture and the Making of a Political Class in Nineteenth-Century Brazil* (2002). He is currently working on a book on Paulo Freire and the politics of literacy in Cold War America.

Fernando Unzueta is associate professor of Latin American literature and cultures and director of the Center for Latin American Studies at Ohio State University. He specializes in the nineteenth century and has published *La imaginación histórica y el romance nacional en Hispanoamérica* (1996) and numerous essays on a wide range of topics, including colonial and postcolonial subjects, the relations between literature and history, the discursive production of national identities, and the emergence of historical consciousness.

Gustavo Verdesio is associate professor of Spanish in the department of romance languages and literatures at the University of Michigan, where he teaches courses on colonial Latin America and indigenous cultures. A revised English version of his book *La invención del Uruguay* (1996) has been published by Temple University Press as *Forgotten Conquests* (2001). He coedited (with A. F. Bolaños) *Colonialism Past and Present* (SUNY Press, 2002) and is the author of numerous articles on colonial Latin America.

Index